Ian Plimer, author, scientist, broadcaster, sceptic, bon vivant is the Professor of Geology at the University of Melbourne. He has published more than 120 scientific papers and books—*Telling Lies for God* becoming a bestseller in 1994—and three books on Broken Hill. His most recent book, *Milos: geologic history* chronicles the 10 000-year history of mining on that Greek island and how the islanders have been at the mercy of geological forces. He has won national and international awards for scientific research, the promotion of science, journalism and humanism. He is patron of Lifeline and Broken Hill's GeoCentre. Professor Plimer has had a weekly ABC Regional Radio segment, 'Talking Rocks', since 1993. This book draws together those programs into a short history of planet Earth.

a short
history
of planet
earth
ian plimer

ABC
BOOKS

Published by ABC Books for the
AUSTRALIAN BROADCASTING CORPORATION
GPO Box 9994 Sydney NSW 2001

Copyright © Ian Plimer 2001

First published July 2001
Reprinted December 2002

National Library of Australia
Cataloguing-in-Publication entry
Plimer, Ian R.
    A short history of planet Earth.

    ISBN 0 7333 1004 4.

    1. Historical geology. 2. Earth. I. Australian
Broadcasting Corporation. II. Title.

551

Illustrated by Paul Stanish
Set in 11/14 Fairfield Light by Midland Typesetters,
Maryborough, Victoria
Colour separations by Colorwize, Adelaide
Printed and bound in Australia by Griffin Press, Adelaide

5 4 3 2

CONTENTS

INTRODUCTION

'Where shall I begin, please your Majesty?' he asked.
'Begin at the beginning,' the King said, very gravely, 'and go on till you come
to the end; then stop.'

Lewis Carroll, *Alice's Adventures in Wonderland*

T his journey and its chronicle is very much a personal view by
one who has had almost a 50-year fascination of the history of
our planet. Geology paints on a very large canvas in vivid
colours. As a natural science it is underpinned by evidence from the
rocks, laboratory, experiments, calculations and models. Geology calls
on chemistry, biology, physics, astronomy and mathematics to integrate
and strengthen this evidence. On the basis of this evidence, the most
likely scenario is constructed. With more evidence, the story written in
the rocks is refined. Like a detective, we visit the scene after the event
and reconstruct the action from a diversity of clues using an arsenal of
weapons. If we revisit the scene of the action with more evidence, then
we may revise our conclusions. In this way geology is non-dogmatic and
has the virtue of slight uncertainty and the celebration of doubt. In the
nineteenth century, geology was called natural philosophy. Although
now more quantitative it still is natural philosophy.

This book is written for a non-scientific audience. As with all sciences,
knowledge in the field is expanding at breakneck speed and I have tried
to explain where we are at in the year 2001. The stimulus for such a
book has derived from communicating the exciting history of our planet
with those who have little or no knowledge of geology, such as my
students, radio audiences and community groups.

In September 1993 a weekly ABC Regional Radio segment on geology was initiated by broadcaster Peter Jeppeson. He taught me some of the basics of presenting science on radio and, for the last five years, I attended finishing school with Gary Bartholomew. He made sure that each week my ABC Regional Radio segment called *Talking Rocks* went to air and forced me to do many retakes until I had explained my science in a suitable form to the listener. To both Peter and Gary I give my heartfelt thanks for the guidance and fun. It is from their efforts that this book arose. Various ABC radio and television programs on matters scientific with Paul Barry, Geoff Burchfield, Richard Glover, Gael Jennings, Helen Richardson, Robyn Williams and Paul Willis have been used to profess my discipline to the community.

The text has had the benefit of editing by John Kerr and criticism and technical editing of all or part of the text was by Pascal Blampain, William Cochrane, Bob Foster, Julian Hollis, John Mitchell, Bruce Skilton and Barry Williams. Their criticism improved much of the text. I thank my best friends and greatest critics, John Nethery and Maja Sainisch-Plimer, for their input, ideas and reading of the text.

1

ONCE UPON A TIME

On Martian meteorite ALH84001, summing up evidence:

None of these observations is in itself proof for the existence of past life.
[But] . . . when they are considered collectively, . . . we conclude that they
are evidence of primitive life on Mars.

NASA scientists, 1996

Our planet is a lonely insignificant piece of rock associated with
an equally insignificant main sequence star called the Sun, one
of billions of stars that are candles in the cosmos. But given the
enormity of time, energy, space and matter, almost anything can happen.
And it has. Planet Earth is the by-product of the death of an ancestral
star leading to the condensation of the solar nebula and planets around
4600 million years ago. Our planet, known to the ancient Greeks as *Gaia*
or *Gaea*, has evolved to a galactic oasis from the nebular nursery.

Planet Earth and we humans are recycled stardust. We are the
product of a long period of pre-solar evolution during which, matter
itself evolved and became concentrated. The formation of the solar
system from primordial cosmic dust may have been hurried along by a
violent blast of radiation from the explosion of a super massive star. A
radiation blast within 300 light years would have flooded the dusty disc
circling the young Sun with enough energy to fuse up to 100 Earth
masses of material into droplets. These, and the dust from which they
formed, are rich in iron which would have very efficiently soaked up
X-rays and gamma rays.

Our Solar System condensed from an interstellar cloud of dust and
gas and the Sun, the planets and many other objects formed during the
next 100 million years. The Sun is the only star in our Solar System

and just one of 100 000 million in our galaxy. The planets in our Solar System lie in a common plane. With minor exceptions, they rotate on their axes and orbit the Sun in the same direction as the Sun's own rotation. This suggests that the whole system originally formed from a single rotating cloud of gas and dust. Pluto is the one planet whose orbit is significantly inclined to that of the other planets and, although its orbit is anomalously elliptical, this fact alone does not alter the idea of a common origin. Neptune at some later time was impacted or affected by the gravity of another planet and changed course into its present 165-year orbit. Some planets, such as Jupiter, might have formed by the collision of comets and, since the beginning of the Solar System, Jupiter has acted as a giant gravitational vacuum cleaner. If it were not for Jupiter having 1300 times the mass of Earth and a very strong gravitational field, Earth and the other inner planets would have undergone a far more intense history of bombardment by asteroids and comets. We see the effects of Jupiter's gravity with the constant gravitational squeezing and pulling of Io, a moon of Jupiter. This constant kneading has heated Io to the point of regular massive volcanic eruptions.

Because the planets in our Solar System are in a common plane, they are occasionally aligned. Some doomsayers with no knowledge of astronomy suggest that a planetary alignment can lead to a civilisation-ending apocalypse with crustal upheavals, tsunamis, earthquakes and winds in excess of 1500 kilometres an hour. You can relax. On Friday, 5 May 2000 there was an alignment of the Sun, Mercury, Venus, Earth, Mars, Jupiter and Saturn and it was just another day in the life of the Solar System. The next doomsday will be in 2438 when the planets will be doing the same thing again.

Earth is different from all other planets in the Solar System. For more than 80 per cent of the history of the Solar System, Earth has had water. It is water that has made Earth different from all other planets. It is water that has supported life on Earth for 3800 million years. It is water that has allowed the recycling of bits of planet Earth over the last 4500 million years to make the continent of Australia.

Our Sun will ultimately make a meal of the Solar System. The planets will come to a fiery end when our parent star swallows them whole. When the Sun's core runs out of hydrogen fuel, it will swell to become a red giant which will balloon out as far as Mars. Red giants lose material at a terrific rate and the stellar wind will drive Earth further away from the Sun. To counterbalance escaping from a red giant, the

Earth will produce a tidal bulge in the Sun which it will try to drag around with it as it orbits. The Sun's envelope will spin faster while Earth will slow and move inward. If the Earth is gobbled up by the Sun, then it will be vapourised before it gets deep into the Sun. We don't know what effect will dominate, but we do know that the end is not quite nigh. In some 5000 million years time the Sun will be a monstrous red glob filling almost all the sky and Earth will be cooked or vapourised. Ashes to ashes. On 51 Pegasi, the first star other than the Sun that astronomers found to have a planet, the atmosphere contains an over-abundance of heavy elements. This makes sense if the star had gobbled up a planet. It has happened on 51 Pegasi and it will happen in our Solar System in only 5000 million years so you had better prepare yourself for the fiery end.

More than 50 planets have been found outside our Solar System. What is the possibility of there being life on planets outside our Solar System? This can be checked by measuring the planetary spectrum for ozone. Atmospheric oxygen derives from life and, in the atmosphere, oxygen combines to form ozone. If another planet contained living primitive bacterial life such as cyanobacteria, space vehicles outside the Earth's atmosphere may be able to detect the waste product from life.

Nomadic planets may be wandering through space free from the gravitational pull of a star. If a cloud of dust and gas is more than 80 times heavier than Jupiter, the cloud will gravitationally collapse and start nuclear reactions that quickly die. All that remains is a brown dwarf. If the dust and gas cloud is less than 14 times as heavy as Jupiter, it will collapse to form a planet. The amount of material is too small to start a nuclear reaction but the planet will emit a very small amount of heat. In the Orion nebula, there are hundreds of points emitting small amounts of heat. At least 150 of these are brown dwarfs and at least 13 are planets. There may be hundreds of millions of nomadic planets roaming our galaxy.

In the meantime, which we are living in for a brief moment, there has been (and will continue to be) fascinating episodes well worth the figuring out and the telling. The past is written in stone and those stones' stories is what this tale is all about. We will get to the saga shortly. Here is as good a place as any to acquaint you with some big-picture themes and constant principles of being a planet. To do that we will visit some other insignificant rocks in space of various kinds—interstellar dust, planetoids, asteroids, other Solar System planets, the moons of those planets, and comets. After the Earth formed out of that cosmically insignificant bit of stardust, some things were certain—its very size meant it would cool down slowly.

The condensation and gravitational collapse of an interstellar cloud into smaller and smaller pieces produced our Ssolar System. We are fortunate that the Sun is a long-lived small single star capable of providing stable planetary orbits for at least 10 000 million years. This long period of time has allowed advanced forms of life to evolve from the concentration of the building blocks of life on the surface of the Earth. If the Sun were a double or multiple star, then there would be no stable orbits for planets. If the Sun was a much larger body, it would have completed its life cycle in a matter of a million years or so, leaving no time for the formation of a planetary system. It is the enormity of time that is the key to a stable Solar System, an evolving Sun, an evolving Earth and life on Earth. Time is the most wonderful four-letter word in the English language.

It is also fortunate that the Sun has been extremely stable over a long period. The life-giving stream of light isn't all that reaches our planet from the Sun. The Sun also emits a relentless current of charged particles, the solar wind, that warps the Earth's magnetic field. At times, the Sun belches out vast balls of ionised gas with potentially devastating effects on Earth. Solar flares occur once or twice a decade. The last big one in 1989 knocked out the power grid in northern Quebec. In 2000–2001, there were numerous communications difficulties from solar flares. Other stars like the Sun produce superflares that are dramatically brighter for minutes to days.

If the Sun had a superflare some 10 000 times brighter than the 1989 event, the ice on Jupiter's moons would melt, the Earth's ozone layer would be lost and the Earth's satellites would be destroyed. This wouldn't matter very much because all life on Earth would have been fried. We do not know why the Sun has not behaved like other normal stars and has not had such a superflare during the history of life on Earth. Whatever the reason, we can thank our lucky star.

It has been speculated that, early in the history of our Solar System, collision of the Sun with another body may have occurred. This may explain why the Sun's axis is some seven degrees different from the rest of the Solar System. If such a collision took place, then it would have been very close to the Sun's equator.

The Solar System was a very inhospitable place early in its history some 4600 million years ago. There was a trend towards gravitational balance but there were large clusters of rock and ice that had no stable orbit and were colliding with each other and with the early planets. Such impacts still occur. The last big one, 65 million years ago, punched out a crater as big as Belgium, darkened the atmosphere with debris and wiped out the dinosaurs. Yet, on the planetary scale, that impact was a mere love-peck.

There was once a rocky planet between Mars and Jupiter that, early in the history of the Solar System, was fragmented into what we now call the asteroid belt. The asteroid belt contains some 20 000 planetoids more than a kilometre across and millions of smaller bodies. Jupiter's very strong gravity sucks up a lot of them like a vacuum cleaner, just as it sucks up a lot of meteorites heading our way. Trojan asteroids orbit Jupiter and have difficulty leaving the strong gravitational field. Apollo asteroids are relatively large, have ellipisoidal orbits, and cross the paths of Earth and other planets. Some 50 Apollo asteroids have been identified. The impacts Earth has had, if the visitor wasn't a comet, were probably Apollo asteroids.

In the very early history of the Solar System the Earth was a molten planetoid, half the size it is today, but growing rapidly by gobbling up rubble that had condensed from the dust cloud swirling around the young Sun.

At the time there was another molten planetary mass, about the size of Mars, in a similar orbit to ours. They collided. The cores of the two fused and the impact splattered much of the outside bits into space, lost and gone forever most of it, but not all.

Some slow-moving bits of Earth were pulled together by their own gravity, and made the early bits of the Moon. Its size and thus gravity were such it orbited Earth and not the Sun.

Meanwhile the Earth grew to about two-thirds of its present size while spinning very fast—each day was 3 hours and the lunar month about 9 hours. Both Earth and Moon grew for 50 million years, impacts— stuff coming from outer space—adding a bit here and there, bulking up both the Earth and the Moon. Earth–Moon pushes and pulls, pushed the Moon further from Earth and the Earth started to spin slower.

The Earth is still growing. Large meteorites and comets impact Earth sporadically and add to the Earth's mass. Meteorites and micrometeorites are continually raining down on Earth. Micrometeorites and meteorites heat up during their fall to Earth, due to the friction of the atmosphere. The heated extraterrestrial visitors lose trapped interstellar gas and volatile chemicals. Today, 40 000 tonnes of interstellar dust falls to planet Earth each year. The extremely small dust particles gently rain on Earth and, because they are too small to frictionally heat during descent, they retain their interstellar gases.

During the first 100 million years of the Solar System, not only did planetary objects form but the planets also underwent gravitational settling. In both the Earth and the Moon, a metallic core gravitationally settled to the centre and left a rocky mantle. You can check this yourself with your own scientific experiment at the bar. Order a Guinness. Watch the separation of the core as the black stout sinks to the bottom of the glass, from the mantle, the overlying froth. This is more or less what happened in the early history of Earth. Of course, one scientific experiment is not adequate proof so the experiment with Guinness must be done very many times in order to show that the results are reproducible.

Planet Earth still has a molten core and this core gives Earth its magnetic field. A swirling vortex of molten iron-nickel alloy has been found 3000 kilometres beneath the North Pole. The vortex is like a giant hurricane and, in a region 2400 kilometres across, moves around a quarter of a degree a year resulting in the wandering of the magnetic poles. Turbulence, fluctuation and eddies in the liquid iron-nickel outer core cause fluctuations in the Earth's magnetic field. Not only does the direction of the magnetic field change but the strength of the field changes. For example, in ancient Roman times, the Earth's magnetic field was half today's field strength.

Sometimes, like a fickle lover, the Earth's magnetic field suddenly reverses. The North Pole becomes the South Pole and the north point of the compass points south. This has happened many times, even when humans have lived on Earth. For example, over the last 50 million years there have been more than 100 magnetic reversals.

If there was a magnetic reversal today, the effect would be widespread. During such a reversal, which may take days to tens to thousands of years, the Earths' radiation shield would be affected and the Earth would be bombarded by ultraviolet radiation. The study of the palaeomagnetic patterns of one specific lava flow shows that during the period the lava was molten, the Earth's magnetic field flipped. Lava is only molten for days to weeks and calculations show that there was a complete magnetic reversal in 15 days.

There would be no television, no radio, no telephones, no computers and no satellite communications. Methods of accurate time keeping would not exist, electricity could not be transmitted and none of the comforts of modern life would work. There could be a mass collapse of western society. In fact, if there were a geomagnetic reversal, the large affluent population centres would be far more affected than places such as outback Australia and third world countries.

The wandering of the magnetic poles and reversal of Earth's magnetic field have been used to reconstruct how the continents have drifted over the last 1000 million years. Each time lava erupts, the magnetic minerals in the lava preserve the Earth's magnetic field at the time of eruption. The reddish-brown iron minerals in soils also preserve the Earth's magnetic field. If the age of the lava or the soil can be determined by independent means, then the position of the old magnetic poles can be located. These pointers to the poles then were dragged across the surface of the Earth as the continents drifted and a reconstruction can show where the continents were at a particular time, the position of the poles at that time and the rate of continental drift. For example, the South Magnetic Pole was located in western Queensland 240 million years ago and it is no surprise that rocks of this age in Australia indicate that conditions were a little chilly. The rates of continental drift vary from 1 centimetre a year to 17 centimetres a year. Over a short geological time span such as 20 million years, continents can move more than 1000 kilometres.

Life on Earth is currently protected by a radiation shield resulting from the Earth's magnetic field. When the outer core of the Earth finally freezes, the atmosphere too will be blasted into space by the solar wind and life on Earth will be fried.

It is fortunate that planet Earth has unusual characteristics such as a magnetic field, molten core, tides and slow spin, all of which are necessary for life on Earth and all of which are, in part, related to the presence of a moon nearby.

Because the Moon is so small, its liquid core froze early in its history. Apollo lunar samples show that the Moon had a strong magnetic field 3900 to 3600 million years ago when magnetic minerals in lunar lavas were frozen into the orientation of the Moon's old magnetic field. The Moon now has no magnetic field. Once the Moon lost its magnetic field, the protective magnetic layer in the atmosphere disappeared and gases in the atmosphere were blasted into space by solar winds. Because there is no transfer of heat from the core to its surface, the Moon is essentially dead.

The Moon is layered. The first layer, about 60 kilometres down, indicates a change in composition from lighter to denser rocks with depth. Such layers and rock compositions are similar to those deep in Earth. This layering of the Moon shows that early in its life it was hot enough to be molten and then to crystallise into layers. Earth, being much larger than the Moon, has larger heat sources and it is still cooling.

There is little excitement on the Moon now. Lunar soil occasionally emits gas, especially from near the crater Aristarchus. This is seen on Earth as light flashes and short-lived clouds. Since formation of the Moon, cosmic dust has rained onto the surface. The dust has been disturbed by impacting and lava flows. These minute dust particles acquire a positive electrostatic charge from bombardment by ultraviolet light. Repulsion between the like charges on the cosmic dust makes the dust levitate. Similar charged particles in Saturn's magnetic field produces the 'spokes' in the rings of Saturn.

On Earth, the constant stressing, straining and breaking of rocks produces numerous earthquakes each day. By contrast, the Moon is almost strain free and there are only very faint tremors. The rare breaking of rocks to produce extremely faint moonquakes occurs at a very great depth in the Moon. By contrast, on Earth, earthquakes result from the breaking of rocks at very shallow depths telling us that the Earth is a healthy dynamic planet. However, those that survived the devastating Richter magnitude 7.4 earthquake on 17 August 1999 in Izmir, Turkey, and the Richter magnitude 5.8 and 7.2 aftershocks on 13 September 1999 and 12 November 1999, might have a different view. The 1600-kilometre long North Anatolian Fault has been active for a long time and slips at an average rate of 2 to 3 centimetres a year. In recent times major Anatolian earthquakes occurred in 1668, 1719, 1754, 1766 (twice), 1894, 1912, 1939, 1957, 1963 and 1967. Calculations show that two events equal to or greater than the 1999 Izmir earthquake are likely to occur within the next two decades beneath the Marmara Sea, south of Istanbul.

The formation of the Earth's magnetic field was the first step in the long march towards life on Earth. A magnetic layer developed high in the atmosphere as a result of the Earth's magnetic field and the planet is protected from bombardment by intense cosmic radiation by this magnetic layer. If planet Earth was not so protected by this magnetic layer, cosmic radiation would destroy life on Earth.

Both the Earth and the Moon continued to separate into layers. The Earth's core separated into two layers and the mantle separated into many indistinct layers. The crust of the Earth separated and is, in effect, floating on the mantle. The mantle is still producing new crust at the mid-ocean ridges such as Iceland and the ocean floor is expanding and being pushed under continents. For example, the floor of the Pacific Ocean is currently being pushed back into the mantle under continents at the edge of the oceans such as at Japan and the Andes.

The Earth's outer core is molten and the mantle of the Earth is kept hot by the breakdown of radioactive elements and by the residual heat from the core. Very slow-moving currents transfer heat from deep in the Earth to the surface of the planet. Although the mantle is almost solid, currents move a few centimetres per year. These currents, called convection currents, rise as plumes and, over time, can produce volcanoes, stretch the crust and eventually break continents.

From 4600 to 3800 million years ago, planets and moons in the Solar System were heavily bombarded by dust, meteorites, asteroids, comets and planetoids. This period, the Late Heavy Bombardment, was followed by more passive times. Impacting still occurs but not with the same vicious intensity as early in the history of Earth.

Craters on the Moon provide a window into what the early Earth was like. Because the Moon has never had running water to reshape, erode and recycle its surface, the lunar craters give us the complete history covering the time of bombardment of the Moon and Earth by comets and meteorites. The oldest meteorite is dated at 4560 million years old, which must be considered the minimum age for the solar system. There are some very large and old lunar craters. Some of the lunar impacts were so large that deep fractures were formed. The rebound from these fractures caused melting deep in the lunar mantle by rapid depressurisation, there were massive outpourings of lunar lava and the huge lunar craters were filled with molten rocks to become a lunar sea. Lunar craters filled with smooth lava can be seen from Earth with the naked eye. Early Earth would have been little different.

The geological record shows that large impacts may have coincided with massive volcanic eruptions, continental fragmentation and mass extinctions on several occasions and that Earth may have been shaped profoundly by these extraterrestrial bombardments. For example, an impact into the ocean would be not cushioned by sea water. A 10-kilometre-sized asteroid would punch through the ocean as if it were a shallow puddle and would break the thin rigid crust of the ocean floor. Fractures would propagate deep into the mantle. Upon rebound, depressurisation would produce partial melting of the mantle, resulting in the release of millions of cubic kilometres of molten rock and the fractured area would be the locus for a mantle plume. This release of molten rock would affect the convection currents in the mantle that carry the plates of Earth thereby inducing the fragmentation of continents.

The dating of lunar rocks and the measurement of lunar craters show that there was a very high rate of planetesimal, meteorite and comet impacts on the Moon between 4500 to 3800 years million ago. There is no reason why the Earth should have escaped this massive bombardment. There is a faint record of this period of increased bombardment in the rocks of Isua in south-west Greenland, which are older than 3800 million years. These rocks contain grains of typical meteorite minerals as do rocks found in the Jack Hills area, Western Australia, which are older than 3600 million years. There are suspicious circular structures more than 100 kilometres in size in some of the very ancient rocks of Western Australia and these may be the rocks that were well beneath impact sites. There is a needle-in-a-haystack search for evidence of massive bombardment of early Earth by extraterrestrial bodies. Even 3800 million years ago the impacting was 20 times greater than at present. The Earth would have suffered the same rate of impacting and much of the material left on the surface of the Earth would have come from space. What are these visitors?

There are 14 bits of the Moon that have been found on Earth, bits blasted out of lunar impact craters. These are composed of broken old lunar crust or lunar volcanic rock, both of which are now familiar lunar rocks. It is surprising that with the thousands of meteorites found on Earth, no lunar meteorite had been found on Earth prior to the Apollo landing in 1969. The first find of a lunar meteorite was ALH81005 in 1981 in the Allan Hills, Antarctica. The first non-Antarctic lunar meteorite found was at Calcalong Creek, Western Australia, and two more have been found in the Libyan Sahara, the largest of which was 1.425 kilograms. The Libyan finds were from different falls yet were only 50 kilometres apart suggesting Earth has been peppered by lunar meteorites spalled off the Moon by small-scale geologically-recent impacts. By considering the immensity of lunar impact craters formed in the period 4500 to 3800 million years ago, there must have been an immense scale spalling off of material from deep below the lunar surface. Although many of these lunar meteorites have been gravitationally swept into the Sun, we would expect to find altered lunar remains in the oldest rocks on Earth. We are still looking.

The scientific collection of cosmic dust, ice from space and meteorites from the surfaces of the Earth and the Moon tells us a little more about the visitors from space. The key year to understanding space was 1969. Not only was the first footprint made on the Moon but also two important visitors from space hit the Earth. A large meteorite, in the order of 2 tonnes, landed near the village of Allende, in northern Mexico, and the Murchison meteorite landed in northern Victoria, Australia.

Meteorites tell evocative stories about deep space. Both the Allende and Murchison meteorites are rich in carbon and contain millimetre-sized spheres of silicate minerals. Both these meteorites are 4500 million years old, the age of the Solar System. These meteorites are samples of the very early solar system. This type of meteorite, termed carbonaceous chondrite, contains the building blocks of life in the form of amino acids and other large organic molecules typical of living organisms. However, the geometry of the amino acids is the same as that from non-biological material. The visitors from space were adding the building blocks of life to Earth but were not adding life itself from elsewhere in space.

The Allende meteorite held another message. It told of a supernoval explosion that pre-dated the Solar System's supernoval-explosion origin. Supernovae (or supernovas) fuse light elements to make heavy metals. It had pea-sized calcium-aluminium silicates that revealed a great deal about such explosions, and the origin of the Universe, the Big Bang, the Solar System and our world.

There are three types of meteorite: common stony meteorites, rare stony-iron meteorites and equally rare iron meteorites. Stony meteorites contain silicate minerals. Silicate minerals abound on Earth. The other two contain iron-nickel alloys similar to those in Earth's core. Meteorites contain a host of rare minerals that can only form in oxygen-free environments. For example, silicon carbide, diamond and graphite. As 99 per cent of the elements that make up the Earth were created in the nuclear hearts of stars that burned out long before the Solar System was formed, and everything down here is composed of this recycled stardust, ancestor to the Sun and Earth and our physical being, and are truly a hitchhiker's guide to The Galaxy and any other galaxy you care to mention, they are worth a look.

Xenon is a rare gas on Earth and it has a number of forms, called isotopes. Rare to the point of long gone on Earth, the light isotope is common in many meteorites—they may be material preserved from before the birth of our solar system.

Diamonds, fairly rare on Earth, are the most abundant pre-solar system mineral in meteorites. Some diamonds and silicon carbide in meteorites contain the light isotope of xenon. In the solar system the ratio of carbon 12 to carbon 13 varies a bit, between 88:1 to 92:1. The ratio in meteorite carbon—in silicon carbide crystals for the most part—varies from 2:1 to 7000:1. Only nuclear reactions in stars can produce such isotopes and the range of their isotopic forms lead us to believe that they must have several origins, that is, be made by several sorts of stars.

One suspect looks particularly guilty, the carbon-rich red giant. No other star type has a carbon 12 to 13 ratio of between 20:1 and 80:1. Red giants bloat up to five times the size of the Sun, and develop relatively cool—for a star—atmospheres which allow silicon carbide, diamonds and other minerals to form, and strong winds which blast gas and dust into space. After they do that, they become white dwarfs.

Supernovae are 10 times as massive as the Sun and collapse to form ultra-dense neutron stars or black holes. But the shockwave of the collapse blows out energy of scarely comprehensible (but measureable) proportions and, we think from the peculiar isotopes in meteorites of such an origin, grains of graphite, corundum and other minerals.

Meteorites are wonderful sources of information. Apart from telling us the age of the Solar System and that there was once a planet similar to Earth between Mars and Jupiter which was smashed to pieces, meteorites provide us with samples of material that we cannot collect from deep in Earth or from the solar system. Antarctica is the best collecting site on Earth for meteorites. However, there are numerous meteorites in outback Australia, probably about one per square kilometre, and the best collecting locality is the Nullarbor Plain.

Old impact craters are extremely difficult to identify because they have been modified by weathering, erosion and sedimentation. Such water-driven processes exist on Earth but not on other masses in the solar system such as the Moon and Mars. Each year, one or two new

Earthly impact craters are found as a result of geophysical studies associated with oil exploration.

Early in the Earth's history, the separation of the core resulted in the extraction of metallic iron, nickel, cobalt, iridium and other metals from the mantle. This is why the iron-rich meteorites, representing the core of an old rocky planet, contaminate the Earth with iridium. Upon impact, the host rocks and meteorite are fragmented and the impact dust is contaminated with extraterrestrial iridium. It is these millimetre-thick layers of shocked minerals, meteorite minerals, glass spheres and iridium-rich rocks that are the smoking gun for a meteorite impact.

Our planet is an oasis in space, delicately balanced in its orbit. If we were a little closer to the Sun, there would be no liquid water on Earth. With no liquid water, carbon dioxide could not dissolve in seawater and be removed as calcium carbonate—limestone—precipitated on the sea floor. Earth would then be like Venus with no water and a carbon dioxide-rich atmosphere which has induced a runaway greenhouse. If the Earth was a little further from the Sun or had a different atmosphere, liquid water and carbon dioxide would freeze.

How did the Earth form an atmosphere? Has the atmosphere stayed the same? Some extraterrestrial material is added to the atmosphere and gases are lost from the upper atmosphere by supersonic solar winds stripping material into space. But such changes have had little effect on the Earth's atmosphere. If Earth had inherited its atmosphere directly from solar nebulae, then its composition would be similar to the solar and cosmic abundances. However, our atmosphere is completely different from solar and cosmic material. Our atmosphere has far more oxygen and nitrogen and far too little hydrogen and helium to be cosmic gas. It is probable that the Earth's early atmosphere derived from volcanoes expelling gas trapped deep within Earth. However, a small part of the atmosphere may be the result of material brought to Earth by comets composed of dirty ice.

Hot springs tell us a lot. Today, they are common wherever new parts of the Earth's crust has formed. Hot springs are simply the surface sign of circulating groundwaters meeting new hot volcanic rocks. They expel gases and hot water, as they have done since the beginning of time on the planet, almost exactly like a radiator does for a hot car engine. Early Earth would have been far hotter than it is now because the radioactivity of the

Earth was greater then than now. Radioactivity is always most intense at the start. Radioactivity, by its nature, simply gets less over time. But whenever, wherever, a hot springs exists, it isn't a big deal in itself. Most of the water—and the gas—is simply recycled from hotter parts of the crust. But not all of it—often there are traces of material from deep within our planet, where the material volcanoes throw up comes from.

Today's hot springs show that some of Earth's atmosphere has come from gas-expelling volcanoes. This might have happened as one huge degassing event or a few burps over time or a continuous rumble of little burps, or all three. We don't know yet.

The early history of the Solar System involved the gravitational attraction of dust, meteorites and comets to form larger planetary masses. This process is still taking place. We saw the spectacular impact of the comet Shoemaker-Levy 9 on Jupiter on 16 July 1994. The massive gravity of Jupiter sucked in the comet and water, carbon disulphide, carbon dioxide and other materials were added to Jupiter. The planet accreted into a slightly larger mass. The impact of Shoemaker-Levy-9 was equivalent to 27 million Hiroshima bombs. The scour mark was the size of the Earth and debris was ejected into Jupiter's orbit. If Shoemaker-Levy-9 had hit Earth then our life-supporting warm wet volcanic planet would disappear.

Early in the history of Earth, a passing icy comet might have been captured by the Earth's gravitational field to crash onto Earth. Collisions of comets and asteroids in the Asteroid Belt between Jupiter and Mars bounce debris out of orbit. A cometary impact with Earth would be hard to detect and would have added huge amounts of water to our planet. Such comet impacts still occasionally occur. German medieval literature records that Earth was impacted by cometary material in November 1531 and November 1556. Every November, the Earth passes through the Beta Taurid stream of cometary material, broken off from the comet Enke. If planet Earth was to be wiped out by a massive cometary impact, the chances are that it would be in November. Guy Fawkes Day seems to be most appropriate.

We know more about one impact than any other. In remote Tunguska, Siberia, at 7.16 am, 30 June 1908 there was a massive explosion and fireball high in the sky. The local Ivenk tribe thought it was the wrath of Agdy, their God of Thunder, and Russian Orthodox Christians thought it was the beginning of The End and prayed. Only 800 people saw the fireball, windows were broken, people thrown 3 metres, wooden buildings damaged and passengers on a Trans-Siberian Railway train heard the bang though they were 350 kilometres away.

A seismic shock wave was recorded around the world. An atmospheric shock wave travelled twice around the Earth. The fine cosmic debris that dusted the Northern Hemisphere's high atmosphere reflected over-the-horizon light so that the sky was lit up after midnight.

But no crater at Tunguska. Thousands of trees fell in a butterfly-shaped area the size of London, leaving trees still standing at the centre, though stripped of boughs and leaves, while the rest splayed out in a radial pattern.

Experiments, atmospheric nuclear testing data and computer simulations show such a pattern is consistent with something travelling at 30° from the south-east and exploding high in the atmosphere. It has been calculated that the explosion of an extraterrestrial visitor 70 metres wide travelling at 25 kilometres per second took place at an altitude of some 8 to 10 kilometres. The explosion converted kinetic energy to thermal energy and there would have been a temperature of 100 000 °C at the site of the explosion. The ground beneath the explosion was seared and forest fires started in what had previously been pine and birch forests in waterlogged peat. It is the explosive equal of 1000 Hiroshima bombs—minor as these things go. If it had arrived six hours later it would have destroyed St Petersburg. Tunguska-sized or larger events occur somewhere every 300 years on average, and during recorded history, about 15 seems reasonable, with around 12 in oceans and the rest on land. Smaller events happen a lot more frequently. Planet Earth regularly takes hits and has near-misses from comets and asteriods. Every time you step outdoors a little cosmic dust settles on you.

As for Tunguska itself, the smart money is on the relics of a comet, probably from the Beta Taurid stream. There was little extraterrestial debris at the site and the lack of a crater favours a comet. Peat gets its nutrients from the atmosphere and the peat of 1908 has unusual carbon and hydrogen isotope signatures that hint of a cosmic source. Chromosomal abnormalities, cell deformations, reduced shapes and sterile buds form in plants there to a greater degree than any human-induced pollution or nuclear fallout effects.

Planet Earth has been cooling down for the last 4500 million years. Volcanoes and hot springs are still bringing heat from deep in the Earth to the surface. Early in the Earth's history, the landscape would have been not unlike that of the Moon. The cratered surface would have been stretched and pulled apart, violent earthquakes and volcanic eruptions were an everyday occurrence and the planet would have been shrouded in vapour and dust derived from the constant impacting. The temperature of the steamy carbon dioxide-rich atmosphere would have been so high that no water could condense into rain droplets. As the temperature of the atmosphere started to fall, it would eventually have rained. The first misty rains would have hit hot rocks and would have been converted back to steam but eventually both the surface of the Earth and the atmosphere were cool enough for rain to fall and for there to be running water to accumulate at the surface. The first rain, with dissolved carbon dioxide and sulphuric gases would have been extremely acid.

There was a window of opportunity for the appearance of life on Earth between 4150 and 3800 million years ago. This occurred after the last of the asteroid-sized ocean-vapourising impacts 4150 million years ago. Such impacts released so much energy that the atmosphere was heated to 1700 °C for a few months before steam condensed back to form the oceans. These impacts occurred every 10 to 100 million years. Any life that formed between these impact events would have been cooked and each major impact would have reset the clock on the timing of the appearance of sustainable life. Once ocean-vapourising impacting stopped, smaller impacts would have vapourised the photic zones of the oceans and high surface temperatures would have existed for hundreds of years. The photic zone, the upper 200 metres of ocean water, was vital for the survival of photosynthetic organisms needing sunlight. This has lent support to the theory that life started in the deep ocean.

Impact craters would have filled with hot water from rain and volcanic hot springs. Although the Sun was not nearly as bright as now, the greenhouse atmosphere of steam and carbon dioxide would have warmed the planet and kept the surface warm enough for water to be liquid. Corrosive hot spring waters would have eaten away at rocks to form a primitive soil but there were no animals, no plants, no lichen, no algae and no bacteria. Nothing. Just a rocky, scarred and barren surface.

As rainfall and water running over the hot surface became a regular occurrence, then the shifting of gravel, sand and mud down watercourses would have changed the face of Earth. The oldest known rocks which were once mud, silt, sand and gravel occur in Greenland. They are 3800 million years old. Although these old water-worn sediments on the first continents have since been twisted, buckled and cooked, they contain carbon compounds of biological origin. Carbon compounds of biological origin not only have a specific ratio of carbon 13 to carbon 12 but have an organisational structure of rings and chains unique to life. The Greenland rocks tell us that 3800 million years ago there must have been a solid crust which was undulating to allow erosion by water. Furthermore, as there was no vegetation on the land and rain was extremely acid, weathering would have been very intense and erosion far greater and faster than today. The fact that there was water 3800 million years ago shows that the atmosphere did moderate global temperatures and allow weathering and running water. Some of the iron-rich sediments such as iron-rich carbonate rocks and iron-rich oxide rocks show that the atmosphere had a very low oxygen content and carbon dioxide was being cycled from the atmosphere to form rocks.

The organisation of life into more complex colonies took no more than 300 million years. There are fossils of bacterial colonies called stromatolites which occur in 3500-million-year-old hot spring precipitates in Western Australia. Stromatolites occur from 3500 million years ago to the present. Modern stromatolites can be seen today in the warm coastal waters such as Shark Bay, Western Australia. For the next 3000 million years after the first appearance of stromatolites, only simple single-celled life thrived on Earth.

Early life was prokaryotic, then, about 2700 million years ago eukaryotic organisms such as photosynthetic algae appeared. Prokaryotic cells lack a wall around their nucleus and eukaryotics have that wall. Rocks of about 2700 million years ago hint at the presence of large sterane molecules that are decay products of cholesterol and similar compounds produced by eukaryotes, and by 2100 million years ago, the rocks have distinct eukaryotic fossils. Eukaryotes diversified 1100 to 900 million years ago, the first multicellular animals appeared 700 to 543 million years ago, and this profound change was the foundation for the explosion of life 540 to 520 million years ago.

As soon as there was running water on the hot surface of Earth, there was life. The same scenario is expected on Mars. The exact mechanism of converting complex organic molecules into self-replicating molecules or simple cells has not yet been synthesised in the laboratory. However, on all the wet rocky volcanic planets, life is the fastest way to process chemical energy and information. The reason why there is life on Earth is that for 3800 million years, Earth has been at an appropriate distance from its source of warmth such that the water was neither completely converted to steam nor completely converted to ice. During the 800-million-year-period that Mars had running water, there was probably also life on Mars. During the period of massive impacting from 4500 to 3800 million years ago, carbonaceous chondrite meteorites such as the Allende meteorite covered the surface of the primitive Earth with the building blocks of life.

Even the rather small 2-tonne Allende meteorite contained 100 kilograms of complex organic molecules. Meteorite messengers from space contain more than 50 different amino acids, of which eight are common protein-building types. Halley's Comet may contain up to 25 per cent organic material. Even interstellar space contains organic molecules such as hydrogen cyanide, aldehydes and alcohols. In the 1950s Stanley Miller recreated the early Earth's atmosphere in a jar and, not having lightning at his ready disposal, passed a high voltage spark through the jar. He produced amino acids. Here was the first evidence that the building blocks of life could have been created on a barren Earth. Other possible early atmosphere compositions can also produce complex organic molecules after a high voltage discharge. However, the next step was not achieved. Amino acids could not be combined to form self-replicating molecules which evolve into complex cells. There was no shortage of materials for the building blocks of life on Earth. Other meteorites brought catalysts such as platinum to the surface of Earth and corrosive hot springs formed clays and zeolites that can also act as catalysts. Earth was ready for life. Although the Earth's surface was still hot, the mixture of catalysts and a great diversity of complex organic molecules was a scene set for the formation of self-replicating molecules.

Some meteorites and impact debris contain buckyballs, tiny cages of carbon molecules containing some 60 or more carbon atoms. Trapped inside these cages are extraterrestrial gases pulled out of interstellar space. Such finds pretty well show that complex organic compounds can survive the plunge to Earth, that very complex carbon compounds form in space and hint that buckyballs could have formed in the atmospheres of old stars, red giants, in the twilight of their lives.

Some scientists have even suggested that Earth was seeded by life from elsewhere in space. The eminent astronomer Sir Fred Hoyle and Chandra Wickramasinghe proposed in 1980 that simple life forms were formed in space and brought to Earth by comets. Some scientists became apoplectic and others uncharitably suggested that Hoyle was on the downward slide from the pinnacle of his career. Now, a quarter of a century later, this outlandish idea is quite acceptable to many scientists who suffer the same mortal frailties as anyone else on Earth when confronted with an idea ahead of its time.

In 1994 the tell-tale signature of the amino acid glycine was detected in the interstellar cloud of Sagittarius B2. Such clouds are where stars, planets and comets form. In early 2000 Indian scientists used computer models to show that interstellar clouds can produce vast amounts of adenine, one of the four amino acids that form DNA. Because of the amount of energy emitted from interstellar clouds, the expected weak spectral signal of adenine is swamped. As NASA now has a large amount of information on the conditions in space, experiments replicating the conditions in interstellar clouds can now be undertaken. The work by Allamandola and colleagues at NASA using synthetic starlight, high vacuums, ultra-cold temperatures, gas and interstellar dust has produced very common biochemicals. The great surprise was that tiny spheres which resemble empty cells were also formed. With a bit of cometary re-organisation, these biochemicals could fill the spheres and, after cometary impacting with Earth, such spheres are ready to spring into life.

RNA may have been the first self-replicating molecule because, like DNA, it is composed of chemical bases that spell out the genetic code but, like protein, RNA is capable of a remarkable array of chemical reactions. RNA molecules can split and produce an enzyme that can act as a catalyst for replication. This splitting occurs in the laboratory at temperatures of 40 °C, a pH of 7.5 to 9 and some magnesium present in solution. Such conditions exist in hot springs and the RNA world of early Earth may have existed in between the layers of clay minerals, inside the tubes of zeolite minerals or in the fractures and pore spaces of volcanic rocks. Both clays and zeolites form from the action of hot springs on volcanic rocks and both minerals are catalysts. Did these minerals catalyse RNA into a self-replicating molecule? It is probable that the ability to replicate was acquired long before the first cell appeared on the scene. Another intriguing study with RNA showed that when RNA is added to a mixture of nucleic acids in the presence of zinc, sequences up to 40 bases in length are copied with an error rate as low as 1 per cent.

Life may have begun as a weird molecular hybrid, half protein and half RNA. It has been argued that the death knell for pre-biotic RNA is because RNA's backbone is composed of sugar groups that are unstable and do not easily form chains. However, this may not be true for RNA's chemical relative, the chimera-like peptide nucleic acid (PNA). The bases of PNA are joined together with sugar-free links like those in proteins. Some 80 per cent of plausible pre-biotic chemicals transform into PNA backbone sub-units, especially at a temperature of 100 °C, a crustal temperature that was common on early Earth.

The next stage in self replication could have involved the development of proteins from amino acids. Later still, DNA must form to take over as the genetic library. The production of membranes, which allow the orderly management of an energy supply and metabolism, would then be necessary. This DNA, common to all life, is very strong evidence that all life derived from a common ancestor. Since the first life there has been great biodiversity. At present, at least 5 million distinct species exist and, over time, there have been hundreds of millions of species. The first cells on Earth were primitive, had poorly developed metabolic systems and could only survive if they were surrounded by nutrients which they could absorb. Again, a hot spring environment provides these conditions.

Those uncomfortable with an extraterrestrial source for the building blocks of life need look no further than volcanoes and their associated hot springs. Methane and heavier hydrocarbons, complex organic compounds and amino acids are belched out from volcanoes. Science is poised to make the ultimate step towards our first ancestor and I expect that simple self-replicating life will probably be synthesised within the next 50 years.

Jupiter has two thirds of the planetary mass of the Solar System. Jupiter's composition resembles that of a small star. Its internal pressure is huge. Its magnetic field is immense and stretches millions of kilometres into the solar system. The planet is electrically active and pours billions of watts of electrical energy into the Earth's magnetic field each day. Jupiter has 16 moons and a huge complex atmosphere which bristles with lightning and swirls with huge storm systems. The largest atmospheric storm on Jupiter has probably lasted for 300 years.

The Galileo Spacecraft has given us a much better understanding of Jupiter and its moons. Launched on 18 October 1989, it entered Jupiter's orbit on 7 December 1995. The closest and largest moon, Io, is a remarkable place. It is constantly squeezed, stretched and heated by Jupiter's immense gravity. As a result, the moon's tortured innards are twisting and turning and volcanoes are constantly erupting at the surface. These strange volcanoes enrich the atmosphere in sodium and it appears that this atmosphere is around the moon's equator. The rest of the atmosphere is swept away by electric fields generated on Io as it passes through Jupiter's magnetic field. Sodium ions swept off Io form a cloud around Jupiter.

Another one of Jupiter's moons, Europa, appears to have a liquid salty ocean between and beneath a cracked icy crust. The crust of ice is 10 to 15 kilometres thick. The lack of craters on Europa shows that the crust is a mere 10 million years old and is constantly being reworked. With constant reworking, all old craters are destroyed. The crust is like crazy paving where ice has broken into a jigsaw of tabular blocks. Between the blocks is a dark red ice which was soft when the blocks broke and moved. The movement pattern of the ice shows that the ice moves over a liquid and not over a solid. Pits, domes, ridges and dark spots can result from brittle ice riding on a thicker ice layer that is warm enough to deform and flow, as glaciers do on Earth. Warmer ice shoulders its way to the surface creating the crazy paving pattern and Europa's tides have created chains of crescent-shaped cracks, each 100 kilometres long, which stretch across the surface.

The gravity of Europa and Jupiter's strong magnetic field have created electrical currents inside Europa which, in turn, create a magnetic field within Europa. Although gravity measurements of Europa show that a light material such as ice or water extends down to 100 kilometres before rock takes over, a conducting shell in salty water a few kilometres beneath Europa's icy crust makes sense. Although the surface temperature of Europa at −145 °C is too cool for life, the enormous gravitational field of Jupiter kneads away at Europa's interior, warming it with squeezing and pulling. Europa has a thin oxygen-bearing atmosphere and an ionosphere derived from its weak magnetic field. Such a dynamic watery moon might be the place for primitive life which requires water, nutrients and no sunlight. We now know that such life still exists on Earth and was probably the earliest life on Earth. If such life appeared on Earth, why not on Europa? Another one of Jupiter's moons, Callisto, may also have a subsurface ocean which could contain life.

We get a clue to the seeding of Earth from elsewhere in space by considering the plight of the world's unluckiest dog. On 28 June 1911, a perfectly innocent dog in Nakhla, Egypt was quietly minding its own business when it was flattened by a piece of a larger meteorite which had just exploded into 40 pieces in the atmosphere. These pieces fell to the ground. This was no ordinary stony, stony-iron or iron meteorite that vapourised the canine critter. It was not even a rarer type of stony meteorite such as a carbonaceous chondrite. It was one of only 13 known Martian meteorites that led to the dog's dreadful demise.

Another Martian meteorite called ALH84001 was a piece of the surface of Mars that had been impacted so intensely by a large meteorite that a fragment of the Martian crust was thrown out of the gravitational field of Mars 16 million years ago. The fragment went for a long trip in space, during which time it was bombarded by cosmic rays before it was caught in the Earth's gravitational field and fell on the icy surface of Antarctica 13 000 years ago. This 1.94 kilogram meteorite, collected in Antarctica in 1984, was re-examined by NASA in 1996 with state of the art equipment. It told a great story.

The meteorite contained minute quantities of the thin carbon dioxide-nitrogen Martian atmosphere trapped in the pores and cracks. From visits to Mars, we have measured a very thin atmosphere dominated by carbon dioxide. The red planet may well have started its planetary history with a thick carbon dioxide atmosphere. Our nearest neighbour was either a greenhouse or the atmosphere may have existed as clouds of frozen carbon dioxide, dry ice. Such dry ice in the Martian upper atmosphere would be at $-100\ °C$ and the very small particle size would scatter infra-red radiation back to the surface to give temperatures of $25\ °C$, warm enough for liquid water. Early Mars may well have been a far more benign place than early Earth and might have been perfect for the first life in the solar system.

The Martian meteorite ALH84001 also had globules of calcium carbonate that had the chemical signature of life and minute filament-shaped tubes of magnetic iron oxide and iron sulphides that were possibly fossils of bacteria. This might be the clue for early life on Mars that many scientists expected. The calcium carbonate globules were rich in polycyclic aromatic hydrocarbons (PAHs). Biological matter can be converted to PAHs after death or by gentle heat, the best example being the black crust on a well-done steak. PAHs are not unique to ALH84001 and have been found in many meteorites that formed without life. Did the PAHs in ALH84001 form by non-biological methods or result from contamination on Earth? The NASA scientists concluded in 1996: 'None of these observations is in itself proof for the existence of past life. [But] ... when they are considered collectively, ... we conclude that they are evidence of primitive life on Mars.'

This discovery led to a great flurry of speculation about whether the filament structures were fossils, whether the chemical signature was from another source, whether ALH84001 had been contaminated by micro-organisms in the atmosphere or Antarctica, and whether life can exist in extreme conditions. It was initially argued that, because of the very small size of the filament-shaped tubes in ALH84001, the genetic material for reproduction of life could not be stored in such a small volume. Since the investigation of ALH84001, similar structures which could be bacterial fossils have been found by NASA in the Nakhla meteorite. These structures resemble bacterial flagellae.

However, there has been a recent discovery of filament-like bacteria of the same size as possible Martian bacteria fossils in rocks from deep oil wells. The samples were from more than 3 to 5 kilometres beneath the sea bed on the north-west shelf of Australia and were cooked to 115 to 170 °C. These minute virus-sized bacteria, called nanobes, were dormant in rocks for hundreds of millions of years, had little selection pressure and may represent a missing biosphere deep in the Earth's crust. They occur in the pores of rocks and in the spaces between clay layers. Nanobes are the size of the postulated fossil bacteria in ALH84001, contain a cell wall, DNA and reproduce. The nanobes are the smallest life discovered to date on Earth and certainly don't conform to our current understanding of life. We therefore must change our view of life on Earth. What is even more bizarre here is what happened when nanobe-bearing rocks were examined with a scanning electron microscope. This required the samples to be in a vacuum, blasted with high speed electrons and X-rays and heated to a high temperature. After scanning electron microscopy, colonies of nanobes started to grow in the samples. If minute bacteria such as nanobes seeded Earth from Mars or elsewhere in space, the scanning electron microscopy operating conditions show that they certainly could survive space travel and entry into the Earth's atmosphere.

A diversity of geologists, mineralogists, chemists, crystallographers and microbiologists undertook research on ALH84001 for three years. Some studies showed that rare chemicals were added to ALH84001 by impact shock on Mars and not by contamination from the Earth's atmosphere. The chemical signature formed in a closed system at high temperatures and not by interaction with the Earth's atmosphere with ALH84001. Volcanic rocks from deep in Earth have micro-organisms of similar shape to the proposed micro-organisms from ALH84001. There is still no consensus regarding the controversial claims of fossil micro-organisms in ALH84001, illustrating the extreme difficulty in recognising obscure and new types of life. Scientists are an argumentative sceptical lot and these qualities guarantee a dispassionate evolution of knowledge. Time and a few well-planned Martian missions will tell.

If life ever existed on Mars, would clues be visible from Earth? The immediate answer is no, but, upon reflection, yes. A discovery in a salt lake, Salda Gölü Turkey, of magnesium carbonate-rich mounds built by rare living stromatolites, single-celled cyanobacteria, might just be the clue to life on Mars. Stromatolites typically precipitate distinctive layers of calcium carbonate. If life on Earth emerged some 4200 to 3800 million years ago, the then predominant rock types on the surface of Earth would have been magnesium-rich volcanic rocks. Such ancient rocks are still preserved in Greenland, Western Australia, Canada and South Africa. Seepages, hot springs and lakes associated with these rocks on early Earth would have precipitated magnesite (magnesium carbonate) or hydromagnesite. Such environments, although very rare, still exist on Earth and the presence of large white mounds of living stromatolites composed of hydromagnesite in Salda Gölü might be an analogue for Martian life or early life on Earth. White Rock near the margin of a 90-kilometre wide crater in Sabaea Terra on Mars could be magnesium carbonate precipitated where ground waters seeped into an ancient evaporating crater lake. White Rock and a similar area of white rock on the western margin of Juventae Chasma on Mars could be a complex of stromatolite mounds.

With our knowledge of life on Earth, nanobes and possible fossil bacteria in ALH84001, what is the possibility of there being life on Mars? Some years ago, we might have argued that given the modern Martian atmosphere and the absence of surface water, there is little chance of life still being on the surface of Mars. Most life on Earth is and always has been microscopic bacteria. The total biomass of plants and macrofauna (including humans) is minuscule compared to the total biomass of bacterial micro-organisms. Newly discovered forms of life, such as nanobes, and bacterial life in a great diversity of extreme environments suggest life on Mars might not be out of the question. If life is to be on Mars or elsewhere, it is most likely bacterial, like the most abundant life on Earth which has survived the tests of time and all sorts of extreme environments.

Evidence of past liquid water on Mars has recently been found, of subsurface aquifers, scars from flows of water-bearing slurry and ice. Deep valleys on Mars fill with morning fog and nightly frosts are burned off once the Sun gets higher. Colonies of bacterial life on Mars might now be in subsurface aquifers or fractured rock deep below the surface of the red planet. Given the evidence for surface water on Mars for at least the first 800 million years, the smaller size of the planet, its distance from the Sun and its more rapid cooling history, life might well have emerged on Mars before it did here. With the knowledge of the crater size and impact intensity on the Moon, we are able to calculate the order of events on the Moon. By using material collected from the Moon, we now have a much more precise history of lunar impacting and can use the same methods for Mars.

The impact history and age of events on Mars can be roughly calculated from the size and intensity of impacting. During the Martian Noachian Era 4600 to 3500 million years ago, Mars was a wet planet. From the Martian Hesperian Era 3500 to 1800 million years ago to the present, there was no surface water. A Northern Ocean on Mars probably occupied the northern lowlands during the Noachian Era and river patterns with terraces, layered sedimentary rocks and channels have been recognised. Old lake systems have been recognised in the highlands. These former wet sites are the places worth exploring for fossil Martian life.

The possibility of there being life on Mars has been one of the most tantalising scientific speculations since the time of Galileo. The possibility of advanced life on Mars has captured the imagination of the public, especially those with cranial hardware and software problems. For example, in 1877, the Italian astronomer Giovanni Schiaparelli recorded *canali* on the surface of Mars. A combination of poor Italian (*canali* are channels, not canals) and a fertile imagination led various Americans to paint pictures of a planet running out of water and an advanced civilisation forced to build gigantic irrigation ditches to transport polar water to the more equatorial, temperate plains. Once this idea gripped the popular imagination, the seasonal changes of colour on the Martian surface were interpreted as the annual growth of lichens, not the boring effects of wind-blown dust.

Photographs taken by Mariner 6 and 7 in 1969, Mariner 9 in 1971 and landings by Viking 1976, Sojourner 1997 and Mars Global Surveyor

1999-2000 missions showed that there are no advanced civilisations, no face on Mars and no evidence of previous great feats by extraterrestrials. Just a dead planet with two little moons.

On Mars, there are extinct volcanoes. The largest, Olympus Mons, is three times bigger than Mt Everest and even the smallest of the triplet of the Tharsis volcanoes dwarfs Hawaii, the largest volcano on Earth. The new volcanic rock erupted on Mars needed to be cooled into solid rock, the most efficient mechanism was probably water-cooling. Such water-cooling leaves its mark on the surface as hot springs. A huge equatorial rift zone the distance from Perth to Sydney stretches across Mars. The red planet has polar caps of solid carbon dioxide, evidence of water and large deserts with extensive plains pitted with meteorite impact craters. The red planet is red because of the constant dust storms which, at times, engulf the whole planet. Martian dust storms are very little different from those on Earth. In 1997 the Mars Pathfinder observed five dust storms up to 80 metres wide and 350 metres high visible for 7 minutes suggesting the surface of Mars is constantly reworked.

The Martian atmosphere is a tenuous veil rather than the thick blanket which cloaks Venus and Earth. At the surface of Mars, the atmosphere has a pressure of 1 per cent of the Earth's atmosphere at sea level. Mars is cold and arid but its surface has the tell-tale signs that liquid water once raged through flood channels, dendritic valleys and mud flows. Ice may have moved as glaciers. Water still exists on Mars as daily frost and fog. The March 1999 pictures taken by the Mars Global Surveyor created great excitement. Fresh water-cut gullies were observed and these are unscarred by impacting and not covered by dust. They occur on crater and valley walls as deep V-shaped channels a few kilometres long. The gullies have a collapsed region at the top and a pile of debris at the bottom. This suggests that they formed relatively recently during sudden floods. Such features on Earth form from water. On Mars, these channels could form if the water table is more than 100 metres deep thereby keeping water liquid by the pressure of the overlying rock. When exposed on a steep slope, this water freezes. More water then builds up behind the dam until it eventually bursts through the ice, and a flash flood carves a channel.

The carving out of such features on Mars by water has been questioned. It is also possible that such features could form from outbursts of liquid carbon dioxide rather than water. If this is the case, then Mars could have been cool, dry and lifeless for the last 3500 million years. The collapse of steep unstable terrains on Mars could have been facilitated by a flow of liquid carbon dioxide, dust and rubble which could carve out channels. But these features appear in the coldest regions of Mars, near the poles and on shady slopes. Furthermore, the cruel irony is that these channels occur on such steep unstable slopes that they would not be accessible by a human in a spacesuit or a robot. Notwithstanding the unimaginable difficulty in checking these sites on Mars, wherever there is liquid water, organic molecules and energy on Earth, there is life and such observations increase the probability of there being life on Mars.

Again, the meteorite ALH84001 reveals another insight into Mars. The modern Martian atmosphere is highly enriched in the heavy isotope of nitrogen whereas no such enrichment is recorded for ALH84001. Solar wind preferentially removes light nitrogen and the Martian atmosphere would have been isotopically layered and enriched in heavy nitrogen. The meteorite ALH84001 looks as though it came from a time when the atmosphere had not been removed. The Global Surveyor has shown that Mars no longer has a magnetic field but, in its youth, the field was very strong. The internal energy, heat, that drove its magnetic dynamo run out early in Martian history and, as long as there was a magnetic field, the planet was protected from solar wind. Once the magnetic field disappeared, solar wind decomposed the Martian atmosphere and oceans and dispersed it in space.

The 1200-million-year-old piece of Mars which fell to Earth as the Nakhla meteorite contains high levels of water-soluble materials such as sodium, chloride, sulphates, magnesium and calcium. Such salts fairly closely mimic the salts in the Earth's ocean. An evaporating brine may have deposited these salts in the cracks of the Martian surface. These surface rocks were later blasted from Mars by impacting and fell on Earth. Again, there are tantalising clues that Mars once had water and may well still have water.

How can Mars have liquid water? It is $-53\,°C$ on the surface and reaches only $25\,°C$ at midday at the equator in mid-summer.

Mars probably had a carbon dioxide-nitrogen atmosphere early in its history. Despite humans pumping out carbon dioxide for a few hundred years of late, carbon dioxide's glory days are long over, now making up less than 1/1000th of the air we breathe. Liquid water renders carbon dioxide unstable, dissolves such an atmosphere during the weathering of rocks and locks it up as carbonate minerals on the sea floor. We have the proof beneath our feet: limestone, for example. If Mars too had such an atmosphere and its atmospheric pressure was equivalent to 5 or 10 times modern Earth's, then the greenhouse effect would have been easily sufficient to hold water on a warm wet planet. Clouds of solid carbon dioxide too could have kept early Mars warm, even at much lower pressures. But if that was once the case, where are the carbonate rocks and other sediments?

Earth's internal heat engine pushes the crust around and recycles water and rocks in a process called plate tectonics. Plate tectonics may have operated on Venus too. But the internal fires within Mars just couldn't get the crust moving. Carbon dioxide production began to lag behind carbon dioxide destruction in new carbonate minerals, and the atmosphere eventually shrank dramatically. The thermal emission spectrometers on the Mars Global Surveyor spacecraft looking for telltale carbon dioxide emissions from carbon-oxygen-bearing rocks didn't find any on the surface, but meteorites smashing their way deep into the planet perhaps did: all Martian meteorites contain faint traces of carbonates.

The death of the atmosphere on Mars is most likely due to a combination of events and processes. Mars went through a torrid time called the Late Heavy Bombardment which would have eroded it rapidly. Not having the recycling capacity of Earth, what was lost was gone for good. What was left was stripped away by ions of the solar wind travelling at 400 kilometres a second. In what very little is left, and in meteorite ALH84001, there are a lot of isotopes of rare gases like xenon 129, supporting the idea Mars lost its atmosphere early in its history.

Minute amounts of water in a 12-gram Martian meteorite found in Antarctica formed 4500 million years ago in molten rock deep within Mars were examined. The isotopes of oxygen and hydrogen suggested 70 to 80 per cent of Mars' water had already left the planet.

Although Mars did have running water, there is no evidence it had it long. Short sharp local events like an outburst of groundwater could have triggered a short warm wet period, maybe all that was needed for life to appear on the planet. Life as we understand it, needs water, but maybe it doesn't need as much as we have thought. On our own planet we are finding bacteria in surprising environments, as we shall see.

There is one last intriguing possibility to be raised on the origin on planetary life: seeding. The very presence on Earth of these rare Martian meteorites proves large impacts can blast material from one planet to the next and so on. We are in a Martian impact splash zone. The mechanism of seeding is a reality. Investigations of nanobes strongly suggest they, for one lifeform, might survive a space flight. It also suggests we don't have to worry too much about a manned mission returning with rocks from Mars and starting a pandemic or minor mass extinction. Have large impacts on Earth seeded, say, a moon on an outer planet? Have we nieces on Io? Whatever, our knowledge of primitive life here and Martian geology strongly suggests, one way or another, records of primitive life in rocks and perhaps living things will be found on Mars and possibly elsewhere in space.

On Earth, life is being found in more and more bizarre environments. Primitive bacterial life on Earth can survive at temperatures from $-15\,°C$ to $+170\,°C$. Early life on Earth thrived in environments above $80\,°C$ and life still thrives in terrestrial and submarine hot springs in acid, toxic waters. Bacteria not only occur on the surface but also in the dark at the bottom of the deepest coldest oceans, in toxic metal-rich hot springs and in hot pressurised rocks at a depth of 5 kilometres. Bacteria have been resurrected from watery inclusions in 250-million-year-old salt beds and from 120-million-year-old opal from Lightning Ridge. Even the clouds contain bacteria. For every cubic centimetre of water condensed from clouds, there are 1500 bacteria.

At Paralana in the far north Flinders Ranges of South Australia, bubbles of helium and radon from radioactive decay surge through a highly radioactive toxic hot spring. The heat and toxic chemicals come from natural nuclear fission. The water is alkaline and at $62\,°C$. The water contains more than fifty species of bacteria, some of which are non-photosynthetic and derive their energy from the hot water. Mats of cyanobacteria thrive in this hot highly radioactive water, cover the floor of the thermal pool and precipitate carbonates and bicarbonates. The cyanobacteria are rich in uranium. The cyanobacteria have found a niche where they are protected from multicellular animals that might make a meal of them and DNA tests show that the cyanobacteria have the same genetic characteristics as bacteria that thrive in the cooling systems of nuclear power stations. The Paralana hot springs are a window into the past on Earth, Mars and elsewhere.

If you undertake science in unusual places, then unusual results can be expected. Bacteria thrive beneath modern glaciers. There is water beneath some 500 metres of ice at Lake Vostok, a 14 000 square kilometre frozen lake on the Antarctic Plateau which formed some 25 million years ago. Life is constrained by the supply of carbon and energy and, in the cold dark isolation of Lake Vostok, both are likely to be scarce. However, Lake Vostok may be part of the Earth that is being wrenched into a rift and the floor of the lake could have numerous hot springs. In the deep ocean, such hot springs form oases for living communities of bacteria and strange complex creatures. Organisms are not fussy whether the carbon comes from an oil seep or old organisms from former times and organisms don't care whether energy is from the Sun, chemical reactions or hot springs. It is all carbon and energy. Such an unusual habitat on Earth might be just the setting envisaged for life on Europa, Jupiter's fourth-largest moon.

Life can emerge on any wet rocky volcanic planet. The first life on Earth was minute rod-shaped, filamentous and spheroidal bacteria-like cells. The spheroidal bacteria are very similar to algae. It has long been known that primitive bacterial life on Earth needed no oxygen, obtained nutrients dissolved in water and thrived in water at more than 80 °C. Close relatives of such life still exist in bogs and swamps. In fact, we walk around with our very own large intestinal bacterial colonies which are very similar to the oldest life on Earth. Life which generated nutrients from sunlight (photosynthetic) or chemical energy (chemosynthetic) were the next forms of life to appear on Earth. Thermophilic bacteria are found in almost all hot springs on land. Unlike ancient hot springs, modern hot springs abound in oxygen. Many are strongly acid, rich in highly toxic metals such as mercury, arsenic, antimony, selenium, tellurium and thallium. What looks like brown and green mud in the hot springs are really thermophilic bacteria which thrive in extremely acid water at temperatures up to 120 °C.

In 1977 another new form of primitive bacterial life was discovered in hot springs in the medial rifts of the mid-ocean ridges. Mid-ocean ridges are rift zones resulting from the tearing apart of the ocean floor and the injection of molten rock from deep in the mantle onto the sea floor. By this very rapid geological process, ocean basins expand. Circulating sea water cools the new volcanic rocks. The hot water leaches metals from rocks and debouches as hot springs into the ocean through chimneys. The high temperature hot springs (black smokers) contain myriads of particles of iron, zinc and copper sulphide minerals which are carried out of the chimney by very hot water. Lower temperature white smokers contain particles of barium and calcium sulphates. The largest known active black smoker chimney, affectionately known as Godzilla, was 45 metres high. Godzilla collapsed onto the sea floor and, within five years, grew back to more than 20 metres high. Black smokers naturally pollute a large a part of the ocean and may well be the future sites for the mining of copper, zinc, silver and gold.

Black smokers occur at depths of 2 to 5 kilometres below sea level. In this dark environment, toxic acid hot springs can be 420 °C and the water pressure is tremendous. Thermophilic bacteria thrive in such an environment though the sea water temperature near these springs is around 2 °C. In black smokers, more than 300 species of bacteria live in a toxic brew at high temperature and high pressure. Such bacteria are capable of metabolising rotten-egg gas, a process which is the sea floor equivalent of photosynthesis. Feeding off these bacteria is a recently-discovered ecosystem comprising worms, crabs, shrimps and fish. Fossilised black smokers have been found in rocks of all ages on Earth. One would suppose that this was hardly the place for life yet these hot springs contain thermophilic or heat-loving bacteria in an oxygen-poor environment.

The recently-discovered fossilised thread-like micro-organisms in 3000-million-year-old fossilised black smokers in Western Australia are little different from those in modern black smokers. Such ancient fossils strengthen the idea that life on Earth began in black smokers deep beneath the sea. These hot springs would have been ideal for nurturing life: they provided a constant supply of nutrients and energy, and were protected from the ultraviolet radiation and asteroids bombarding the Earth's surface.

In drill holes deep in the Earth's crust, thermophilic bacteria have been found in the cracks of hot rocks under very high pressure. Thermophilic bacteria gain energy from the hot springs or hot rocks and obtain their nutrients from the dissolved materials in the hot springs or the surface of minerals in the cracks in rocks. It is the general consensus that if there were present or past life to be found on Mars, then it would be thermophilic bacteria. When the Viking mission landed on Mars in 1976 with the mission to search for past and present life on Mars, thermophilic bacteria had not been dis-covered on Earth!

The first life on Earth need not have first formed at the surface in a soupy mixture of clay, water and organic material as has been commonly assumed. Life could have formed beneath the surface in hot springs or volcanic lakes like those in New Zealand, Yellowstone National Park or Iceland. The recent discoveries of heat-loving bacteria in extremely hostile environments deep in the Earth and in acid hot springs have revealed another possibility for the origin of life on Earth. Life on Earth might have started in wet fractures in hot rocks at depth, hot springs at mid ocean ridges or in volcanic environments. Hot springs and cracks in rocks supply carbon dioxide, methane and nitrogen gases necessary for organic molecules and there is a supply of the necessary trace elements such as potassium, sodium, phosphorus, manganese, iron, nickel, zinc, selenium and molybdenum. Seems a perfectly sensible place to start the game of life by being away from the photic zone, which periodically was vapourised by impacting, and protected from solar radiation.

The appearance of life on Earth was no accident: it was a certainty. It was the inevitable consequence of changes to the crust, atmosphere and oceans of a wet rocky volcanic planet. Water is a unique banana-shaped molecule which allows it to be the matrix of life. Maybe the meaning of life is an understanding of water in biological processes. Since the first life on Earth, the four parts of the planet comprising the crust, atmosphere, oceans and life have been interacting. All of the great changes on Earth have occurred as a result of the interaction of these parts. When we add time, then anything is possible.

While the planet was getting on with the business of forming life and cooling down, new crust was forming by melting and removal of the lighter components from the mantle. The early Earth's crust was hot because of the excess heat from the radioactive decay of uranium, potassium and thorium. The Earth's mantle was some 300 °C hotter than at present and volcanoes spewed out very high-temperature lavas in the first 2000 million years. Such lavas do not occur today. When the first surface on Earth solidified, it was barren. No plants, no animals, no running water. The Earth was receiving about 30 per cent less radiation from the early Sun, which was faint, but the crust was receiving probably four times as much heat from the depths as at present. The rate of spin of Earth was probably three times the present rate, centrifugal forces would have concentrated the crust at the equator and the shorter length of the day accelerated surface heating and cooling. Calculations suggest that the atmosphere had at least 4 per cent carbon dioxide, which although the early Sun was faint, would have given a surface temperature of at least 11 °C. The high quantities of water vapour and ammonia in the early atmosphere would have raised this surface temperature.

The early crust has been intensely and repeatedly cooked, folded and broken, and the remaining pieces of the very old jigsaw almost defy reconstruction. The crust became thicker as more and more volcanic material was erupted during the cooling of the Earth. It is still cooling. Because the Earth's crust has had thousands of millions of years of constant recycling, there are only very small remnants of this early crust left as pieces of the jigsaw in Western Australia, Greenland, Canada and South Africa. There are some veiled clues about the early history of the Earth written in stone. The oldest dated material on Earth is 4400 million years old. Most old rocks have been remelted and recycled. Recently, a 40-square-kilometre area of rock 4010 million years old has been found in Canada. In Canada, Australia, South Africa and Greenland there are probably other undiscovered small blocks of material which have not been recycled. The consistent age of meteorites of 4550 million years suggests this is the minimum age for the Earth and the Solar System.

The early history of Earth we can deduce from both Earth and lunar studies. There is one line of evidence to show that the Moon is made of green cheese. Lunar rock 10017 has a shock wave velocity of 1.84 kilometres per second. This velocity is an indirect measurement of the composition of rocks. A study of the shock wave velocities of cheese shows that there are variations such as 1.65 km/sec (Münster, USA), 1.72 km/sec (Emmental, Switzerland), 1.75 km/sec (Cheddar, UK), 1.75 km/sec (Provolone, Italy) and 1.83 km/sec (Gjetost, Norway). The Moon is therefore made of green cheese. What's more, it is made of Gjetost, a Norwegian green cheese! Although there is one piece of evidence to suggest that the Moon is made of green cheese, there are numerous other bodies of evidence which show that this is not the case. A lunar composition of green cheese is not coherent with evidence from direct sampling, lunar mapping, lunar magnetism, lunar gravity, orbital features and the reflection of sunlight from the Moon. If the Moon is indeed made of green cheese, then all other observations and measurements must be in agreement with a cheese composition. They are not and, accordingly, the theory that the Moon is made of green cheese is rejected. This is the way science works.

Measurements of moonquakes show the Moon's crust to be 60 kilometres thick. The light coloured highlands are of a rock which once existed as a scum on the molten Moon. These rocks separated 4600 to 4100 million years ago and were essentially solid crust 4350 million years ago. Then the solid crust was continually pock marked by impacts that punched through and released large amounts of basalt lava from within the mantle to flow over the surface, filling the craters and creating darker lunar seas that we see easily from Earth.

Early in its existence gravity pulled molten iron into a core, giving the Moon a magnetic field. Radioactive heating in the mantle sent a single plume of molten rock to the surface, hence the concentration of seas on one side of the Moon. The core cooled and became solid, so the Moon lost its magnetic field.

The story of Earth is very similar. Heavy liquid iron would have trickled down to the centre of Earth to form the core. This concentration of mass towards the centre of Earth would have resulted in Earth spinning faster with shorter days. In the Earth-Moon system as the Earth's spin slowed, the Moon moved further away from Earth. The mantle concentrated above the core and lighter material or material that was not stable in mantle rocks moved out to the crust to form a scum. Unlike the Moon, the Earth did not expel all of its volatiles and many of the original Solar System gases are still trapped in the mantle. The volatiles within the Earth are still being expelled and their presence prevented the Earth from building a thicker crust. Although the inner core froze, the outer core is still liquid and provides the Earth with a magnetic field. The slightly fluid mantle has very sluggish large convection currents carrying heat from deep in the Earth to the upper mantle. Some of the heat in our planet has derived from the original heat from the solar system and most of it now derives from the heat released by the radioactive breakdown of potassium, uranium and thorium deep in the Earth. It is these massive convection currents which break up continents and stitch them back together again.

The separation of the crust into lighter continental crust and heavier ocean floor crust started at least 3800 million years ago. The earliest fragments of crust are still preserved and are composed of rocks which have been heated, bent and broken many times. Nevertheless, we can see a variety of rocks ranging from once very high temperature lavas similar in composition to the mantle, sodium-rich granite and old sediments including muds, silts, sands and gravels. In the gravels there are fragments of lava that had exploded from volcanoes, hot spring precipitates and feldspar-rich rock rather like the rocks in the lunar highlands. The most important feature is that there was running water on early Earth. There has never been running water on the Moon.

The growth of the Earth's crust was episodic. Continents came and continents went. Periods of supercontinent formation were at 2700 to 2600 million years ago, 1900 to 1700 million years ago and 1300 to 1000 million years ago and very little new crust formed in the periods 2500 to 2200 million years ago and 1650 to 1350 million years ago. The supercontinent Rodinia was fragmented 800 to 600 million years ago and, in the period 650 to 550 million years ago, another supercontinent formed. This supercontinent fragmented between 550 and 450 million years ago, followed by the formation of the supercontinent Pangea 450 to 300 million years ago. Between 150 and 100 million years ago, Pangea fragmented into Gondwana and Laurasia, which in turn fragmented into smaller continents. New supercontinents are now in the process of formation. Continental formation and fragmentation affects climate, ocean chemistry and life, and is the normal healthy process of a cooling dynamic planet.

The volcanic rocks 3800 million years ago were different from those we see today. They were more like mantle than crustal material, far hotter and brought unusual components to the surface. Many lava flows travelled along valleys and melted rocks over which they flowed. Such rocks are very common in Western Australia. Cooling these volcanic rocks was circulating water that then erupted at the surface as geysers and hot springs, precipitated muds and silica terraces (sinters) and became home for colonies of thermophilic bacteria as today.

The fragments in 3800-million-year-old gravels in Greenland tell us the Earth irreversibly changed. Life had appeared. By 3800 million years ago, the Earth had evolved a solid crust upon which there was running water, primitive bacterial life, hot springs and shallow marine environments. The Earth's temperature had moderated because the atmosphere was rich in carbon dioxide and water vapour created a greenhouse. This atmosphere was very poor in oxygen.

Today, the complete volume of the oceans circulates through crustal rocks every 8 to 10 million years, cooling the new hot crustal rocks. Compared to today, some 3800 million years ago the crust was hotter and the oceans far smaller, hence the circulation of the oceans through new hot rocks would have been very rapid.

Atmospheres surround some planets and, because of gravity, are densest at the surface. The Earth's present atmosphere of nitrogen, oxygen and a little carbon dioxide is unique. Venus and Mars have atmospheres composed largely of carbon dioxide and the outer planets have atmospheres composed of hydrogen, helium and methane.

In the lower atmosphere on Earth, the concentrations of oxygen and carbon dioxide are controlled by life, volcanoes and other geological processes. The concentrations of carbon dioxide, hydrogen and ozone in the Earth's upper atmosphere are controlled by reactions in the stratosphere controlled by solar radiation. Gases such as ozone are broken down by solar radiation. The production rate of ozone is about the same as the breakdown rate and a narrow zone of slight ozone concentration at 25 to 30 kilometres altitude absorbs UV radiation from the Sun.

The Earth's atmosphere was born of primordial gas which escaped from the mantle. Such gas still escapes from volcanoes. Carbon dioxide from the last few thousand years of volcanic activity is produced commercially from the Mt Gambier area, South Australia. Sediments that formed 3500 million years ago can tell us about the Earth's atmosphere at that time. Minerals formed in the sediments are a response to running water interacting with the atmosphere and surface rocks. Very ancient sediments are characterised by oxygen-poor minerals which shows that the Earth's atmosphere had no oxygen early in its history. The ancient atmosphere contained nitrogen, carbon dioxide, water vapour, carbon monoxide, ammonia, methane, hydrogen sulphide, sulphur dioxide, hydrochloric acid and rare gases such as argon, neon, krypton, xenon, hydrogen and helium. Such an atmosphere would have kept the Earth warm and water liquid. Acid rain deeply weathered new crust and erosion was greater than today.

Some of these rare gases still lurk deep in the mantle, clues to the primordial cloud that formed the Solar System. For example, the Earth's atmosphere contains heavy xenon whereas the Sun contains light xenon. Lighter xenon isotopes escaped from planet Earth early and heavier xenon atoms accumulated as they were formed by the decay of radioactive atoms in the mantle. Deep drill holes and inclusions in minerals which came from a great depth contain a high proportion of light xenon, suggesting Earth retains some xenon left over from the raw material that formed the planet 4500 million years ago.

Other rare gases in the atmosphere and mantle show that, as expected, Earth underwent maximum degassing during its first 50 million years.

Samples from the upper mantle show that degassing is not complete and is continuing.

Most hot springs and volcanoes release a mixture of recycled surface water and gas mixed with water and gas from deep within the Earth. Modern volcanoes that expel deep level water and gas release no oxygen. The most common gases released from deep in the Earth by volcanoes are nitrogen, carbon dioxide, water vapour, methane, helium and hydrogen sulphide. In early Earth, chemical reactions in the mantle involving iron released hydrogen, carbon monoxide and methane and, in a younger Earth with metallic iron concentrated in the core, these reactions now release carbon dioxide, water, nitrogen, hydrogen, hydrochloric acid and sulphur dioxide. Because the timing of early degassing of the Earth is not exactly known, we are not exactly sure of the composition of the first atmosphere but it was hot, steamy and contained little or no free oxygen.

Imagine a glass of champagne. Even better, pour one. Watch the bubbles rise. Depressurisation and warming releases dissolved carbon dioxide as bubbles. Exactly the same happens in the Earth. Gases ascend fractures in the mantle as a result of depressurisation and warming by hot currents or plumes of slowly flowing superheated partially molten rock. Oxygen is not one of these gases.

There are other ways of determining which gases are deep within the Earth. Some minerals like diamond require very high temperatures and pressures to form, equivalent to a depth of 150 kilometres. Lavas from this depth within the mantle are contaminated with diamond as the molten rock rises to the surface. The solid diamond contains small gas and liquid bubbles, samples of the mantle from 150 kilometres down. Nitrogen, carbon dioxide, water vapour, methane, helium and hydrogen sulphide are the most common gases in diamond. Each diamond field in the world has diamonds with unique solid and gas inclusions, thereby making it very difficult to sell a synthetic diamond as a natural stone or to hide where a stolen stone came from. Oxygen is not a gas found in diamond.

As the Sun evolved into being a main sequence star, its core became denser and hotter as hydrogen was converted to helium by nuclear fusion. The early Sun had a luminosity of some 30 per cent less than now and, over time, luminosity has increased in a steady state. The low luminosity of the early Sun was such that the Earth's average surface temperature would have been below 0 °C from 4500 to 2000 million years ago. But, there is evidence of running water and oceans as far back as 3800 million years ago. This paradox is solved if the Earth had an enhanced greenhouse with an atmosphere of a lot of carbon dioxide and methane. Warming is also aided by a decrease in the amount of solar energy reflected by cloud cover. To conserve angular momentum in the Earth-Moon system, the early Earth rotated faster with a 14 hour day which decreased the cloud cover by 20 per cent.

When the first life formed on Earth and for the first half of its history, the atmosphere was very different. If volcanic degassing gave us most of the gases for the primitive atmosphere, then why does the modern atmosphere contain 21 per cent oxygen?

The climate of ancient Earth is a jigsaw with most pieces missing. In the oldest sediments on Earth, at Isua in Greenland, finely laminated iron-rich sediments formed in warm shallow marine conditions. This implies low wind velocities to preserve such delicate layers. This is consistent with a carbon dioxide-rich atmosphere in which temperature differences with latitude are small, as are the corresponding wind velocities. The earliest salt beds and stromatolites appear about 3500 million years ago, pointing to a warm climate too. By looking at the chemistry of sediments, the rates of weathering and erosion can be calculated, and all studies suggest that in the first 2000 million years, chemical weathering was intense. The abundance of shallow marine carbonates and the preservation of iron-depleted soils suggest a warm wet tropical climate, consistent with a carbon dioxide-rich atmosphere.

Although there were minor glacial events 3000 and 2400 to 2300 million years ago, the global temperature might have only dropped 2 or 3 °C to induce chilling. Two major cataclysmic events occurred early in the history of the Earth and the Moon. The eruptions of large quantities of superheated lava in Australia, South Africa, Canada and Greenland 3470 to 3460 million years ago seem to have been triggered by massive impacting when a large part of the Earth's early crust formed. An even greater cataclysmic event occurred 3200 million years ago. There was extensive volcanism on the Moon with huge volumes of lava filling the impact craters. On Earth, the bombardment formed craters several hundred kilometres in diameter and volcanic rocks filled the craters. The land surface was punched down and these lower areas were filled with sediment which was stripped off areas which had popped up.

AS OLD AS TIME

Miranda used to say that everything begins and ends at exactly the right time and place ...

Joan Lindsay, *Picnic at Hanging Rock*

When a geologist refers to old rocks, how old is old and how is time measured?

Geology is the history of nature. A geologist is like a detective who visits the scene of the crime after it has been committed. From the few clues left, the detective pieces together what happened and when. The detective then tries to understand the history of events. The geologist arrives at the scene millions to thousands of millions of years after the event, observes, measures, gathers clues, collects samples, and uses sophisticated technology to extract as much information as possible from the samples. The geologist then tries to understand what happened. As with the detective, if there is fresh evidence then the geologist's understanding of the events is modified. Nature can be very fickle and clues are normally concealed; the scene of the events needs to be visited many times and looked at with different eyes. Nature has left us only a dim and discontinuous record with which to work. Experienced detectives extract more clues from the scene of a crime than a lay person. So, too, with natural science.

Natural science is like a jigsaw puzzle. However, in nature, at least half the pieces have been concealed. Many pieces of the ancient jigsaw are lost. Often newer or older jigsaws must be put together to understand the key one.

If a geologist wants to understand the history of Earth, then there must be a reading of the rocks by making basic observations and measurements. If there are drill holes or mines, then a better three-dimensional picture can be put together. Samples need to be collected for testing and the age of rocks needs to be determined by using the clocks in the rocks. Well before radioactivity was discovered, a geological time scale was constructed by using fossils. This time scale has been confirmed by accurate measurements of rock ages.

There are five main methods of accurately determining the age of a rock. They are independent and rely on totally different processes. A combination of these methods can be used to look at the complete history of planet Earth from deep time to the present.

The most common method is to use the decay of a radioactive element such as uranium, thorium, potassium, rubidium or carbon. Another method involves measurement of electrons captured in minerals as a result of a long period of bombardment by particles from solar and cosmic radiation. The ever-changing magnetic field of the Earth is also used to determine when magnetic minerals formed thereby dating the host material. Over time, biological material such as amino acids undergo decay and by measuring the chemicals in old biological material, it is possible to calculate the length of time the biological material has been suffering decay. As bones age, nitrogen is lost and fluorine gained from groundwaters. The use of carbon dating (radioactive decay) combined with amino acid breakdown and bone chemistry change gives three totally independent methods of determining the age of bones.

The last method of age dating is a simple measurement of tidal or seasonal cycles. Such cycles are well preserved in some sediments and not only have these been used to measure time but they have been used to calculate Earth-Moon rotation and gravitation in former times. In summer there is far more runoff into glacial lakes and sandy sediments are deposited on the lake floor. In winter there is little or no runoff and a much thinner muddy layer forms. By counting the doublets of sediment layers, the summer-winter cycles in sediments in glacial lakes can be used to understand ancient climates and to measure the length of time the glacial lake was active. Dendrochronology involves the measurement of the annual growth rings in trees. Not only can time be measured but, by using the isotopes of carbon, oxygen and hydrogen, the nature of ancient climates can be deduced.

GEOLOGICAL TIME SCALE

Eras	Periods and systems	Derivation of names
CENOZOIC Kainos or Cenos = recent Zoe = life(Recent life)	**QUATERNARY** Recent or Holocene Glacial or Pleistocene **TERTIARY** Pliocene Miocene Oligocene Eocene Paleocene	 Holos = complete, whole Pleiston = most Pleion = more Meion = less (i.e. less than in Pliocene) Oligos = few Eos = dawn Palaios = old
MESOZOIC Mesos = middle (Middle life)	**CRETACEOUS** **JURASSIC** **TRIASSIC**	Creta = chalk Jura Mountains *Threefold* division in Germany
PALAEOZOIC Palaios = ancient (Ancient life)	**UPPER PALAEOZOIC** PERMIAN CARBONIFEROUS DEVONIAN **LOWER PALAEOZOIC** SILURIAN ORDOVICIAN CAMBRIAN	 Permia, ancient kingdom between the Urals and the Volga Coal (carbon)-bearing Devon (marine sediments) Silures, Celtic tribe of Welsh Borders Ordovices, Celtic tribe of North Wales Cambria, Roman name for Wales
	<u>PRECAMBRIAN ERAS</u> PROTEROZOIC ARCHAEOZOIC or ARCHEAN	 Proteros = earlier Archaeos = primaeval

Physicists have discovered that, over time, radioactive elements will decay into other elements with a different degree of radioactivity, or into stable non-radioactive elements called radiogenic or daughter isotopes. Measurements, calculations and experiments have shown that each radioactive element decays at a predetermined rate that is consistent over time, and it is this phenomenon that makes radioactive decay an accurate tool for the dating of things of great geological antiquity. If you have a known amount of a radioactive element, after a certain period half of the atoms in it will have decayed to the lower state; after the same length of time again, half of the remaining atoms will have decayed and so on. The name given to this measurement parameter of radioactive substances, is their half-life. Each radioactive element has its own characteristic half-life ranging from microseconds to many billions of years. Generally, the higher the radioactivity, the shorter the half-life.

A minute amount of uranium 238 in rocks eventually decomposes to lead 206. The lead 206 is the end product in a decay process that includes some 13 other decomposition products. If one of the 13 decay products such as radon gas escapes from the rock, the radioactive age will be lower. If there is some lead 206 retained in the rocks from the primeval Earth, the age will be too large. These possible errors are eradicated by cross checking with other radioactive decay series and measuring the lead 206 in lead-rich rocks such as Broken Hill lead-zinc-silver ore.

It takes 4468 million years for half the uranium 238 to decompose to lead 206. The rate of change of uranium 238 to lead 206 is known from experiments, nuclear reactors and the Sun, so all that has to be measured in the rock is the amount of lead 206 and uranium 238 and the age of formation of the rock can be calculated. Uranium 238, the heaviest natural substance on Earth, has been used for armour-piercing weapons and as a counterweight in the tail of modern jet aeroplanes.

Like all scientific measurements, this process must be repeated by cross checking. Traces of uranium 235, the material used in nuclear reactors and bombs, occurs naturally in all rocks. It takes 704 million years for half the uranium 235 to decay to the end product, lead 207. This figure is very accurately known and no nuclear reactor could be controlled if this figure was wrong. By measuring the amount of lead 207 and uranium 235 in the rock and by using the known rate of decay, the age of the rock can be calculated.

Minerals which contain small amounts of uranium and thorium are bombarded by particles as uranium and thorium decay over time. Bombardment leaves a trail of damage in the mineral crystal called fission tracks. The older the mineral, the more fission tracks. Furthermore, if the mineral undergoes an event of heating after formation, the mineral reorganises and the fission tracks are destroyed. In this way, fission track dating can be used to date heating and cooling events in rocks.

Half the thorium 232 in rocks decays to the end product lead 208 in 14 010 million years. Half the rubidium 87 decays to strontium 87 in 48 813 million years. Half the potassium 40 decays to argon 40 in 1250 million years. By measuring the gas argon in rocks, the proportions of argon 40 and argon 39 can be computed to determine when a rock was heated to above 300 °C, another method to calculate when rocks were heated and cooled. Half the samarium 147 decays to neodymium 143 in 106 002 million years and half the rhenium 187 decays to osmium 187 in 41 606 million years. In short, there are measurable elements in rocks of any age, elements that in numerous independent scientific cross checks have proven to give an extremely accurate age when a rock formed. We don't expect to find ages on Earth older than 4500 million year because that's the stardust age of our solar system.

Such methods can only be used for rocks that were once molten or had been cooked up to very high temperatures. Not only can these methods give the age of rocks, they can also be used to look through geological processes because many rocks are recycled and inherit characteristics from earlier times. If these techniques are used to date a rock that was once molten, then by looking through time, we can calculate what material was melted, for the sake of an example, in a mudstone. By looking through time, we can also measure when and where this mudstone formed, how many times it had been cooked up, when it had been heated in the past and what the climate was like in the dim distant past. Other tricks of the trade are that we can calculate when an area was uplifted to form mountains. Minerals are a logbook that records a long sequence of events in history. For example, detailed dating of rocks from the Broken Hill district and the latest scientific studies show that there is a hazy and long history of events. Most of the rocks in the Broken Hill area formed from volcanic rocks 1690 million years ago. These volcanic rocks were melted from material which was formed 1740 million years ago and there is some evidence that these 1690-million-year-old rocks formed by melting of small amounts material up to 3100 million years old.

Our planet is constantly bombarded by cosmic rays that form materials such as chlorine 36 in water, beryllium 10 on the land surface and carbon 14 in the atmosphere. Half the chlorine 36 decays to argon 36 in 310 000 years, half the beryllium 10 decays to boron 10 in 1.5 million years and half the carbon 14 decaying to nitrogen 14 in 5730 years. These materials are used to date more recent events.

For example, we can use chlorine 36 to date how quickly polar ice forms and melts, how quickly lakes, rivers and harbours are filled with silt and the age of groundwaters. Groundwaters in many parts of the world formed when there were warmer wetter climates. Groundwater is actually fossil water and hence it must be used with great care. In the Great Artesian Basin of Australia, groundwater is 2 million years old. If the water is wasted, we just can't sit around for millions of years waiting for the aquifer to be recharged in future times when we next have a warmer wetter climate.

The northward pushing of Australia under South East Asia carries surface beryllium 10 to a great depth beneath Indonesia. By measuring the beryllium 10 and boron 10 in modern Indonesian volcanic rocks, we can calculate that bits of Australia started to be melted beneath Indonesia about 50 million years ago and we can show that Australia was initially moving northwards at 1 centimetre a month. This incredibly fast rate of continental drift has now slowed to about 5 millimetres a month. Nevertheless, the collision of the Australian continental landmass with South East Asia has resulted in millions of years of catastrophic earthquakes and volcanoes in Indonesia. Furthermore, with the beryllium 10, we can show how quickly Australia was being eroded over the last 20 million years and this gives us a good window into how quickly climate fluctuates from icehouse to greenhouse.

As a result of more than 2000 nuclear blasts since 1945, minute quantities of radioactive fallout have spread across planet Earth. On the land, this radioactive fallout resides in the soil. Fallout material such as radioactive caesium 137 is used to monitor and measure post-1945 soil erosion and land degradation. We humans have left our geological mark on the planet which appears as this thin radioactive layer in soils and sediments derived from soil erosion. This will be detectable for many millions of years to come.

Carbon dating is much maligned by those whose agendas are threatened by a truthful representation of the age of earthly things. Atmospheric carbon dioxide contains known relative proportions of three carbon isotopes, radioactive carbon 14, stable carbon 13 and stable carbon 12. Any living organism (including us) absorbs these isotopes in the same proportions and, on the death of the organism, no more carbon is absorbed. The carbon 14 decays to nitrogen 14 at a known half-life rate, the carbon 12 (and 13 for that matter) stays constant. Thus the proportion of carbon 14 to carbon 12 found in organic remains gives a method of measuring the time since the death of the organism. Just to check if there has been contamination of the sample, carbon 14, carbon 13 and carbon 12 are all measured as part of good housekeeping.

In order to appreciate carbon dating, buy a large drink. Pour half of it into a second glass. Pour half of the remaining drink into a third glass. Again, pour half the remaining drink into a fourth glass. Do this experiment another two times and then see how much drink is left in the first glass. Very little. The same with carbon 14. Half the carbon 14 decomposes after 5730 years, after another 5730 years, half again has decomposed. As with the drink, after the original amount of carbon 14 has been halved five times, there is so little carbon 14 left that it is very difficult to measure. This limits the accurate use of carbon 14 dating to fewer than 40 000 years which, in geological terms, is only yesterday. Material which formed after 1945 has been contaminated by carbon 14 derived from radioactive fallout and hence cannot be dated. Attempts to carbon date material older than 40 000 years of course produce a carbon date of 40 000 years. Carbon dating, like all techniques, has its limitations, but its limitations are well known, and dates given by this technique, as with all of the others, are always expressed within margins of error.

Carbon dating depends on measuring the amount of carbon 14 in organisms. The carbon dioxide that plants absorb contains traces of radioactive carbon. When the plant dies, the carbon 14 starts to decompose. By measuring the amount of carbon 14, the time when the plant stopped acquiring carbon 14 can be calculated. So far so good. Carbon 14 dates from Egyptian sites, for which there were very reliable historical dates, did not correspond. This was the first hint that the carbon 14 in the atmosphere, held in carbon dioxide, was not constant over time. By using precise historical and tree ring dates, carbon 14 dates can now be corrected.

However, this raised an interesting sideline. Why does the carbon 14 content of the atmosphere change? Carbon 14 is made by bombarding atmospheric nitrogen 14 with cosmic rays, those particle bullets that come from the Sun and distant supernovae. Cosmic rays from the Sun are controlled by the activity of the Sun's magnetism. It appears that the Sun has a 200 year cycle of magnetism with the most recent peaks being around 1500, 1700 and 1900. These peaks in solar magnetism coincide with peaks in the production of carbon 14 in the atmosphere. Furthermore, the peaks in carbon 14 production coincide with advances in glaciers suggesting that the Sun may be responsible for changes in climate on Earth.

Beaches can be used to show another dating method. Anyone who has been sunbaking gets sunburnt and a darker skin. Go down to the beach and have a very good look at all the partially naked bodies, purely as part of a scientific observation, of course. By just looking at a person, we can tell if they have been in the sun for hours, days or weeks.

Minerals, especially quartz, also get sunburnt and we can measure how long a mineral has been exposed to sunlight. Quartz exposed to sunlight captures electrons and these are trapped in the mineral. By heating the quartz in the laboratory, it emits light and the amount of light emitted is related to the number of electrons and hence the time that the quartz was exposed to sunlight. This is often used to measure the age of old beaches, campsites and soils which have been exposed to sunlight for a long time.

When rocks are heated above 580 °C, the iron oxide mineral magnetite loses its magnetic properties. When rocks such as lavas cool, the magnetite inherits the Earth's magnetic field at 580 °C. If we measure the age of the lava, using a method such as potassium-argon dating, and measure the magnetic field of the magnetite crystals in the lava, then we can calculate where on Earth the lava erupted. Using this method, palaeomagnetic dating, we are able to show the history of magnetic reversals, especially around the mid ocean ridges. Furthermore, the position of the Earth's magnetic poles is not the same as the Earth's geographic poles and, over time, it appears that the magnetic poles wander. This apparent polar wandering is not because the position of the magnetic poles change greatly but because the continents are drifting.

Geology is the history of deep time. The techniques available now can measure when a rock formed, the age and type of the unseen material from which the rock formed, the post-formation history of heating and cooling of the rock and the date when the rock was lifted from depth to the surface. As we have seen, we can measure time very accurately using a great variety of different methods that are crosschecked as part of good housekeeping. The enormity of time is almost incomprehensible. Given time, then almost anything can occur on Earth, and it has.

Accurate dating methods were only possible after the discovery of radioactivity. In the nineteenth century, although such methods were not available, there was a consensus among scientists that the planet was very old. Exactly how old was old, was not known.

Up until a few hundred years ago, the principal accounts of Earth history were mythical or religious; for example, Babylonian, Druidic, Egyptian, Hindu, Norse and Sumerian. The first attempt to calculate the age of the Earth (and the Universe) was made by St Augustine in the fourth century. The 6000-year-old age of the Earth, constructed by St Augustine from the genealogy in the Bible, makes an appearance in Shakespeare's *As You Like It*. The age was modified by Johannes Kepler in 1598 in *Mysterium Cosmographicum*; he calculated the date of creation as 11 am Sunday, 27 April 3877 BC. We don't know whether Kepler, the Professor of Mathematics at Graz in Austria, was using European summer time or Greenwich Mean Time!

Until the late seventeenth century, most European Christians believed the biblical creation story literally. The first book of the Old Testament outlined a timetable of events for Earth history. In 1654 Archbishop James Ussher used biblical chronology and added up all the lifespans of the descendants of Adam. In *The Annals of the World Deduced from the Origin of Time*, Ussher came up with a slightly different date. Ussher calculated that the Earth was created at 9 am on Sunday, 23 October 4004 BC (Greenwich Mean Time). Ussher further calculated that Adam and Eve were expelled from the Garden of Eden only 18 days later and Noah beached his ark on Mt Ararat on Wednesday, 5 May 1491 BC.

Soon after the Ussherian date was published, the Vice-Chancellor of Cambridge University, Dr John Lightfoot checked the calculation and announced that creation occurred at 9 am, Friday, 17 September 4004 BC. The Ussherian age of the Earth was entered as a marginal note in the King James edition of the Bible in 1701 and there it stayed. It is still there. Despite the enormous scientific advances over the last 350 years, the Ussherian dates of creation and Noah are still adhered to as a matter of faith by the modern young Earth creationists.

The Industrial Revolution started in the late eighteenth century.

There was a technological revolution and miners and engineers were acquiring a great knowledge of rocks through which they tunnelled. Regular sequences of rocks were identified within which there was a regular sequence of fossils of now-extinct animals. For example, the canal engineer William Smith was able to show that distinctive fossils are found in the same sequence of rocks over a very large area of England. Simultaneously in the Paris Basin, Jean Baptiste Lamarck, Georges Cuvier and Alexandre Brongniart were able to show that there had been extinctions of life and that there were abrupt changes from marine to terrestrial sequences of rocks.

In 1788 the Scottish farmer and businessman James Hutton made an observation at Siccar Point on the east coast of Scotland near Edinburgh that changed forever the view of the Earth and showed that the Ussherian age was not consistent with the evidence for all to see. Hutton found a sequence of gently-tilted sandstones which overlay nearly vertical shales and sandstones. The surface between the two sequences is called an unconformity. Hutton deduced a sequence of seven events at Siccar Point:

1. Rivers eroded an ancient landscape, shifting fragments of the bedrock as sediment down to the sea.
2. The material carried by the rivers accumulated at the bottom of the sea to form a sequence of muds, silts and sands which were buried and eventually became horizontal layers of rock.
3. These rock layers were uplifted out of the sea by movements inside the Earth. In the process, they were turned from the horizontal to the vertical, contorted and folded back on themselves.
4. Rivers flowed off the uplifted and contorted rock, wearing down the surface to a flat plain.
5. Subsequently, the flat plain subsided and became the site of accumulation of a new sequence of sands, carried by rivers from high ground elsewhere.
6. Another period of Earth movements uplifted and tilted the new sequence of sediments.
7. Rivers today are again wearing away the uplifted rock, creating the present landscape.

What clearer evidence was needed to show that rocks are a record of deep time? The clearest way to understand geological time is to map an area. Document the rock types, where the intrusions of granite and other igneous rocks occur, where the unconformities occur, where the rocks tilt, where the rocks are broken or folded and plot all these features onto a topographic map or an aerial photograph. Without using radioactive dating or fossils, a logical reconstruction of the order of events shows that the planet could not possibly be just thousands of years old. Unconformities occur throughout the geological sequence on Earth showing that at one place on Earth erosion was taking place eventually producing an unconformity and, at another place, sedimentation was occurring. The same occurs today. Unconformities are used to reconstruct old mountain chains and to look at the constant recycling of crustal material.

In 1862 William Thomson (later to become Lord Kelvin) used mathematics to calculate the age of the Earth. He assumed that the heat of the Earth is from the creation of the planet, that the Earth is cooled by conduction and that the Earth's atmosphere has remained at about the same temperature. By using the temperature of a molten basalt (1100 °C), the thermal properties of rocks and the temperature gradients in deep mines, Kelvin tried to calculate how long the Earth had been cooling. He initially suggested that the age was somewhere between 20 and 400 million years and, with more refined calculations in 1897, he settled on an age of between 20 and 40 million years old. Only a few years later, when radioactivity was discovered, it was shown that Kelvin's assumptions were incorrect and the Earth was billions of years old.

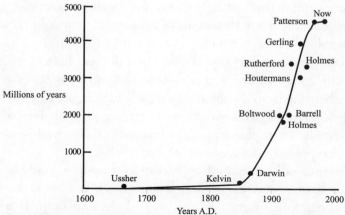

As science evolved from 1654 to the present, the age of the Earth underwent revision.

The same common sense can be used today to get crude estimates of the age of the Earth. Measure how long it takes for a few different layers of sediment to be deposited, measure the thickness of the rocks preserved in the rock record and then back calculate. Measure the volume of rock removed by erosion in a canyon, measure the rate of sediment flow in the canyon's rivers and back calculate. Measure the salt load and amount of water in the Earth's rivers, measure the salinity of the sea and back calculate. This was done by the Irish geologist John Jolly in 1899 and he calculated an age of the Earth of 99 million years.

Measure the volume of a granite intrusion, measure the thermal properties of granite, conduct experiments on the time required for granite to grow large grains, conduct experiments to show the temperature and pressure of granite crystallisation and calculate the time taken for molten granite to cool to solid granite. Whether this experiment is done using the measured hundreds of cubic kilometres of granite or hundreds of thousands of cubic kilometres of folded metamorphic rocks, the answer is the same. The planet is not thousands of years old. It is billions of years old. The problem with all these calculations is that the rate of natural processes such as weathering and erosion change with time and calculations are an underestimate.

Young Earth creationists would claim there is a scientific dispute about this matter: either the planet is a few thousand years old or it is billions of years old. They are wrong. There is no scientific dispute, nor are these claims two sides of any rational debate. The first claim is a matter of belief; a belief that is not supported by one scintilla of scientific evidence. The second claim is based entirely on scientific evidence and this evidence comes from many entirely independent scientific techniques. The Earth is many thousands of millions of years old. There is no compromise.

If the planet is a mere 6000 years old, then the half-lives of uranium 238, uranium 235, thorium 230 and numerous other isotopes would have to be changing from an initially extremely high figure to an average half-life of 6000 years. This would result in the present day half-life increasing rapidly from year to year, a feature not observed in almost 100 years of repeated measurements of half-lives.

The only way that the young Earth creationist position could be true would be if a preposterous lie had been written in the rocks by a supernatural being in whom they ask us to lodge our faith. If true it would be a misplaced faith. In the nineteenth century, there was a view that the Devil left all those apparently old fossils lying around just to test our faith. Clearly the view of creation 'scientists' is a theological and scientific turpitude. In fact, the creationist position denigrates those with genuine religious beliefs.

3

BEFORE THE OXYGEN REVOLUTION

Lavoisier decided that air was made up of two gases. The one-fifth that combined with mercury in his experiment was the portion that supports life and combustion: this he called *oxygen*. The remainder he called *azote*, from Greek words meaning 'no life'.

Isaac Asimov, *Asimov's New Guide To Science*
Azote was abandoned when it was identified as nitrogen in 1771

The early Earth was molten. Around 4300 million years ago there was a layered core and large-scale convection of heat in the mantle. A dozen or so polygonal mantle convection cells formed a crust which, very soon after solidification, was dragged down into the mantle for recycling. As convection slowed by planetary cooling, recycling slowed and a crust derived from the partial melting of the mantle formed. This lighter more buoyant crust started to form the first continental crust. The early crust underwent both chemical and mechanical erosion and was surrounded by a moat of water. The continents grew steadily between 3900 and 2800 million years ago, became flatter and thicker and became sufficiently brittle to be fractured. Basalt lava poured out of the fractures and deep basins formed.

The most ancient rocks preserved on Earth occur in Australia, Greenland, South Africa and Canada, relics of the old crust which have escaped recycling. The oldest rocks in Australia occur in Western Australia. These rocks are 3600 to 2800 million years old and are a good sample of the Earth's early crust. In the Pilbara area the early crust was at least 25 kilometres thick and composed of interlayered ocean floor basalts, high temperature mantle-like lavas, silica-rich hot spring precipitates, quartz-bearing volcanic rocks including lavas and products of volcanic explosions, iron oxide-rich hot spring precipitates called banded iron formations, and sediments derived from the weathering and erosion of this sequence of rocks. The small quantities of banded iron formation tell us that for short periods of time there was just enough oxygen locally in the atmosphere or water to convert soluble iron into insoluble iron, iron oxide. The mantle-like lavas become solid at very high temperatures. The fact that they only occur in the oldest rocks on Earth shows that the Earth has been cooling and the crust has been thickening.

This ancient sequence of rocks has been folded double, bent, broken, slipped sideways for many kilometres, heated and changed by numerous flushes of hot fluid. Nevertheless, some original features can be seen in the rocks which were once volcanics and these are the same features seen in modern volcanics and furnace products. In rocks that were once sediments, we see ripple marks, old sand banks, mud cracks and flow marks from currents telling us that the volcanic debris underwent reworking. The same features are seen in modern settings. In many Western Australian rocks 3500 to 2800 million years old which were once sediments, stromatolites are common.

Stromatolites are accumulations of biological precipitates and, from chemical studies of the stromatolite fossils, it has been calculated that biochemical evolution was advanced and the sea temperature was about 25 °C. They need water currents and sunlight and the oldest were anaerobic autotrophs with mucus sheaths. They lived on stable shelf-type marine environments. They could cope with high salinity, desiccation and high sunlight intensities. With time, stromatolites migrated to lagoons and near-shore marine environments and, 2500 million years ago, expanded into tidal and deep subtidal environments. Between 2200 and 1200 million years ago, stromatolites expanded in numbers and complexity and then dramatically declined about 500 million years ago, possibly because of grazing of algal mats by the earliest metazoans or a decrease in the amount of carbonate dissolved in sea water. Stromatolites still survive in very restricted ecosystems.

A shift from a predominantly oceanic to a continental geological flavour took place 3100 to 2900 million years ago in South Africa, 2800 million years ago in Western Australia and 2700 to 2600 million years ago elsewhere in the world. The constant process of weathering, erosion, sedimentation, cooking and bending of rocks, and melting of

5000 million years ago
4800
4600
4400
4200
4000
3800
3600
3400
3200
3000
2800
2600
2400
2200
2000
1800
1600
1400
1200
1000
800
600
400
200

present

crustal and mantle rocks to form volcanoes is the process by which planet Earth recycles material. Much of Western Australia was planed flat by erosion 2800 million years ago and, in some places, this 2800-million-year-old erosion surface can still be seen. The Earth had changed. Forever.

That second irreversible change saw small single-celled bacteria, the only life on Earth for 1000 million years, have competitors. Some 2700 million years ago new eukaryotic organisms appeared. Eukaryotic cells are photosynthetic and their appearance suggests that there were now small amounts of oxygen gas accumulating in the atmosphere. Their appearance heralded something more sinister: genocide. Before the appearance of eukaryotic cells, prokaryotic bacteria were having a raging party on Earth. Waters teemed with brilliantly coloured bacteria living off the sulphurous gases and carbon dioxide spewed out of volcanoes. Others were freeloaders living off the amino acids and other complex chemicals formed in the atmosphere by lightning and UV light. Smarter bacteria were fermenters, breaking down large molecules and using the energy. Even smarter bacteria were making glucose from the chemical cocktail that existed in the oceans. The population boomed on an Earth with seemingly unlimited resources.

One of the greatest thicknesses of the first ancient rocks with a continental chemistry is seen in the Witwatersrand Goldfield of South Africa. The Goldfield was discovered in 1886 and more than 50 000 tonnes of gold has been produced from 16 different layers of ancient continental sands and gravels. The Witwatersrand has produced more than half the gold mined throughout the course of human history. The 3100- to 2700-million-year-old continental sequence of rocks of the Witwatersrand Goldfield are part of a 12 kilometre thick sequence of muds, sands, gravels and limey rocks. These old sediments contain traces of micro-organisms, distinct tidal flats, alluvial fans, deltas and feeder rivers and a 5 kilometre thickness of volcanics. In fact, bacterial mats on these deltas and tidal flats preferentially sucked up gold and these are one of the major sources of gold from the Witwatersrand Basin. These rocks of the Witwatersrand Goldfield contain bacterial colonies, rounded grains of fool's gold—pyrite—and rounded grains of the uranium oxide, uraninite. Gravels formed at the surface and there was a lot of mixing of water with the atmosphere. Grains were rounded during transport and then left to chemically react with water and the atmosphere. In today's oxygen-rich atmosphere, neither pyrite nor uraninite can exist in surface gravels. Pyrite rapidly rusts to iron oxide and releases sulphuric acid. Uraninite rapidly dissolves in water. For pyrite and uraninite grains to have been rolled along a river and not rusted or dissolved could only have taken place where there was no oxygen. The bacteria that thrived in these areas 2700 million years ago did not need oxygen in the atmosphere.

Exactly the same gold-bearing pyritic gravels are found in Brazil and at Nullagine, Western Australia. Although the Brazilian and Australian gravels are not nearly as rich in gold and uraninite as those at Johannesburg, such widespread gravels indicate that the oxygen-poor atmosphere was not a local South African phenomenon but was an expression of a global oxygen-poor atmosphere.

The famous gold deposits of Western Australia, such as Kalgoorlie, all formed in a very narrow time interval between 2640 and 2630 million years ago. At this period of time, the crust was heated, bent and broken. Compression of the crust squeezed carbon dioxide and pore water from the ancient crustal rocks in Western Australia. This hot potent water scavenged gold, sulphur, arsenic, tellurium and selenium from the rocks, moved up major fractures and deposited the gold where the fractures were in contact with chemically reactive rocks. The whole process probably resulted from the collision of continents 2640 million years ago.

The crust and upper mantle of planet Earth is a thin solid skin which lies on slightly less solid hot rocks. All we have used and will use for the short time that we humans are on planet Earth comes from the crust. During the 1000 million years from 3500 million years ago to 2500 million years ago, most of the crust of planet Earth formed. Since then, the Earth has been recycling the crust and the upper mantle. Molten rock from the Earth's mantle becomes solid at or close to the surface as new crust. New crust is exposed to the elements, is weathered to soil which is then washed down streams and rivers to be deposited in lakes, rivers, deltas, beaches and on the continental shelves.

It is these very old soils and sediments that record what Earth was like thousands of millions of years ago. Soil forms by the interaction of air, water and rock, and the type of soil reflects the original rock type, climate, water chemistry and composition of the atmosphere. Ancient soils are a great window into unravelling the past atmosphere. By looking at 3500-million-year-old rocks that were once soils, we can see that

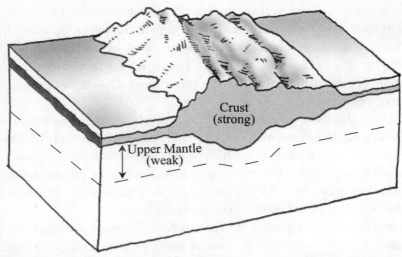

Crust
(strong)

↕ Upper Mantle
(weak)

During plate movement,the rigid lithosphere(crust and upper mantle) rides over a more plastic asthenosphere

there were no plants on Earth then. The continents were rather like the surface of Mars. Traces of nitrogen, carbon and oxygen still left in these old soils tell us that the atmosphere had essentially no oxygen, yet bacterial life thrived in these soils. The rain that converted rocks to soil was very acid and ate away at most rocks to form clays.

Although meteorite impacting was less than in earlier times, during the period from 3500 to 2500 million years ago, some very large meteorites hit planet Earth. The impacts were so large that fractures went deep into the planet and tapped molten rock from the mantle. This molten rock solidified in the crust in what are now Greenland and Zimbabwe. Bacterial life, which can survive very extreme conditions, did not become extinct as a result of these catastrophic events. If there were more advanced life forms on Earth, then mass extinctions would have occurred.

Bacterial life flourished and the teeming microbial biota became increasingly complex and interacted with the crust, oceans and atmosphere. When we start looking at rocks that were once oozes and the soils of 2800 million years ago, we can see that the picture was starting to change. There was still very acid rain that continued to attack the rocks to form clay-rich soils. There were no land plants or animals and the rains leached materials from the continents to form salty oceans. However, there were traces of bacteria in the soil, called methanotrophs, and this type of organism needs very small amounts of oxygen. This was the first signal to show that the Earth's atmosphere was changing and that the oxygen content was increasing over time, but there was not yet enough oxygen in the atmosphere to breathe.

The only life on Earth 2700 million years ago was bacteria in hot springs, soils and lakes on the land and in the overpopulated oceans. When organisms decompose after death, they use small amounts of oxygen and 2700 million years ago there was a very delicate balance between the miniscule amount of oxygen and the abundant carbon dioxide in the atmosphere. We know from measurements today that if we did not have a delicate balance in the atmosphere between oxygen and carbon dioxide, we would run out of carbon dioxide in 10 years and all plant life would die. All the oxygen we consume today has been recycled back into the atmosphere over the last 5000 years and there have been calculations to show that during our life of three score and ten years we have breathed exactly the same molecule of oxygen that was breathed by Michelangelo.

There were periods in ancient Australia when there was a mass outpouring of molten rocks. These events, 3510, 3470 to 3420, 3300, 3260 to 3240 and 2700 million years ago, are well recorded in the Pilbara area of Western Australia. Impact fallout layers occur at the same time periods. These fallout layers contain what were glass spheres. Impact on the land has smashed the most common mineral on Earth, quartz. An impact on a continent spreads shocked quartz over a very large area of the planet. The glass spheres derive from the shock vapourisation and condensation of the impacted surface rocks on Earth. What was rock vapour was mixed with meteoritic vapour which gives these tiny glass spheres a characteristic extraterrestrial chemical signature of platinum, iridium, nickel and chromium. Carbon compounds at the surface on continents get pressurised into diamond, a rare mineral in impact debris.

The ancient sedimentary rocks in Barberton Mountain land in South Africa contain impact fallout layers that formed at 3472, 3445, 3243 and 3227 million years ago. Similar horizons which formed at 3460, 2680 to 2600, 2560 and 2470 million years ago are in sedimentary rocks in Western Australia suggesting that some ancient impacting had a global effect. At that time the crust of the Earth was hot and very thin and, because of the lack of shocked quartz, such mega-impacting was probably in the oceans. Mega-impacting occurred at the same time as the formation of widespread, large quantities of molten rock.

Calculations show that in the period 3800 to 2500 million years ago, there must have been 50 craters more than 300 kilometres wide and many up to 1000 kilometres wide. Upon impacting, the crust of the Earth would have been cracked, large faults would have moved and rift zones would have been activated. Most craters would have been greater than 10 kilometres in depth and the mantle beneath the oceans would have been penetrated. The breaking of the mantle results in the spewing out of huge volumes of molten rock. Long-term geothermal effects in the crust from huge volumes of molten rock would have melted and recycled the crust. Such impacting events are so far back in the past in such complicated rocks that they might never be pieced together. To make matters even more difficult, these ancient rocks were later buried, cooked up, twisted and recycled and all that remains are the fallout horizons in some of the ancient sedimentary rocks. The craters are long gone. The coincidence of a number of events of spewing out of molten rocks and impacting is probably not coincidental and the formation of the ancient crust of the Earth may have been greatly influenced by impacting.

Early Earth was a warm wet greenhouse. The rain was acid because of the high quantities of carbon dioxide and sulphur dioxide in the atmosphere. The Sun was far lower in luminosity and must have looked like the present Sun at sunrise or sunset. There was at least 30 per cent less energy pumped out of the Sun and, if it were not for the greenhouse gas-rich atmosphere, our watery volcanic planet would have frozen. Anyone who has experienced a total eclipse knows how quickly the temperature can drop when solar radiation is decreased.

There are clues to suggest that 3000 million years ago a small part of southern Africa was glaciated (Pongola Glaciation). This was a local event, possibly resulting from a continent drifting over a pole at a time of slightly lower atmospheric carbon dioxide. If carbon dioxide decreased, the greenhouse atmosphere would not have been as efficient and global cooling would result.

The first evidence of a widespread global glaciation was 2400 to 2300 million years ago when Laurentia, Baltica, Siberia and South Africa were glaciated (Huronian Glaciation). At least two major ice caps existed at this time and glacial sequences are seen on continents and in the marine sequences surrounding the ancient continents.

As with most climate changes, the origin of this global chilling is elusive. There is no evidence that there were massive volcanic events that blasted ash into the atmosphere resulting in reflection of solar energy and chilling of the Earth's surface. Glaciation could have been due to the coincidence of a polar continent with a slightly lower atmospheric carbon dioxide content. There is little evidence for this theory. Alternatively, there could have been a draw down of atmospheric carbon dioxide from the atmosphere by micro-organisms. Again, there is little evidence for this theory as carbonate rocks would be expected immediately before glaciation and this theory can not explain how the Earth plunged twice in and out of glaciation during the Huronian Glaciation. The rapid growth of continents at this time would have led to increased weathering and the associated increased extraction of carbon dioxide from the atmosphere thereby affecting the Earth's greenhouse. The origin of the Huronian Glaciation is simple: we don't know.

These were the first of many glacial periods recorded which interrupted the long history of warm wet greenhouse conditions on Earth.

Between 2800 and 2200 million years ago there were profound changes to the Earth's atmosphere: oxygen levels rose and the oceans rusted. Although the fossil record is indistinct, the first algae may have started to thrive at this time. They would have extracted carbon dioxide from the atmosphere and excreted oxygen. Soils form from the interaction of rocks with the atmosphere and water and, by looking at the chemistry of ancient soils later converted to rocks, the composition of the ancient atmosphere can be calculated. Soils which formed when oxygen was sparse are green or black whereas soils which formed when oxygen was abundant are red, yellow and brown showing that iron existed in the fossilised soils in its oxidised form. Such soils we see today in our modern oxygen-rich environment. Any excess oxygen not locked up in oxidised soils and surface rocks dissolves in the ocean. Oxygen is not added to the atmosphere from hot springs, mineral reactions or comets. Once oxygen produced by photosynthesis is combined with minerals and removed from the oceans by rusting, excess oxygen accumulates in the atmosphere.

Why did the oxygen in the atmosphere increase? Very early in the history of Earth, bombardment of the oceans by ultraviolet energy converted water into hydrogen and oxygen. Hydrogen, which is very light, was lost to space and the oxygen accumulated in the atmosphere. Some of the oxygen combined to form ozone and an ozone layer started to form. This protective shield slowed the process of splitting water into hydrogen and oxygen but, nevertheless, the oxygen content started to slightly increase. This process still takes place today. However, bombardment by ultraviolet light is not able to explain why the oxygen content has suddenly increased at various times in Earth history.

Some 2600 to 2200 million years ago another irreversible global event changed the face of the Earth. The oceans rusted. What was dissolved iron in the oceans combined with dissolved oxygen in the oceans, formed rust (iron oxide) and sank to the sea floor. There was a time in the Pilbara of Western Australia 2500 million years ago, I think it was a Tuesday, when the oceans suddenly rusted. For this to happen, the atmosphere must have had at least 1 to 3 per cent oxygen. Furthermore, with this level of oxygen, oxygen gas would have reacted with itself to form ozone. The ozone layer would then have formed providing a protective shield to the Earth from ultraviolet radiation. This would have assisted the diversification of life.

Fossilised 2760-million-year-old soils in the Mt Roe area of Western Australia contain traces of organic carbon. At this time, the carbon cycle began shifting away from a methane-rich atmosphere after photosynthesis evolved. However, methane and oxygen could not have both come from the atmosphere otherwise they would have chemically combined. Photosynthetic bacteria in the water supplied the oxygen, while the carbon 13 isotope levels suggest that methanotrophic bacteria were feeding off an atmosphere with at least 20 parts per million methane. This explains a great paradox called the 'faint young Sun paradox'. If some 2800 million years ago the Sun was 30 per cent fainter than it is now, why did the Earth not freeze? Although the ancient atmosphere contained carbon dioxide and water vapour, it needed something else to maintain the Earth's greenhouse. It was methane. If methane was being produced at present day levels and released into an oxygen-free atmosphere, methane levels 100 to 1000 parts per million are plausible. That would have kept the early Earth warm.

These iron-rich rocks, banded iron formations, contain about 30 per cent iron as oxides, carbonates and silicates. Not only did banded iron formations extract oxygen from the atmosphere as the oxygen content increased by thriving bacterial activity but the banded iron formations depleted atmospheric carbon dioxide and flushed dissolved iron from the oceans. Banded iron formations occur on all continents and the largest and best preserved occur in the Gondwana continents (Brazil, Africa, India, Australia). Everywhere on planet Earth, iron oxides accumulated in basins on the ocean floor. The huge iron mines of Australia, South Africa, Russia, Ukraine, India, Brazil, Canada and the US extract iron from the rocks that formed when the oceans rusted. It is ironic that post World War II Australia thought it was running out of iron ore and export restrictions were put in place. Although new discoveries of iron ore were made in Australia during the 1950s, it was not until the 1960s that the magnitude of the iron ore deposits in Australia was realised. The Hamersley Basin of Western Australia contains thousands of billions of tonnes of iron ore and is the greatest producer in the world.

Organisms that do not need oxygen for breathing actually excrete oxygen. For thousands of millions of years, bacteria have been quietly excreting oxygen. In fact the oxygen we breathe today is oxygen excreted by bacteria and other organisms by photosynthesis. At a critical point in Earth history, there was enough oxygen in the atmosphere to force a great change in life on Earth. There was a subdivision into those that did things the old way (anaerobic bacteria which need no oxygen for life) and those that wanted to exploit this new exciting oxygen-bearing ecological niche (aerobic bacteria). This subdivision was far from gentle. It involved mass killing on a scale which has never been surpassed on Earth and a fundamental change in bacterial cells. This led to an explosion of life, one of the many that planet Earth has enjoyed. The explosion of bacterial life resulted in the sudden increase in oxygen in the atmosphere and the consequent rusting of the oceans.

There was a population explosion some 2600 million years ago. Bacteria boomed and food became scarce. There was great pressure to survive. The photosynthesising bacteria, cyanobacteria, had it easy and were harvesting almost unlimited energy from the water they floated in. With sunlight, water, carbon dioxide and other nutrients, they formed bacterial mats and cabbage-shaped clusters. The cyanobacteria excreted oxygen. Soils, rocks and ocean water rusted as the oxygen was sucked up. Once there was no more unrusted iron in the soil, and rocks and dissolved iron in the oceans for rusting, then the oxygen content started to increase in the atmosphere. Up until then, oxygen was unknown in the atmosphere.

This previously unknown gas, oxygen, was toxic for life on Earth. Oxygen creates highly reactive chemicals in cells that literally burn themselves from the inside out. This toxic waste from the cyanobacteria was the ultimate weapon for chemical warfare. There was mass genocide of bacteria. This was on a scale far greater than anything perpetrated by any human turpitude. Most anaerobic bacteria were wiped out and the world changed forever. The few miserable survivors found refuge in specialist niches such as bogs, swamps, hot springs and deep underground. Relatives of those survivors from mass genocide are still hiding in our intestinal folds. We humans now conserve the relics of the oldest and most primitive life of Earth.

Some bacteria got smart and developed the cellular machinery to use oxygen to break down organic material to carbon dioxide and water, and oxygen-loving bacteria set up home inside larger cells. This was a good deal. One cell had food and shelter in return for disposal of toxic waste. These partnerships not only survived the mass gassing of bacteria but changed into a new type of cell with a nucleus surrounded by cellular apparatus. These eukaryotic cells are in all plants and animals. The first clearly distinctly recognisable eukaryotic fossils were widespread 2000 million years ago. Eukaryotes could only survive when there was oxygen in the atmosphere. These were advanced cells with a cell nucleus enclosing DNA and with specialised organs in the cell. RNA studies of living unicellular eukaryotes suggest that they derived from prokaryotes.

This example shows that the history of planet Earth is the story of the interaction of the crust, oceans, atmosphere and life. The only other factor is time. It was inevitable that the Earth's atmosphere would change from a primitive oxygen-poor atmosphere to one with oxygen. The only question was when? The answer: 2800 to 2200 million years ago, when the oceans rusted.

There is other evidence to show that the atmosphere contained oxygen. In South Africa, pebbly soils 2200 to 2000 million years old are present on limestone within which there are caves. The old soil is well preserved and shows the vertical changes, texture and chemistry very similar to modern tropical soils. Such a soil profile tells us that not only did the atmosphere of 2000 million years ago contain oxygen but the climate was hot and humid. These soils were considerably different from those formed 2700 million years ago showing that in the intervening time there had been a complete change to the Earth's atmosphere. This change was oxygenation with oxygen added from bacterial excretion.

Around 2300 million years ago there was global glaciation. Glacial rocks recorded from the Hamersley Basin, Western Australia, India, South Africa and the Lake Baikal area of Russia, show that the glaciation was a global event.

This icehouse lasted for up to 300 million years until both aerobic and anaerobic organisms had added enough carbon dioxide and oxygen to the atmosphere to restore the Earth's greenhouse. There are many possible reasons for climate change and the glaciation 2300 million years ago is the first event of Earth history where climate has probably been changed by organisms. After the icehouse, the oxygen-bearing atmosphere supported extensive development of microbiological life under the protective screen of an ozone layer.

While life was changing the Earth's atmosphere, it was business as usual for extraterrestrial activity. Throughout these early times, Earth was still sporadically bombarded by visitors from space. In the 2470-million-year-old Dales Gorge Member of the Hamersley Basin, there is a faint clue that Western Australia was hit by a large extraterrestrial visitor. Small spheres, once rock vapour, are present in what were volcanic rocks which had been reworked by water and hence it has been suggested that the impact was in the ocean.

The best documented impact at this time was 2020 million years ago. The hit formed the Vredefort dome in South Africa, 120 kilometres south-west of Johannesburg. Although more than 11 kilometres of rock have been removed by erosion since that event, the broken and shocked rocks still remain. The deep crust in the centre of the impact zone popped up like a cork as huge volumes of rock above were vapourised or blasted into the atmosphere by the force of the impact. A comet or meteorite more than 8 kilometres wide formed a crater that could have been up to 250 kilometres across, one of the largest impact craters known on Earth. Much of the ejected material would have covered southern Africa which is possibly why the Witwatersrand Basin near Johannesburg is so well preserved.

Another impact 1850 million years ago at Sudbury, Ontario broke and shocked rocks and established a geothermal cooling system which lasted for 4 million years. The Sudbury impact crater may have been up to 200 kilometres across. Impacting formed fractures that went deep into the mantle and the depressurising and rebound induced massive melting in the mantle. Molten rock rose to the upper levels of the crust and then solidified as huge saucer-shaped bodies of mantle-like rocks in Ontario. It is from these saucer-shaped bodies that the world derives much of its platinum, nickel, chromium and vanadium.

A large basin formed in Western Australia between 2000 and 1800 million years ago as a result of the collision of the ancient Yilgarn and Pilbara Blocks. This basin was unrelated to impacting. Volcanic activity in the 20 000 square kilometre basin has been used to show that part of the basin was like the modern basin between Japan and China and part was like those forming in south-western USA.

4

THE GREAT STRETCH

It is useful to be assured that the heavings of the Earth are not the work of angry deities. These phenomena have causes of their own.

Seneca (4BC–65AD)

5000 million years ago
4800
4600
4400
4200
4000
3800
3600
3400
3200
3000
2800
2600
2400
2200
2000
1800
1600
1400
1200
1000
800
600
400
200
present

T he new thick continental crust started to stretch about 1800 to 1700 million years ago and the stretch marks can be found still on many parts of the Earth. An unanswered question is: was this global stretching related to the massive meteorite impact at Sudbury in Canada 1850 million years ago?

Huge rift valleys formed in what is now Scandinavia, central Europe, Canada, the US, Brazil, Antarctica, Australia and South Africa. Most of these rift valleys formed in the centre or at the edge of ancient continents. The stretching and breaking of rocks resulted in a hot crust only 10 or 20 kilometres thick. This thin crust was stretched so much that great rift valleys formed. New volcanic rocks belched out in the rift valleys and these rocks were cooled by circulating waters. The pulling apart of old continents gave a whole series of new smaller continents separated by new small oceans. Both aerobic and anaerobic bacteria thrived on land and in water but did not compete as they lived in different environments. There were no plants and animals, the continents only had a rocky soil and only bacteria lived in the oceans.

There was a shift in life from simple single-celled organisms to metazoans (multicellular organisms). Metazoans appear to have evolved from single-celled ancestors that adapted for a colonial life with specialist cells undertaking different functions. Some cells concentrated on food gathering, some on reproduction, whereas others permanently engaged in defence. Fossil metazoans in North China, dated at 1700 million years

73

old, are 5 to 30 mm in length. They were large enough to have specialised organs and multicellular structures. They were probably bottom-dwelling multicellular algae. Although the first multicellular organisms appeared at this time, they certainly did not become established until 1000 million years ago. The great diversity of metazoans of this age suggests a number of evolutionary lineages leading to multicellular development.

Rifting 1700 million years ago was a huge global event and was accompanied by the circulation of hot waters which leached much of the Earth's crust. Hot springs disgorged into the rift valleys. The metals and salts carried by the hot springs accumulated on the sea floor in deep rifts in a similar fashion to the metal-rich muds we see today on the floor of the Red Sea. At times the rifts were drained of water and became massive salt pans, later to be covered by mud and sand. At other times, the rifts were so deep that no oxygen could get to the rift floor and the metal-rich muds from the hot springs accumulated into very large masses. Because of the lack of oxygen, the metals were not dissolved in the overlying water. There is a world-wide similarity of rocks in sequences 1800 to 1700 million years old showing that there were global events which resulted in the formation of the same rocks. In fact, many of the world's large lead-zinc-silver ore deposits formed at this time from submarine hot springs. Examples are Broken Hill, Australia, Gamsberg, South Africa, Sullivan, Canada and Zinkgruvan, Sweden.

Finally, the rift valleys were filled with volcanic material and sands, silts and muds. Only 30 to 50 million years after the rifts were filled, the pile of new crustal material was compressed. Some of the rocks were squeezed so hard and became so hot they melted. New mountain ranges were pushed up and the fragments of old continents were squashed back together again to form another series of different continents. The muds, silts and sands contained pore water. Huge amounts of pore water were squeezed out of the rocks and there were many active spas around the new mountain ranges. All this took place around 1600 million years ago and it was followed by a period when the elements ground down the new mountain ranges and spread sand and mud over the land and sea floor.

The same process occurs today. On the land, hot springs are enriched in trace metals and are currently precipitating iron, gold, silver, arsenic, antimony and mercury in sinters—white, porous silica encrustations—and volcanic lakes. The back pressure plate in geothermal power stations contains precipitates from steam and these precipitates contain a few per cent gold and more than 10 per cent silver. Hot springs under the sea precipitate iron, zinc and copper sulphides (black smokers) from waters at more than 250 °C and barium and calcium sulphates (white smokers) from lower temperature waters. Although these submarine hot springs are above the boiling point of water, the water does not boil because of the weight of many kilometres of water. Submarine precipitation occurs where the sea floor is being stretched and pulled apart. Some precipitates such as those in the Manus Basin, Papua New Guinea, are enriched in copper, zinc and gold, and others are enriched in iron, manganese, arsenic, sulphur and mercury minerals. Hot springs in the Guayamas Basin have converted biological material on the sea floor into petroleum and those in the Whakatane Graben, New Zealand, have precipitated arsenic, sulphur and mercury minerals. These minerals are coated in a film of petroleum and the hot spring vents contain a mass of bacteria that can metabolise sulphur. The vents are saturated with mercury which occurs as droplets of the liquid metal and as the sulphide. Well before these vents were discovered, it was known that fish in this area contained exceptionally high quantities of mercury.

This is one of numerous examples of natural pollution. Many sequences of rocks, especially volcanic rocks through which hot waters have travelled, are naturally enriched in arsenic, antimony, thallium, lead, mercury, uranium, tellurium and selenium, all of which can be highly toxic. Weathering of such rocks produces soils and water which far exceeds the allowable World Health Organisation minimum figure. For example, groundwaters from the deltaic sandy sediments of Bangla Desh are the source of potable water from hundreds of thousands of bores. The groundwater is abnormally enriched in arsenic and hundreds of millions of people on the Indian sub-continent are drinking water which exceeds the WHO minimum level for arsenic and are suffering the medical consequences.

Back to the rocks. The circulation of water through a crust breached by stretching or volcanism is the major method of cooling new volcanic rock. Circulating hot waters leach metals which are subsequently precipitated when the hot spring debouches onto the land or the sea floor. Ancient black and white smokers and metal-rich hot spring precipitates have been found in rocks of all ages, showing that water circulation has cooled the new crustal rocks formed just beneath or at the surface of the Earth. Hot springs also release gas from deep in the Earth. Global rifting 1700 million years ago added massive quantities of the greenhouse gases, comprising water, carbon dioxide and methane, to the Earth's atmosphere. The Earth would have had a run-away greenhouse until the rifting activity ceased.

After the first process of mountain building was taking place in parts of Australia, a meteorite hit the Wiluna area of Western Australia 1630 million years ago to form the Teague ring, some 30 kilometres wide. Shocked, broken and fractured rocks are present as are the tell-tale chemical fingerprints of extraterrestrial material. This impact site is now called the Shoemaker Impact Structure in honour of Eugene Shoemaker, who spent most of his working life studying meteorites and Australian impact structures and died in a car accident at Alice Springs in 1997. In an attempt to ascertain whether there was ice on the Moon, a probe containing the ashes of Eugene Shoemaker was blasted into a crater at the Moon's South Pole on 31 July 1999 by NASA's Lunar Prospector. This first burial in space was a fitting tribute to a planetary scientist and comet-spotter. There was no water detected in the plume of debris kicked up by the Lunar Prospector impact.

Rifting of a sequence of rocks results in the thinning and heating of crustal rocks. Volcanic activity, with molten rock derived from the mantle or the heated crustal rocks, follows. Rifting also fractures rock and hot fractured rocks are cooled by circulating waters. These leach the hot rocks and rise to the surface to form hot springs at the fractured margin of the rift. At the surface, hot springs depressurise, mix with aerated surface waters and cool. These processes result in the precipitation of muds rich in metals, silica and clays. Iron oxide-silica precipitates are common in many modern rifts such as East Africa and the Red Sea, and such hot springs precipitates have a diagnostic chemical signature.

An extraterrestrial visitor hit the Goyder area in Arnhem Land, Northern Territory, and blasted out a crater which could have been anything from 7 to 25 kilometres in size. The timing of this impact is uncertain but was between 1400 and 1200 million years ago. In Finland, 1400-million-year-old red sandstones contain micro-meteorites suggesting that there was a swarm of cosmic material which hit Earth some 1400 million years ago.

There was another global round of continental squeezing around 1200 million years ago called the Grenvillian Event. In Central Australia, we see evidence that the rocks were heated to above 300 °C. There was minor movement along fault and shear zones which were used as the conduit for the pumping of hot waters expelled during the Grenvillian Event. Again, bits of continents were stitched back together again and new mountain ranges formed only to be ground down to plains. Central Australia at that time would have been mountainous and mountains of at least a few kilometres in altitude would have been weathered and eroded to plains. We don't know where all the material removed from the mountains was dumped at this time as no rocks which were once sediments are known in the area.

Following the Grenvillian Event, a giant supercontinent called Rodinia formed as a result of the stitching together of land masses on Earth. Rodinia was probably bigger than other giant supercontinents and underwent its inevitable fate: recycling, continental breakup and continental drift followed by another period of stitching back together of the continents. Reconstruction of Rodinia shows that Australia was connected to Africa, China and the US. A part of China was probably wedged between the Australian continent and North America (Laurentia). The breakup of Rodinia was probably triggered by a huge mass of molten rock which rose in the mantle. Rodinia started to fragment about 830 million years ago. By 570 million years ago, it had broken into the large continents of Laurentia and Baltica, numerous small masses and a large sea, the Iapetus. The continents started to stitch back together some 500 million years ago to form a giant supercontinent called Pangea.

Each time there was a stretching event, the continents were fragmented and each time a new mountain range was formed, new continents appeared from the stitching back of fragments of the crust. This process is rather like a large conveyor belt and constantly recycles the crust of our planet. The rising of hot plumes from deep in the mantle results in the pulling apart and stitching together of the rigid crust of the Earth. This process has been taking place for thousands of millions of years on a 400-million-year cycle which correlates with the 400-million-year cycle of major prolonged icehouses 1200 to 1000, 750 to 600 and 320 to 250 million years ago with shorter intra-greenhouse glaciations 780, 440 and 2 million years ago. The plumes are driven by heat derived from radioactivity and major cycles of greenhouse and icehouse are correlated with the pulling apart and stitching back together of supercontinents. Bizarre as it seems, major cyclical natural climate changes are driven by radioactivity from deep within the Earth.

While the crust underwent great changes, the Earth's atmosphere remained rather uniform. However, for the first time on Earth, large amounts of gas started to be stored in rocks. Limestone, composed of calcium carbonate, was becoming a common sediment on the sea floor and as limestone formed, it extracted carbon dioxide from the air. Most of the planet's carbon dioxide is still held in limestone and other rocks and is released during continental collision.

By estimating the amounts of carbon and oxygen in ancient limestone, it has been calculated that both the carbon dioxide and oxygen content of the atmosphere remained rather constant from 2200 million years ago to 700 million years ago. It is intriguing that a constantly changing and evolving planet should have a period of 1500 million years when little was changing in the atmosphere and oceans. Both anaerobic and aerobic bacteria were quietly keeping apart on a planet that had no vegetation and no animals on the land or in the sea. At the time of the Grenvillian Event 1200 million years ago, the abundance and diversity of stromatolites peaked. Earth was a pretty boring place but the dominantly aerobic bacteria didn't really care.

Bacteria are the ultimate survivors. For 3800 million years, bacteria have lived on Earth in all sorts of conditions, super hot, steamy, high pressure, acid, anaerobic and aerobic, yet we humans try to convince ourselves that we are the dominant organism on Earth. Various authors have written about the Age of Trilobites, the Age of Dinosaurs and the Age of Mammals. Wrong. For the last 3800 million years planet Earth has enjoyed the Age of Bacteria. They started the game of life, were the only life on Earth for 3200 million years and they are still here. They live in quantities which dwarf the rest of all life put together. Bacteria are now, have been and always will be the dominant life form on Earth and their metabolic range is such that they can live in habitats from underneath glaciers, clouds and submarine hydrothermal vents and even in the pore spaces of deeply-buried rocks. They can lie dormant in very hostile environments for hundreds of millions of years.

There is a popular view that most of the Earth's biomass consists of plant matter. Wrong. The planet's biomass is dominated by bacteria. For example, bacteria account for 90 per cent of the cells in a human body and over 10 per cent of human dry body weight. We humans are in fact a walking community of critters with a few minerals thrown in for good measure. Some of the bacteria we carry in our bodies are very little different from those that first appeared on the planet 3800 million years ago. Kidney stones are very similar to stromatolites with a layered structure of calcium carbonate minerals precipitated by micro-organisms. Without bacteria we could not digest food or fight off infection. We humans appear to be a walking package of bacteria, eukaryotic cells and minerals which questions about what it is to be human. Are we special, unique or made in God's image?

Blue-green algae are also relics of early life on Earth. If we were really concerned about conservation, we would feel very strongly about green slime as blue-green algae are the best preserved relics of life from thousands of millions of years ago! Some 99.9 per cent of all macro-organisms that ever existed on Earth are now extinct. Most macro-organisms on Earth only survived between one and ten million years before they either became extinct or evolved into another species. Bacteria are the ultimate survivors.

We humans have only been on Earth for 2 million years. We humans mutate slowly whereas bacteria are now mutating so quickly that many drugs such as penicillin are becoming less useful. Never forget that one good healthy bacterial infection can kill you. So, who is the winner of the game of life on Earth: bacteria or humans? Unlike humans, the boring bacteria just keep on thriving, rapidly mutating and have no problems with either ego or sex! When we humans are long gone, there will still be bacteria on Earth and these ultimate life machines will exist until the Sun gobbles up Earth.

A global stretching of the continents about 830 million years ago associated with the breakup of Rodinia again formed large rifts that filled with shallow seas. Volcanoes spewed out lava and large amounts of carbon dioxide. The shallow seas filled with sand, mud and limestone. Rift valleys were common and, after evaporation of the lakes, thick sequences of salt layers were left behind. Later, deltas and lakes blanketed the salt layers with muds, silts and sands. Bacteria thrived on tidal flats which contain fossilised rain drop marks, mud cracks and tidal scour marks. The high carbon dioxide content of the atmosphere would have induced another greenhouse period. This did not worry the bacteria. They went about their daily business of being anaerobic and aerobic, excreting the oxygen we now breathe, engaging in no sexual relationships and keeping away from each other.

There had been a number of cold periods earlier, but then the Earth

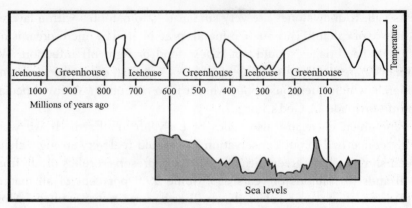

There are 400 million year supercycles of greenhouse/icehouse related to the pulling apart and stitching together of continents.

entered the most savage icehouse in its history. It is not known why the Earth went into an icehouse period. However, this was a period of pulling apart of the continents. What we do know is that in the period 750 to 575 million years ago, the Earth endured at least two alternating icehouse and greenhouse events during this cryogenian time. We also know that climate changes can be induced by volcanicity, solar flaring, orbital changes, the drifting of continents over polar regions and broad cycles of pulling apart and stitching back together of the continents which change the atmospheric carbon dioxide contents. We also know that climate change has been with us for thousands of millions of years before humans appeared on Earth. How do we know that the Earth was in an icehouse 750 to 575 million years ago?

The global icehouse, which actually was a series of alternating icehouses and greenhouses, left its mark. Moving ice collects soil and rocks. The grinding of ice over the land during the most recent glaciation in Europe left very typical land shapes. Very commonly, the rock surfaces are polished. Others are scratched where moving ice has scraped one rock over another. The melting of the ice left a blanket of debris and dammed lakes. European naturalists have long been familiar with the effects of the most recent icehouse which peaked some 18 000 years ago. However, when various Southern Hemisphere natural scientists in the early 1900s claimed that there was evidence of very ancient glaciation in South Africa, Australia and India, these suggestions were mocked and regarded as being ludicrous. Over a few decades, the weight of evidence became overwhelming and there was a quiet reversal of European attitudes.

During this time, there were two major icehouses called the Sturtian and Marinoan glaciations. Before each of these major glaciation events, there were hundreds of fluctuations of sea level from shallow warmer conditions to deeper cooler conditions. Material left behind on the continent after these icehouse conditions is well exposed in the Flinders Ranges of South Australia. In the Flinders Ranges, the Marinoan glaciation left debris up to 1.5 kilometres thick over more than 1000 square kilometres. Identical material is found in the Ngalia Basin, Amadeus Basin and Kimberleys of Australia as well as in Namibia and the Mackenzie Mountains of Canada.

There is a global sequence of rocks at this time showing that the Sturtian and Marinoan glaciations were very intense, major global events. Material left by retreating glaciers or melting icebergs is covered with a limey layer which, in turn, is covered by red shale. Both the limey and shaley rocks formed in very deep water where there were no strong currents. In the limey rocks, both the isotopes of carbon (carbon 13, carbon 12) and oxygen (oxygen 18, oxygen 16) show that temperature was increasing after the glaciation, probably as a result of releasing carbon dioxide from sediments into the atmosphere. The red colour of the shale shows that there was an excess of oxygen, even in the ocean deeps, and the sudden change from continental sediments to deep-water ocean sediments shows that there was no continental shelf. There was so much water tied up in glaciers on the land that sea level dropped by more than 400 metres.

Each time the continent was loaded with ice, sea level dropped and the continents sank under the additional weight of ice. This sinking caused numerous earth tremors. When the ice melted at the end of an icehouse, sea level rose, the unburdened land rose and there were again a series of earth tremors.

At the end of each one of the many icehouses at this time, the ice left extensive blankets of debris across the land. Much of this debris dammed up the meltwaters and lakes formed. In summer, the higher run-off into the lakes deposited a layer of sand on the lake floor whereas in winter, the low run-off deposited a very thin layer of silt. By counting such layers, we can show that some of these lakes were active for up to 15 million years. Bits of ice broke off and floated in the lake and, when the ice melted, the soil and boulders carried by the ice dropped on to the lake floor. These features are very common in ancient icehouse rocks.

During an icehouse, glaciers break off into the sea to form icebergs which melt; soil or boulders carried by the glaciers drop on to the sea floor. Many of the dropped stones are faceted, polished and striated rocks that can be traced to sources within the central Flinders Ranges. Such drop boulder sediments are very common in rocks 750 to 575 million years old and are extremely common in central Australia and the Flinders Ranges.

In some places there is material that was once soil and mud, and the shapes of ice crystals are still preserved in what is now 750-million-year-old rock. Ancient soils with permafrost features such as sand polygons, frost-shattered block fields up to 20 metres thick, frost thrusts, truncated earth mounds and frost-heaved blocks define the bitterly cold times 750 to 575 million years ago. These are very similar to those in modern high-latitude areas such as the Dry Valleys of Antarctica and the arid Arctic. For example, many-sided sand wedges result from the winter contraction cracking of the upper part of the permafrost and infilling of the cracks by windblown sand, alternating with summer thermal expansion of the permafrost that causes upturning of the adjacent material.

Underneath icebergs, the seawater separates into fresh water, which freezes, and salt crystals which accumulate. This still happens today. The crystals of salt then rain down onto the sea floor and in ancient sea floor sediments that formed in an icehouse, it is very common to see moulds and casts of salt crystals.

Much of the North Pole area today is covered by sea ice. There is very little current activity under sea ice and the water becomes starved of oxygen. This oxygen-poor water allows iron to dissolve back from the sea floor sediments into the cold seawater. When the sea ice is broken or moves, oxygen mixes with the seawater, the dissolved oxygen changes the iron to an insoluble form and myriads of crystals of iron oxides rain down on to the sea floor. In the sea floor sediments that formed 750 to 575 million years ago, iron oxide rocks with drop boulders are a rock type which tells us that sea ice broke and melted at that time. Again, these rocks are common, especially in South Australia.

Ice occurred at the equator and at low elevation. How do we know this? When lava freezes, the crystals of magnetic minerals are frozen into an orientation controlled by the direction of the Earth's magnetic field at that time. Some volcanoes erupted during the icehouse. The lavas have a near horizontal orientation of the magnetic minerals showing they were erupted near the equator. Because these lavas are interlayered with rocks that were once glacial debris, the most logical explanation is that there was ice at the equator. In fact, all Sturtian and Marinoan sequences show the same feature indicating that there was a giant equatorial supercontinent covered in ice.

There is a view that although there may have been ice at the equator, the Earth was not necessarily a snowball. There is no evidence that sea ice covered the high latitude areas and it appears that there was no climate zonation with latitude. At present, we enjoy distinct climate zonation. As a result, glaciation is restricted to high latitudes like Greenland and high altitudes like the Alps of Europe.

During this icehouse, inland Australia was part of a continental mass above sea level. In the period from 1600 to 750 million years ago, a thickness of more than 10 kilometres of rocks had been removed by weathering and erosion in some parts of western NSW, South Australia, Northern Territory and western Queensland. The older rocks underwent considerable renewed erosion by glaciers between the period from 750 and 575 million years ago. Thick sequences of glacial sediments were deposited together with sands, silts, muds and limestones. Canyons up to 150 metres deep show that sea level was greatly lowered, especially as continents had sunk under the weight of ice. Great plumes of molten rock in the mantle may have lifted up parts of the crust in South Australia to accelerate erosion and canyon formation.

During this period of weathering and erosion, the character of the sediments changed. The older sediments contained weathered material from ancient rocks 3100 to 1700 million years old but after icehouse, the sediments formed 500 million years ago came from mountain chains pushed up in central Australia 1200 million years ago, Antarctica 600 million years ago and central Australia 500 million years ago. Perhaps these more ancient rocks had been buried.

The first major glacial event in the history of time poses some profound questions. Why did planet Earth chill out? There are a number of theories, the jury is still out and this is the fascinating unfinished business of science. Here are some intriguing theories.

One theory is that the ancient Earth, like Saturn, might have had rings of ice and dust which reflected solar energy. Recent space exploration has shown that there are millions of rings encircling Saturn, far more than are seen from an Earth-based telescope, and they are wafer-thin. Uranus, an outer icy planet, rolls around because of impacting, appears blue because of methane in the atmosphere and has only 11 rings of dust and ice. Did Earth have rings of ice and dust early in its history which would have blocked sunlight? If there were rings, then it is difficult to explain how Earth lurched in and out of two major glacial periods. Recent observations from Voyager 2 and the Hubble Space Telescope have shown that two of Uranus' moons, Cordelia and Ophelia, occur inside and outside Uranus' main rings. They act as gravitational shepherds, keeping the rings from dispersing. If this is the case then it is highly unlikely that the Earth, with one moon, ever had rings.

The Sun and atmospheric carbon dioxide were certainly major factors that controlled ancient climate. The Earth would not have received as much solar energy from the faint Sun as now and that energy received had to be held in a thick greenhouse atmosphere otherwise all water on Earth would have frozen. Fortunately, at that time, the Earth's atmosphere was very high in carbon dioxide and methane and the Earth did not enter a permanent icehouse.

The Earth only escaped from becoming a permanent snowball because volcanoes belch out carbon dioxide. The carbon dioxide is usually scrubbed out of the atmosphere by rainwater which percolates through

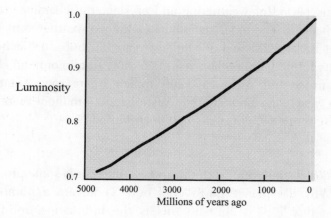

During glaciation 600 million years ago, the sun emitted 30% less radiation than today because solar luminosity has changed with time.

rocks, chemically changes them and then sweeps the products into the oceans. The carbon dioxide becomes locked up in carbonates that precipitate out of seawater and are buried on the ocean floor. Although planet Earth has had liquid water for the last 3800 million years, changes to the Sun, the Earth's orbit or the atmosphere could easily have resulted in the boiling or freezing of all ocean water. We live on the surface of a very fragile wet volcanic planet beneath an ever-changing atmosphere and Sun. A change in solar luminosity could have caused a very rapid climate change 750 million years ago. Depletion in the global atmospheric carbon dioxide and methane 750 million years ago would have plunged the Earth into an icehouse. However, the giant supercontinent Rodinia was breaking up 800 to 600 million years ago and this would have resulted in the release of huge quantities of carbon dioxide from the mantle into the atmosphere.

Atmospheric changes might explain the glaciation between 750 and 575 million years ago. There was little global volcanicity at that time, so little carbon dioxide and methane would have been added to the atmosphere yet carbon dioxide and methane continued to be removed by sediments such as carbonates and muds. During icehouse times, carbon dioxide dissolved in seawater. During the greenhouse times, huge volumes of carbon dioxide were released into the atmosphere. This carbon dioxide was soaked up by limestone that formed in reefs, tidal flats and formed on the sea floor as a precipitate. The limestone reefs at that time formed by an accumulation of limey secretions from algae, as coral had not yet made its appearance on Earth. Such limey rocks are commonly black due to the large amount of organic material derived from the decomposition of biological material. Much of this black biological material is very fine-grained iron sulphide and freshly broken limey rocks commonly leak methane and smell of rotten egg gas released from pores and fractures. By 750 million years ago, bacterial life was having a significant effect on the carbon dioxide in the atmosphere and the balance in the atmosphere between carbon dioxide and oxygen was maintained. A closer analysis of the carbon and oxygen in these limestones demonstrates that at about 575 million years ago, the atmosphere was quickly becoming richer in oxygen.

Many of the rocks formed between 750 and 575 million years ago were once red dune sands deposited by wind action. Not only was this sand deposited on the land, it was blown into the oceans. Red dust in the oceans stimulates algal growth and carbon dioxide is soaked up from the atmosphere. If a significant quantity of carbon dioxide is removed from the ocean then an icehouse can commence.

Mountain building locks carbon dioxide up in rocks too. New mountains undergo very rapid weathering which extracts carbon dioxide from the atmosphere, forming soluble bicarbonates which are swept into the sea and precipitate as carbonate minerals, locking up atmospheric carbon dioxide in sea floor sediments. However, in the period 750 to 575 million years ago, there is no evidence to suggest that large mountain ranges formed. In fact, there is evidence to the contrary: the frost wedging, frost heaved block and glacial-marine nature of the glacial debris in South Australia indicates that glaciation was at sea level.

Rapid continental drift opens up ocean basins and pumps out massive quantities of carbon dioxide from mid-ocean volcanoes. If the equatorial supercontinent Rhodinia broke up around 770 million years ago it would have left smaller continents near the equator and close to monsoonal rain. Renewed weathering of the micro-continents by warm rain could have scrubbed carbon dioxide out of the atmosphere.

The balance between drifting continents resulting in carbon dioxide release and the uplift of mountain ranges resulting in the uptake of atmospheric carbon dioxide affects the global carbon dioxide budget.

The drift of a continent over a pole may induce a local glaciation event but the evidence suggests glaciation from 750 to 575 million years ago was at low latitudes as well as low altitudes. It has been suggested that continental drift was rapid 750 million years ago, the continents were glaciated and later received their magnetic fingerprint when at the equator a short time later. Detailed magnetic measurements indicate that this explanation is a little far fetched.

Today, periodic changes in the Earth's orbit are one of the factors driving cyclical climate change. These orbital changes, called Milankovitch cycles, combined with other factors such as mountain building, continental drift, volcanicity and the resultant changes to ocean currents have given us at least 23 separate glacial events over the last 5 million years. However, the Earth's rotation has changed over time and, early in Earth history, rotation was greatly affected by impacting. It is possible that Milankovitch cycles might have influenced climate 750 million years ago. However, the Earth's rotation and Milankovitch cycles were different 750 million years ago from those which we measure today. In fact, the faster rotation of the Earth may have dampened the effect of Milankovitch cycles.

The obliquity or tilt of the Earth's axis is currently 23.45° but there is no evidence that it has always been so. Some have suggested that during the times of snowball Earth, the tilt was closer to 70°. This idea sounds like creative science fiction but an unbalanced planet, irregularities in the Earth's mantle-core circulation or a glancing blow by an asteroid could change the tilt. Impacts and glancing blows were far more common then than now. Indeed, some planets (Venus, Uranus and possibly Mars) of equivalent or larger size in our solar system exhibit obliquities of 70° or more.

Tilting the Earth to 70° gives large parts of the hemisphere constant sunlight for three months, day and night. On land, temperatures would be constant and hotter than 45 °C in summer but, because land cools very rapidly, during the three months of constant darkness, temperatures would plummet. Anyone who works in the outback in winter knows how quickly temperature drops at the end of the day and how cold it can get at night. By contrast, 700 million years ago the Earth was 90 per cent ocean. Water has a very high heat capacity and, because of the tilt, the Earth would have remained warm. Constant sunlight for three months would not overheat the oceans and, during the three months of constant darkness, they would not freeze. Hence continents at the equator could ice over and oceans at the pole would not freeze.

Computer simulations show that with a 70° obliquity and a 5 per cent reduction in the solar constant, permanent snow and ice cover in areas of between latitude 30° North and 30° South. Bear in mind too that solar luminosity has increased about 30 per cent over the 4500 million year lifetime of the solar system. If this increase was regular, then 600 million years ago the solar luminosity was about 4-5 per cent less, and at 750 million years ago 6-7 per cent less, than now.

How did Earth straighten up from 70° to 23°? If a large enough mass accumulated at a pole, the Earth could untilt. Around 570 million years ago most of the continents were clustered around the South Pole. Calculations have shown that it would take about 100 million years to return the Earth to a tilt of between 20° and 30°.

Although the only known glaciation at that time appears to have formed at equatorial regions, there is a view that the whole planet was a snowball with the continents glaciated and the sea covered by ice. A fascinating story has evolved from connecting geological observations from all over the planet. The continents were clustered around the equator when global cooling began. Polar ice caps may have grown on water and not continental land masses and expanded uninterrupted towards the equator. The white ice caps reflect more sunlight thereby accelerating global cooling. Because modern Earth has high latitude continents, such a scenario could not occur today.

On a snowball Earth or a planet with the equatorial continents covered in ice, there would be no evaporation, no rain and no chemical weathering of rock. Volcanic carbon dioxide would simply build up in the atmosphere, enhancing the greenhouse effect and warming the Earth until there was enough heat to melt the ice. Carbonate rocks that precipitate out of seawater have a carbon 13 to carbon 12 ratio that reflects the chemistry of seawater. If there is plenty of photosynthesis in the oceanic algae, carbon 13 increases in seawater and in the carbonates precipitated from seawater. However, carbonates in seawater formed during snowball Earth times have the carbon 13 to carbon 12 signature of volcanic carbon dioxide. Photosynthesis was not taking place. There was a biological shutdown during the times of extreme cold.

When the icecaps melted and oceans warmed, water vapour would have been added to the atmosphere which contained at least 350 times more carbon dioxide than the modern atmosphere. In the space of a few hundred years, the planet went from the coldest climate ever experienced on Earth to the warmest one. Atmospheric temperatures were 40 or 50 °C, acid rain fell in torrents, super-cyclones were a common event, the fine rock powder left behind by glaciers was weathered by the carbon dioxide-laden acid rain and the oceans were flooded by carbonates—the ultimate product of chemical weathering.

There were two major cycles of snowball Earth and possibly up to five icehouse cycles altogether at this time. The last icehouse event finished 575 million years ago, a very significant point in Earth history, the time that soft-bodied multicellular life suddenly filled the oceans with the appearance of the Ediacaran fauna. And very soon after there was an explosion of life and the birth of all major biological groups.

Towards the end of this long glacial period, an extraterrestrial visitor came to South Australia. About 590 million years ago an asteroid 4 kilometres in diameter travelling at 90 000 kilometres per hour hit a shallow sea in what is now the Gawler Range of South Australia, some

430 kilometres west of Adelaide. A crater 85 kilometres in diameter and 4 kilometres deep was formed and is seen as the present day Lake Acraman. The impact produced an earthquake greater than 10 on the Richter scale and the shock waves travelled at 3 kilometres a second through the rocks and stirred up mud and sand on the sea floor.

The unusual 1600-million-year-old red volcanic rocks from the Gawler Range were blasted out and fell as dust and boulders in an area blanketing most of South Australia. This blanket now occurs in the sequence of red deep-water shales. If the debris blanket had not fallen into quiet deep-water muds, then it would have been destroyed by currents, abrasion during reworking and reaction with air. If the debris blanket had fallen into deep ocean waters when multicellular life thrived on Earth, the sediments would have been reworked many times by bottom-dwelling metazoans before the sediment was converted to rocks. All traces of the debris horizon would have been destroyed. It is a geological coincidence that the debris blanket, only millimetres to centimetres in thickness, is preserved. It can still be seen in the Flinders Ranges, especially at Brachina, Bunyeroo and Parachilna Gorges, in sediments which formed as a result of the rapid sea level rise after the Marinoan glaciation.

The blast debris crashed into water about 200 metres in depth and took about an hour to settle. Impact fallout is composed of pieces of the Gawler Range Volcanics, shocked grains of quartz, rounded fragments which were once glass, a high content of iridium and a high content of material typical of outer space. An hour or so after the fallout debris had settled, 100 metre high tsunamis churned up the debris into ripples and raced towards landmasses. The whole process from impact to the churning over of the sea floor by tsunamis took no more than 9 hours, a blink of the geological eye. At that time, there was a local minor mass extinction of primitive life in South Australia and a slight rebound immediately after the impact. The impact dust cloud would have blocked out the Sun over much of the Southern Hemisphere for many years. The giant tsunamis would have scoured the Australian continent.

The asteroid which hit at Acraman was quite small but if such an asteroid hit the same place again, all life in South Australia and probably all of Australia would be wiped out. After the initial intense earthquake, a lateral blast would flatten everything for hundreds of thousands of square kilometres and then the sonic boom would hit. Searingly hot fallout would rain onto continental Australia and the surrounding oceans, vegetated areas would explode into fire, sunlight would be blocked, darkening the Earth for weeks to years and we would give our neighbours a wet welcome with giant tsunamis. There would be another minor mass extinction on Earth.

Other smaller meteorite impacts occurred in Australia sometime between 900 and 545 million years ago. These ancient impact sites are now preserved as geological structures with shattered and shocked rocks. Identified impact sites are the Glikson structure (Savory Basin, Western Australia, 18 kilometres wide), Kelly West (Tennant Creek, Northern Territory; 8 to 20 kilometres wide), Spider (Kimberley, Western Australia; 13 kilometres wide) and Strangeways (Northern Territory; 26 kilometres wide).

Primitive life survived both impacting and the global icehouse. It blossomed after the icehouse and it is reasonable to assume that micro-organisms eeked out an existence in isolated ecosystems on snowball Earth. During the rigours of snowball Earth, the few surviving creatures would have huddled around sources of geothermal warmth and remained genetically isolated for millions of years. Also, there was a population crash and a mass extinction among bacteria.

Recent finds show that life might not only have hidden in isolated protected ecosystems but might have become dormant during the icehouses. A dormant prehistoric virus has recently been found in the Greenland ice sheet. The virus, the tomato mosaic tobamorovirus, is a common plant pathogen. This discovery suggests that other viruses, such as strains of flu, polio and smallpox, and micro-organisms may have been entombed for up to 400 000 years in polar ice. Such finds indicate that simple life can survive the most hostile environments on Earth and remain dormant for exceptionally long times.

Bacteria and algae were still excreting oxygen and, as soon as the planet started to change from a snowball to its normal greenhouse state, there was a rapid increase in biological activity. Multicellular life appeared. Changes in the sulphur and carbon isotope content of seawater show, a progressive increase in the efficiency of organic carbon recycling. These isotopic fingerprints derive from the appearance of multicellular organisms and reworking of sea-floor sediments. The planet was poised to make another great irreversible change. There was an explosion of life. As soon as snowball Earth ceased, the Earth was a greenhouse packed with empty biological niches.

5

NEW LIFE AND BIG KILLS

'The Lord was inordinately fond of beetles.'

Sir Julian Huxley, evolutionist, commenting on the Creator's tastes.

When the glacial period ended 575 million years ago, the explosion of life was quick. In fact, the explosion of life was only an explosion of skeletal life: multicellular organisms, which reworked sediments on the sea-floor appeared well before 575 million years ago. Bacteria no longer had all ecosystems to themselves. The transition from the Precambrian Era (older than 545 million years) to the Palaeozoic Era (545 to 251 million years ago) is frustratingly obscure and, in most parts of the world, occurs as an erosional boundary. In the late Precambrian, there is good evidence that multicellular organisms reworked sediments on the sea-floor and, in the Palaeozoic, these multicellular organisms are preserved as fossils.

The coherent story of the history of life has been generated by reconstructing a story from fragmentary clues whose survival depends on chance. The fossil record, a wonderful misnomer, has no birth certificate. Fossilisation is a very rare process. Fossils are isolated patches on an incomplete patchwork quilt. We know the size of the quilt, represented by deep time, but there is no way we could know every patch let alone the colour, pattern and texture of each. The history of life will always be incomplete. However, fossils are exciting because of the endless surprises, the links between organisms and the changes over time from a common ancestor.

Life started as a very long slow march over some 3500 million years from the first cell to this spectacular explosion. The first life (hetero-trophs) on Earth obtained energy and nutrients from their surroundings, possibly hot springs, quickly followed by autotrophs 4100 to 3800 million years ago which were able to manufacture their food and then, by 3500 million years ago, anaerobic prokaryotes were wide-spread and stromatolites, probably constructed by cyanobacteria, had appeared. Sulphate-reducing bacteria were also present by 3500 million years ago, although probably in very restricted environments. By 2400 million years ago, oxygen levels in the atmosphere had increased enough for eukaryotes to appear, although the oldest eukaryotic fossil is 2100 million years old. Multicellular life evolved 1700 million years ago, soon after the appearance of eukaryotic life and, by 1500 million years ago, unicellular eukaryotes were the dominant life form. Stromat-olites peaked in abundance and diversity 1200 million years ago, then declined. Soft-bodied metazoans increased rapidly in numbers from 1000 to 550 million years ago, culminating in the dominant Ediacaran fauna, 600 to 543 million years ago. The first hard outer skeleton appeared 550 million years ago.

Most major animal groups appeared in the fossil record 540 to 530 million years ago. There were a few stragglers such as vertebrates and land plants. The first vertebrates appeared 530 million years ago and land plants colonised continents 470 million years ago. Catching the first fish has been a major problem for palaeontologists. The fossil record of fish is good from the present to about 430 million years ago, poor from 430 to 480 million years ago but two distinct fish fossils have been found in the famous 550-million-year-old fossil beds at Chengjiang, China. Amphibians 370 million years ago, reptiles 330 million years ago and insects 310 million years ago added to the complexity of the symphony of life. Mammals 214 million years ago and flowering plants 150 million years ago were late starters. Hominids 4 million years ago are a Johnny-come-lately, barely worth mentioning. All life contains DNA indicating a common ancestor.

The warmer, watery oxygen-rich planet was far too pleasant just for bacteria and algae. In the Flinders Ranges in the upper part of the Bunyeroo Formation, there is good evidence that the sediments on the sea floor had been burrowed and reworked. We can't exactly put our finger on the time when soft-bodied multicellular life started to become

Biological Time Scale		
CENOZOIC	Recent	Modern man
	Pleistocene	Stone Age man
	Pliocene	Great variety of mammals
		Elephants widespread
	Miocene	Flowering plants in full development
		Ancestral dogs and bears
	Oligocene	Ancestral pigs and apes
	Eocene	Ancestral horses, cattle and elephants appear
	Paleocene	
MESOZOIC	Cretaceous	Extinction of dinosaurs and ammonites
		Mammals and flowering plants slowly appear
	Jurassic	Dinosaurs and ammonites abundant
		Birds and mammals appear
	Triassic	Flying reptiles and dinosaurs appear
		First corals of modern types
PALAEOZOIC	Permian	Rise of reptiles and amphibians
		Conifers and beetles appear
	Carboniferous	Coal forests
		First reptiles and winged insects
	Devonian	First amphibians and ammonites
		Earliest trees and spiders
		Rise of fishes
	Silurian	First spore-bearing land plants
		Earliest known coral reefs
	Ordovician	First fish-like vertebrates
		Trilobites and graptolites abundant
	Cambrian	Trilobites, graptolites, brachiopods, molluscs,
		Crinoids, radiolaria, foraminifera
		Abundant fossils first appear
	Late Precambrian	Scanty remains of primitive invertebrates,
		sponges, worms, algae, bacteria
	Earlier Precambrian	Rare algae and bacteria back to at least 3 800
		million years for oldest known traces of life

Distinctive life characterises the geological time periods showing the
3 800 million year history of the evolution of life.

widespread but it is during the period when the Bunyeroo Formation
was deposited as mud on the sea floor.

Before the metazoans took over, the sea floor was dominated by slime that held the bacterial empire together. Slime, a mixture of polysaccharides and proteins, surrounded clay flakes and grains of sand. The slimy mats were the perfect way for microbes to exploit the environment, taking nutrients from the water above, the sediment below and the waste of other organisms. But the slime disappeared when the metazoans arose. An armada of multicellular animals chewed their way through it. Such slime is now restricted to environments too extreme for metazoans. In hot springs, the rings of colours around vents come from the different bacterial pigments which capture the Sun's energy or protect the bacteria from UV radiation. At Paralana hot springs in the northern Flinders Ranges, the high temperature and abundance of toxic elements make the environment unattractive for metazoans but the sediment on the floor of the pool is covered by a mat of green cyanobacteria. Slime loves hot springs. In very saline environments, such as the tidal flats at Shark Bay, Western Australia, sticky micro-organism mats, half cyanobacteria and half algae, still trap layer after layer of lime mud to give the distinctive mounds called stromatolites.

Before the metazoans, the sea floor would have been covered with mats with a tell-tale elephant-skin texture. Sand volcanoes, small outbursts of sand from water-saturated sediments were constrained and occur only as fossilised upward bulges. Gas bubbles could not travel freely to the sea and were trapped beneath the mat. Sediments which were deposited after the expansion of metazoans have been continually churned into a soup by burrowing and crawling animals and hence are easily shifted by currents, waves and tides. Sediments deposited before the appearance of metazoans are extremely delicately layered. Such layers, less than a millimetre thick, can be traced for tens of kilometres. After the metazoans, such finely layered sediments were extremely uncommon and only occur in very restricted settings such as glacial lakes, oxygen-poor deep sea sediments and oxygen-poor lakes.

Almost 'immediately' after the first evidence of churning over sediments, all sorts of alien looking soft-bodied animals appeared. Evidence of this odd assemblage of animals, the Ediacaran fauna, was first found in silty rocks at the Ediacara Hills, near Lake Torrens. It is more common for fossils to be found in muddy material because mud forms in quiet water conditions. Tidal silts and sands were washed over mud flats where ancient life had died or was entombed. Silts and sands form where currents are active; one does not expect to find jellyfish-type fossils in

Typical Ediacaran fauna

 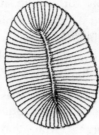 

Parvancorina   Dickinsonia   Rangea

such rocks. Europeans rejected the Antipodean discovery of strange fossils in such old rocks. The first Ediacaran fossils, discovered in 1946 by Dr Reg Sprigg, were dismissed as marks left on sediments by currents. It took 30 years before there was universal acceptance that the presence of such ancient and highly advanced life forms in the Antipodes was the link between bacterial and more highly organised life on Earth.

Ediacaran fauna has now been found etched in stone on all continents and more than 40 species of flatworms, coelenterates, annelids, soft-bodied arthropods and soft-bodied echinoderms have been identified. Looping and spiral trails in sediments up to several millimetres thick and trails of faecal pellets show that the Ediacaran fauna were soft bodied with a well-developed nervous system, asymmetry and a one way gut. Were some of the Ediacaran fauna very distant cousins to modern life? Why did the Ediacaran life become extinct? Was the Ediacaran fauna an early biological experiment?

It is not really known why the Ediacaran fauna is preserved in silty rocks. In younger sequences, we only see hard-bodied animals preserved in silty and sandy rocks. This suggests that the first multicellular life on Earth may not have been completely soft-bodied like jellyfish and may have been coated with something hard. Something like chitin, the material of our fingernails. There was a view that the Ediacaran fauna may have been a failed experiment that died out when ecosystems were flooded as a result of the later explosion of life. However, not only was the Ediacaran fauna the first abundant multicellular life on Earth but Ediacaran fossils in Namibia show that the Ediacaran fauna survived after the explosion of life of Earth. Furthermore, the shape of many of the Ediacaran animals is very similar to modern soft corals, arthropods, echinoids, flatworms and jellyfish. These subtidal marine animals were probably our original multicellular ancestors.

Ediacaran fauna probably formed an alliance with slime. The leaf-shaped animal *Charnia* had a curious small disc at its base. This disc probably helped *Charnia* cling to the mats to resist the waves, currents and tides. Slime may have formed a death mask which could explain the unique preservation of Ediacaran fossils. Some have tell-tale elephant-skin type textures and faint films of rust on their surfaces. The rare fossils are usually preserved as indentations in the layers of rocks above and below the vanished carcass. Many have raised bumps on the lower layer and hollows on the upper layer. Such features could form if sand from wave action or a storm was swept over a slime mat, a new mat grew and Ediacaran life was trapped beneath the mat decayed. The peaceful coexistence between slime mats and the Ediacaran fauna did not last long. As the metazoans tightened their grip on the world, the slime retreated into isolated ecosystems.

The oldest known metazoan with a hard outer skeleton was *Cloudinia*, a tubular fossil found worldwide which first appeared about 550 million years ago. Soft-bodied metazoans disappeared about 543 million years ago. There was an explosion of marine invertebrates between 545 and 530 million years ago. The number and diversity of organisms increased, matched by a sharp increase in the churning over of sediments by burrowers. As a result, buried organic matter was returned to life rather than being locked up in sediments. Organisms developed hard appendages for digging and burrowing but the reason why hard parts were developed in so many groups of animals at about the same time in Earth history is puzzling. Hard parts were developed independently and composed of different substances by different groups of animals. Possibly the development of hard parts was for defence, such as the hard outer armoured skeleton of trilobites. Hard parts improved feeding such as in brachiopods where a shell enclosed the filter-feeding cells that operated like a vacuum cleaner. Hard parts might have assisted locomotion or structural support such as it does in echinoderms and corals.

The major groups of marine invertebrates reached their peak by 530 million years ago. The seas were dominated by trilobites (60 per cent) and brachiopods (30 per cent). It is quite possible the total number of species on Earth was greater then than now. Evolutionary turnover was very fast. For example, the average longevity of a trilobite genus at that period of time was only 1 million years. By 500 million years ago, most of the common invertebrate classes that occur in modern oceans were all established. Bryzoans, graptolites, cephalopods, crinoids, echinoderms, molluscs and corals appeared at this time and began to increase in numbers. Marine algae and bacteria continued to be the important plant forms.

In the shallow warm seas soft-bodied life thrived and experimented with different ways of feeding and locomotion. Most conceivable methods of transport were tried except wheels! Dead organisms sank to the sea floor, where muds, silts and sands covered them and they were ready for fossilisation. Fossilisation rarely took place: bacteria had a wonderful time scavenging all this new food that was dropping onto them.

Major earthquakes can trigger submarine debris flows of sediments from the continental shelf. These debris flows dislodge fragments of the continental crust and the mass of material cascades from the shelf to the ocean deep, often along submarine canyons. In 1929, an earthquake at Grand Banks off Newfoundland triggered a huge submarine debris flow. Twelve submarine cables were broken in 23 places. Nearly all the breakages occurred in pairs, near the edges of a trough-like submarine canyon where the cables were already tensioned under their own sagging weight. This submarine canyon is in line with Cabot Straight, which is in itself a deep submarine valley cut into the continental shelf. The cables near the epicentre on the continental slope broke instantly and

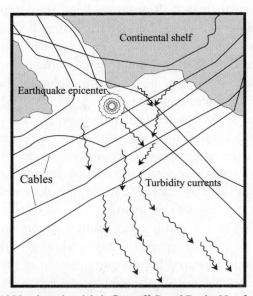

The 1929 submarine debris flow off Grand Banks, Newfoundland.

cables further away broke in a delayed sequence over a 13-hour period. By using the timing of cable breakage, calculations showed the submarine debris flow was travelling at 80 kilometres per hour and, over a distance of 200 kilometres, had slowed to 60 kilometres per hour. The debris flows traveled nearly 500 km. The breakage of cables and pipelines by submarine debris has occurred many times since 1929.

A submarine debris flow almost 540 million years ago left us with well-preserved samples of life on Earth. A large block of the continental shelf broke off and slid into deeper water where the bacteria population was far less active. This block was quickly covered with sediment and the fossilisation took place to give us the Burgess Shale in the Rockies of Canada. These fauna were either doomed to extinction or evolved into other forms.

The amount of carbon dioxide in the post-icehouse times was very high. During the icehouse from 750 to 575 million years ago, the atmosphere contained about 5 per cent carbon dioxide and as the Earth rebounded from the icehouse, atmospheric carbon dioxide content increased rapidly. The exact maximum content 545 million years ago is unknown but it was greater than 4 per cent and less than 30 per cent, possibly in the order of 18 per cent. Today, the atmosphere contains almost 0.0365 per cent carbon dioxide. Atmospheric carbon dioxide reached a maximum about 520 million years ago, declined until 470 million years ago and then increased. It again declined from 450 million years ago until 380 million years ago, increased, and then declined again from 360 million years ago to 300 million years ago when there was only 1 per cent carbon dioxide in the atmosphere. Carbon dioxide was being extracted from the atmosphere by plant life exploiting the land and by the ever-diversifying micro-organisms.

The explosion of life took place in a warm oxygen- and carbon dioxide-rich environment. After the explosion, more than 100 major groups of life started to compete for resources. Some formed shells or skeletons. Carbon dioxide was on offer for any organism that could use it. Most organisms used the carbon dioxide to make calcium carbonate shells and calcium phosphate skeletons.

A study of DNA in modern life has painted a more complex picture of the ancestry of modern species. This work shows that the major groups of organisms appeared before the explosion of life and that the explosion might merely reflect the sudden appearance of shells and skeletons.

A faint clue suggests the composition of the atmosphere had something to do the with explosion of life. Muscles need ATP (adenosine triphosphate) before they can operate and ATP can only exist in oxygen-rich conditions. If shells were to open and close for feeding and protection, they needed ATP. This again underlines the idea that oxygen in the atmosphere had increased. During the icehouse from 750 to 575 million years ago, the atmospheric oxygen increased from about 0.5 to 3 per cent. The current oxygen content of the atmosphere is 21 per cent. The oxygen content continued to increase rapidly and, at the explosion of life 545 million years ago, it was in the order of 5 per cent, and 25 million years later it was 13 per cent. This rapid increase in oxygen was due to the warmer conditions which allowed oxygen-excreting micro-organisms to thrive. There were no plants on the land masses doing their job then. The atmospheric oxygen content was constant from 520 to 350 million years ago and then increased from 13 per cent, 350 million years ago, to 21 per cent, 120 million years ago. This increase was driven by the appearance, diversification and expansion of land plants. Three times in the history of planet Earth the atmospheric oxygen has been substantially changed by life on Earth: 2800 to 2400 million years ago and again 700 to 520 million years ago due to micro-organisms, and 350 to 120 million years ago due to land plants.

Competition was fierce during this explosion and organisms started to eat each other. Nothing has changed. It is still eat or be eaten. Most of the organisms that had suddenly appeared in the explosion have become extinct and only a rare few have not needed to adapt. This explosion took place in the oceans, while the land was still barren and rocky. After 3300 million years of being the only life on the planet, the bacteria suddenly had numerous other life forms as neighbours, competitors and colleagues. Notwithstanding, bacteria retained their position as top of the pile of life and still do.

The type and diversity of life 530 million years ago was far different to life on Earth now. Some species became extinct, some adapted and others have evolved into something totally different. With increasing time, fossil life looked more and more like present life.

Since the explosion of life 530 million years ago, there have been five major mass extinctions: 430, 368, 258, 214 and 65 million years ago. There were also numerous minor mass extinctions of multicellular life.

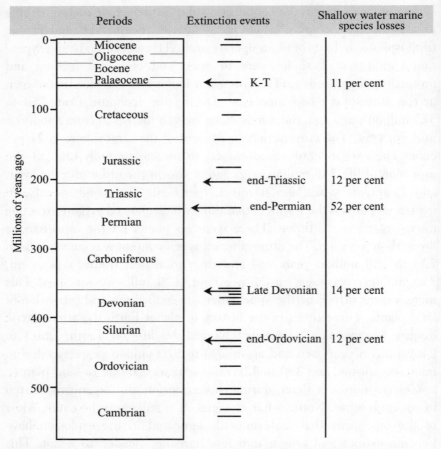

Periods	Extinction events	Shallow water marine species losses
Miocene		
Oligocene		
Eocene		
Palaeocene	← K-T	11 per cent
Cretaceous		
Jurassic		
Triassic	← end-Triassic	12 per cent
Permian	← end-Permian	52 per cent
Carboniferous		
Devonian	← Late Devonian	14 per cent
Silurian		
Ordovician	← end-Ordovician	12 per cent
Cambrian		

The five major mass extinctions and numerous minor mass extinctions of life over the last 600 million years.

Major mass extinctions are rare events with the most likely cause being impacting from extraterrestrial bodies, 70 per cent of which are asteroids and the rest comets. Only large extraterrestrial bodies can cause a mass extinction with the minimum size for a mass extinction-causing asteroid being about 10 kilometres wide. Impact of a 10-kilometre-diameter extra-terrestrial would blast out a crater of 150 kilometres across. At least 65 per cent of life disappears in a mass extinction.

For the last 530 million years hard-shelled marine animals are abundant in the fossil record. By looking at the fluctuating fortunes of these animals, it was shown that Earth takes 6 to 10 million years to recover from a mass extinction. The time lag was not related to the size of the extinction. It measures how long it takes to recreate diverse ecosystems with a wide variety of niches.

Minor mass extinctions can be caused by smaller extraterrestrial impacts, climate change, changes in the ocean or atmospheric chemistry, changes in ocean temperature, disease, volcanism or continental drift. There is a strong suggestion that minor mass extinctions occur every 26 million years, hinting that the periodic orbit of asteroidal swarms close to Earth might be implicated.

However, calculations show that only 5 per cent of the asteroids which cross the Earth's orbit have been recorded. A recent 1 kilometre-sized asteroid, 1989FC, was only twice the Moon's distance from Earth. This was a close shave. It was only spotted after it had passed through the Earth's orbit! We are probably living in a period of extinction of large fauna and some vegetation. However, there is no evidence to suggest that we are living in a period of mass extinction.

Mathematicians have calculated that the species on Earth will occasionally end up in a fragile state in which a minor climate change will start a series of events that wipes out most life. The pattern of extinctions over time is fractal. That is, major mass extinctions are rare, minor mass extinctions more common. The fossil record is a long list of losers. By looking at the ecology in which a species became extinct, the reason for the extinction can be determined.

For example, the tropical oceans today are rimmed by coral reefs that contain much of the world's biodiversity. Since the explosion of life, extensive reefs have been with us for half of geological time. They have changed from algal- to coral-rich and have disappeared during the five major mass extinctions, only to re-appear. Death of coral reefs is normal. Coral reefs form complex ecosystems that easily reflect changes in the environment. It alarms the tourist industry when some reefs today show signs of bleaching, the beginning of degeneration. Some have ascribed this to global warming but this contradicts the geological data. Coral reefs have survived geological periods with considerably higher and lower temperatures than we face now or in the immediate future, and sea level fluctuations of up to 10 metres above and more than 100 metres below the present level. Corals, like other organisms, are well capable of adapting to changing environments and the geological past shows that global warming is not a threat to coral reefs. In fact, the opposite. The geological past shows us that with a warmer climate, higher sea level and a greater area of shallow water ecosystems, coral reefs thrive.

Coral reef death occurs when there is a great drop in sea level and there is very little warm water on the continental shelves.

If we wound back the clock and started the biological record again, the organisms that would evolve would be different from those presently listed. This is because of the randomness of external events. If there had not been a random mass extinction 65 million years ago followed by a minor mass extinction 55 million years ago, we mammals might be still hiding from dinosaurs in our burrows.

A sobering conclusion. There are a few certain things in life. Death is one. So too is extinction of species. More than 99.9 per cent of all multicellular species that have ever lived on planet Earth are now extinct. Although life has been on Earth for 80 per cent of time, complex life has existed for only the last 20 per cent of time. Extinction is normal, species survival or species conservation is not.

While complex life on Earth was enjoying the benefits of evolution and extinction, there were a few remarkable exceptions. Some organisms survived the pressures of mass extinctions and evolution, and have lived relatively unchanged for hundreds of millions of years. Why? Have they found the elixir of survival? Have these organisms had all the lucky breaks and been able to spectacularly out-survive their evolutionary peers? What can the continued existence of these organisms tell us about evolution over deep time? If these supreme survivors remain unchanged for million of years, is it really valid to argue that a change in the environment can be damaging to life on Earth? Charles Darwin called such organisms 'living fossils'. The average multicellular organism lasts between 1 and 10 million years on Earth and, in response to the huge changes in biological and physical environments, there has been a massive turnover of life.

For the last 550 million years, the possible ancestor to all vertebrates has been unchanged. Lancelets, which live in marine sediments and look a bit like a fish, have hardly changed since the explosion of life. Rather than being an ultimate survivor, lancelets might have been held in suspended animation for 550 million years because they had too few genes to improve their design.

For the last 500 million years *Neopilina*, a transitional genus between a mollusc and a worm, has lived unchanged. The lamp shell *Lingula* has lived for 450 million years and may have survived the environmental trauma of mass extinction by burrowing in the sea floor sediments to get out of harm's way.

The deep-sea coelacanth has been on Earth for 400 million years. They were once found in a great diversity of environments and, for the last 200 million years, these environments have been shrinking. Only two small populations of coelacanths remain, off the Comoros near Madagascar and around Sulawesi in Indonesia. These cobalt blue and speckled white fish are about the size of a human, live in deep dark cool water and are solitary hunters in the deep ocean. Because the coelacanth has a very specialised diet, it has a specialised habitat and lives in submarine volcanic caves. Furthermore, it has the lowest oxygen consumption among all living vertebrates and, as a result, has a low food requirement and survives in parts of the ocean where no predators live. Although enormous and rapid environmental changes have taken place on the surface of the Earth and in shallow marine environments, environmental changes in the deep ocean have been gradual, giving coelacanths time to adapt.

The nautilus is the sole survivor of a group of molluscs related to the octopus that dominated marine life 300 million years ago. Nautilus is long-lived and breeds slowly compared with their living mollusc relatives so natural selection is slowed down. The nautilus may not be the ultimate survivor, it might just be trapped in an evolutionary time warp. By contrast, cockroaches are great ecological generalists and, for 250 million years, have been able to live in a great diversity of environments and climates. They are highly adaptable and opportunistic. Other organisms have been far more specialised ecologically and hence far more prone to extinction than the somewhat more catholic cockroaches.

Good luck rather than bad genes or evolutionary changes also plays a part in survival. The tuatara, a reptile called *Sphenodon*, now only lives in New Zealand. However, 200 million years ago it was worldwide. When New Zealand drifted away from Gondwana 80 million years ago, its sphenodontia population was isolated on the island landmass. New Zealand either lost or never had mammals and the tuatara thrived whereas, elsewhere in the world, mammalian competition resulted in its extinction.

Horseshoe crabs have been scavenging for 200 million years and, in the modern world, appear to be far more resistant to pollution than other arthropods. Maybe this is the secret of their success? Over the last 140 million years, crocodiles have evolved into a great diversity of now extinct crocodilian animals which had a great range of sizes, shapes and habitats. Crocodiles were clearly able to evolve into other types but modern crocodiles remained unchanged for 140 million years.

On the continents, ginkgo trees would have been a familiar sight for dinosaurs 100 million years ago. Ginkgos are able to survive in hostile environments. For example, they thrive in cities and cope well with atmospheric pollution. Impala, unchanged for 7 million years, saw their close relatives, the wildebeests and hartebeests evolve into 32 distinct species, most of which are now extinct. The secret to the success of the impala is that they are not too fussy about what they eat and, as Africa greatly changed during alternating greenhouse and icehouse conditions, the impala just adapted their diet to the ever-changing ecosystems. Other antelopes became extinct and new species arose in response to the rapid changes in the ecosystems.

What is the secret to survival on Earth? To be a generalist like the cockroach or a specialist like the coelacanth? A fast breeder like *Lingula* or a slow breeder like nautilus? A simple organism like a lancelet or a complex organism like the crocodile? Being in the right place at the right time like the tuataras? A physiology which can take a real battering like the horseshoe crabs or ginkgos?

The ultimate question is: Do we humans have what it takes to become a living fossil? Are we humans on the path to extinction like most other organisms that have lived on our earthly Ark? We have the knowledge to avoid our own extinction but will we use this knowledge?

Another global event took place between 505 and 470 million years ago. This is known as the Pan African Event or, in Australia, the Delamerian Orogeny. In Africa the event was so intense that large volumes of older rock were melted, rose in the crust and solidified as granite. At that time, Australia and Africa were part of a giant supercontinent. Europe and South America were also bent and molten rocks squirted into the older rocks during the Pan African. In Western Australia the Pan African event bent and folded the older rocks in distinct zones. In South Australia, the Pan African Event was not as intense and a zone of bending and minor amounts of melting of rocks took place in an arc from the Mt Lofty Ranges through Burra to Olary and to Broken Hill. In this zone, the crust was again heated to above 300 °C, new minerals formed, and water driven out of the pores and fractures in the rocks lubricated the movement of large blocks along large faults and shear zones. Major fault zones then moved again and were the pipelines for the loss of large volumes of water from deep in the crust. The new minerals formed at this time suggest that the Pan African event pushed rocks down to a depth of 5 kilometres.

For 80 per cent of time on Earth, the continents looked like a moonscape. No vegetation. No animals. Just rocky outcrops and soil. Weathering was intense during the predominantly warm wet times, soil erosion was enormous and the only life on the continental land masses was a diversity of bacteria. Concurrent with the Pan African mountain-forming event was the colonisation of the continents by land plants. One of the great challenges is to understand the evolution of algae into land plants. The history of the Earth shows us that plants have only colonised the landmasses over the last 20 per cent of time. For 98 per cent of time, there was no grass on the continental landmasses. Life was expanding and diversifying and, for 100 million years, plants were the only large species on the continents.

For the 300 million years following the explosion of life, the planet was a warm wet place. Climates, on the whole, were warmer than now although there were wide climate variations possibly related to the formation, fragmentation and drifting of continents. As a large number of new life forms appeared and the warm oceans were full of life, a slight problem arose. There was a mass extinction only 115 million years after the explosion of life.

Although mass extinctions are a normal part of life, such major mass extinctions are not well recorded in the fossil record before 545 million years ago because the planet was populated by single-celled organisms. Such life forms are very poorly preserved in the fossil record. The extinction of some bacterial species might not be noticed. Furthermore, bacteria are very resilient and mass extinctions would be more difficult than with more advanced life forms. The 430-million-year-ago event was the first recorded major mass extinction of multicellular life. About 85 per cent of multicellular species were wiped out. Mass killing of life is far easier when there is a great biodiversity with life in numerous ecological habitats.

It is not known why there was a major mass extinction some 430 million years ago. What is even more tantalising is why did some organisms die and others live? How did the survivors actually survive? There are no known massive impacts or volcanic events recorded in the rocks 430 million years ago and the chemistry of sediments formed in the seas and on the land does not indicate that anything odd happened.

Immediately after the mass extinction, there were vacant ecosystems. Competition for these niches was aggressive. Unlike the new warm oxygen-rich environments that had encouraged an explosion of life 545 million years ago, no new lifeforms filled these vacant niches. There were very rapid modifications of existing forms of life.

Vascular plants expanded over the continents. A vacant ecosystem had been created by the mass extinction and this was opportunistically filled. Suddenly, ferns, trees and other greenery spread over the continents. This, in turn, resulted in a very rapid increase in the amount of oxygen in the atmosphere. Mudstones in 430-million-year-old rock in eastern Victoria contain mudcracks, raindrop marks and scours from water currents. Such features are the same as those seen on modern mud flats. The eastern Victorian mudstones contain fossil footprints straddling a central zone of scraping, from a belly or tail, perhaps indicating primitive attempts to leave the sea for a life on land.

Life in the oceans rapidly changed. More complex fish and shells were forming and developing better protection systems, better methods of transport and more creative ways of living. Many sea-dwelling animals were living at the limit of their survival and the total destruction of isolated populations was common.

Life continued to diversify and expand. There were deserts, lush forests and coral reefs, all of which have stories to tell. For example, coral has a daily growth pattern and the corals from 400 million years ago tell us that there were 390 days in the year and the days shorter, confirming the planet's rotation has been slowing for at least 400 million years. Slowing rotation has given us shorter years and longer days over time, with the result that the Moon is slowly moving away from the Earth in order to conserve energy in the Earth-Moon system. In a few thousand million years, give or take a few days, the orbital system will have decayed to the point where the Moon is released from the Earth's gravity into the clutches of the Sun.

An intriguing study in the Flinders Ranges on rhythmically-layered tidal sands and muds, formed 620 million years ago during a massive glacial event, gives us a day-by-day account of the tides. By using celestial mechanics, it has been calculated that 620 million years ago the day was 21.9 hours long and the Moon was moving away from the Earth at 2.16 centimetres per year.

The Sun, although 400 times larger than the Moon, is 400 times further away. The Moon sometimes appears to be bigger than the Sun, which is essential for a perfect eclipse. A total eclipse occurs on Earth every 18 months, a celestial coincidence. Because the slowing down of the Earth's rotation and tidal effects cause the Moon to recede from the Earth, the Earth has enjoyed total eclipses for the last 150 million years and will continue to do so for the next 150 million years. After that, there will only be partial eclipses. Earth is the only planet in our Solar System where a total eclipse is visible, although there are over 60 moons associated with the other planets.

The Earth's rotation is still slowing down. At 8.45 am on 15 April 136 BC Babylon was plunged into darkness. The Moon had passed in front of the Sun to form a total eclipse which tracks an arc of darkness 250 kilometres wide across the surface of the Earth. Although the 136 BC eclipse occurred in Babylon, calculations show that it should have occurred in Mallorca, Spain. The only valid explanation of this paradox is that the Earth's rotation has slowed down.

Australia will experience total eclipses on 4 December 2002 and 23 November 2003. Good eclipse-watching sites in 2002 will be in the late afternoon in South Australia in an arc from Ceduna to Marree.

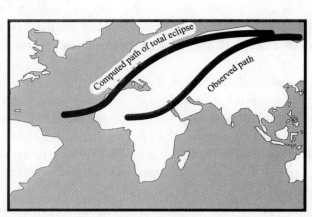

The computed and observed eclipse track on 15th April, 136 BC.

On 14 March 1879, Albert Einstein was born in the city of Ulm, Germany. On 11 August 1999, the skies above his birthplace darkened as the Moon eclipsed the Sun. One of the central predictions of Einstein's general theory of relativity was that the Sun's gravity would bend light from distant stars twice as much as Newton predicted. This bending of light could be tested with stars whose light passes close to the Sun on the way to Earth and such stars are only visible in the darkened sky at the time of a total eclipse.

Einstein's theory of relativity was written in the darkest days of World War I. The theory was enthusiastically supported by Professor Arthur Eddington of Cambridge. Eddington made measurements on the west African island of Principe during the total eclipse of 29 May 1919 and announced to the world in September 1919 that Einstein was correct. Albert Einstein became a celebrity and a household name and more popular than Charlie Chaplin. Politicians and film stars in the 1920s queued to be photographed with him, thanks to a total eclipse. The irony is that Eddington's measurements were not very accurate, the gravitational shift in the stars was very small, Eddington did not prove relativity beyond reasonable doubt and his interpretations were coloured by his enthusiastic embrace of Einstein's ideas. More accurate modern eclipse measurements later confirmed relativity.

Herodotus and Plutarch recorded eclipses and the Greek poet Archilochus describes an eclipse of 650 BC in a poem and Ptolemy documented eclipses dating back to 720 BC in his *Almagest*. From Babylonian, Chinese, European and Arab records, we have some 300 documented total eclipses since 700 BC showing eclipses every 18 months 11.5 days. The first eclipse was documented on carved bamboo from the tomb of King Wei Xiang, who ruled China around 500 BC. These writings tell of a day, calculated as 21 April 899 BC, when dawn broke twice.

Ancient records show that in 500 BC the day must have been 50 milliseconds shorter than today. The Moon's gravity stretches the Earth, a bulge forms (especially in the oceans) and the Moon pulls on this bulge as the Earth rotates. The end result is the Earth's spin slows and the Moon recedes from the Earth. This slowing down of the spin is partially counterbalanced by a slight speeding up as a result of post-icehouse conditions.

The huge weight of polar ice during the last icehouse created a bulge in the Earth at the equator. Once the ice completely melted, the equator became slimmer and the planet started to spin faster thereby shortening the day about 0.5 milliseconds a century. However, after a glacial event, water is transferred from ice at the poles to the sea. Sea level rises and, as a result, the Earth spins a little slower thereby making the day longer. The end result of both lengthening (sea level rise) and shortening (slimmer equator) the day is that the day has been getting 1.7 milliseconds longer each century but this figure oscillates between 1.4 and 2.0 milliseconds. This oscillation occurs every 1100 years in accord with a 1100 to 1500 year oscillation of slight greenhouse and icehouse. Such changes, although slight, can have a large effect over hundreds of millions of years.

The rotation of Earth slows for other reasons. For example, El Niño causes a reversal in the Pacific Ocean current and affects the world's winds. Winds near the equator that blow from east to west slow down whereas westerly winds, such as the jet stream, speed up. The result is that the atmosphere spins around the Earth faster and faster in the same direction as the Earth's rotation. As the atmosphere speeds up, it steals momentum from the Earth hence the Earth spins slower and the days become longer. In the 1998 El Niño, the days dragged on relentlessly for an extra 0.4 milliseconds and we all enjoyed the extra tenth of a second in the year 1998. Did anyone notice?

Since the last glaciation, the atmosphere has been warming and slowing the rotation of the Earth. It has been calculated that if the Earth's atmosphere increased by 0.79 °C per century, then the Earth's rotation should slow by 0.56 milliseconds per century and it has been suggested that a more accurate method of measuring global warming might be by measuring the decrease in the Earth's rotation. This is the theory. In practice, there are numerous other factors which affect rotation such as the rise and fall of mountain chains or the rise of molten rock beneath the surface.

Strange as it seems, ancient tidal mud flats, fossil corals, historical eclipses and modern El Niño records agree that the Earth is slowing down with age.

Siljan in Sweden was struck with two huge extraterrestrial bodies 368 million years ago. There were two waves of mass extinctions of multicellular life and marine species were particularly hard hit. This was the second of the major mass extinctions on Earth that occurred since the explosion of life. The best-known impact site was under water and a crater 53 kilometres in diameter is still preserved. The impact melted the floor of the sea, a waterspout carried bits of the sea floor, molten rocks and meteorite fragments high into the atmosphere. The crater floor was compressed, shocked and rebounded. Minerals which form only at extremely high pressure were left on the floor of the crater and much of the impact site was melted and vapourised. Melted and vapourised rock rained down on Earth as glass. The sea floor peeled like an orange to give a deep crater and a lip from the blasting out of crater floor material. Shock waves went through the planet and rocks on many parts of Earth were triggered into melting and breaking. The shock waves went deep into the Earth, surface grains of quartz were shocked into another form of quartz which we now create at nuclear bomb test sites and tepee-like structures were formed beneath the impact site. The tsunami engulfed all of Scandinavia, vegetation was flattened and Scandinavian life was destroyed. A layer of sand and gravel with bits of glassy material and meteorite fragments was left behind and the backwash filled the craters with sediment.

There was so much material blasted into the Earth's atmosphere that sunlight could not penetrate to the Earth's surface. Earth became a cold dark place. Vegetation which relies on photosynthesis and floating marine organisms died. The food chain collapsed and this led to a major mass extinction of life forms which thrive at the surface of the continents and oceans. Most of the life that survived was in the Southern Hemisphere, in the ocean deeps or underground. Immediately after the mass extinction, amphibians appeared, filled vacated ecosystems and thrived on land plants established 100 million years earlier.

Life which did not become extinct after the Siljan impact still had a few more trials and tribulations. More massive extraterrestrial bodies hit planet Earth. These formed a 15-kilometre-sized impact crater 360 million years ago at Kaluga, Russia and a 54-kilometre-sized crater 357 million years ago at Charlevoix, Canada. Organisms weakened by the Siljan impact were pushed to extinction by the Kaluga and Charlevoix impacts.

Oil drilling in sedimentary basins has given many clues about old impact sites. Oil drilling east of Shark Bay in Western Australia gave some faint clues of a 120-kilometre-diameter circular structure, which only appears from gravity and magnetic measurements. This was recently drilled with a view to ascertaining whether it was a major impact site. A structure this size indicates that the extraterrestrial visitor was big enough to cause a mass extinction. The re-drilling of the structure, the

Woodleigh Impact Structure, showed typical impact shock features, glass and debris. Preliminary dating shows that the date of the Woodleigh structure could be the same as the Siljan impact.

There is a 7-kilometre-wide impact structure at Piccaninny, Kimberleys, Western Australia, which contains fragmented rock. The impacting took place at or before 360 million years ago. A little later, also in the Kimberleys, appears a tell-tale iridium concentration in muddy rock coincidental with minor mass extinctions. This again suggests life might have been affected by an impact. There may have been an extraterrestrial cluster that hit Earth between 360 and 370 million years ago.

After the major mass extinction 368 million years ago, there was a period of global aridity. Red dune sands and salt lakes were abundant, amphibians left tracks on the sediments and fresh water lakes teeming with fish dried out to give us some of the most spectacular fossil fish beds on Earth.

In the period 370 to 250 million years ago the atmosphere was so rich in oxygen it was very close to combustion. Lightning would have caused local combustion of the atmosphere. At this time the fossil record shows the sudden appearance of insects such as giant dragonflies with wingspans of over 70 centimetres. Such large bodies could only have been possible if there were high quantities of oxygen diffusing through the insects' passive respiratory tubes. Furthermore, an atmosphere with 35 per cent oxygen would have been considerably denser thereby facilitating flight. When the atmospheric oxygen content dropped 250 million years ago, the giant dragonflies became extinct. The sudden appearance and disappearance of organisms over geological time is a reflection of the constantly changing environments and is the normal business of a dynamic planet.

The time from 330 to 250 million years ago was one in which vegetation thrived. Initially, the Northern Hemisphere was a cool moist place with large swamp areas on plains, deltas and lakes. The massive expansion of continental vegetation caused the Earth's atmospheric carbon dioxide content fell. Perhaps 18 per cent 570 million years ago, it was only 1 per cent 300 million years ago. Almost all of this carbon dioxide still remains in rocks such as limestone and carbon-rich materials which extracted carbon from the atmosphere like coal, petroleum and black muddy rocks. Life–excreted oxygen rose from 0.05 per cent

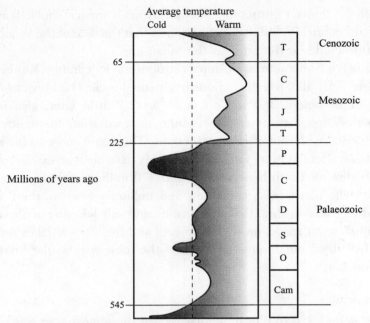

Estimates of the surface temperature changes over time showing that,
for the history of time, there has been continual climate change.

600 million years ago to 13 per cent 350 million years ago. While all
this was going on, reptiles made a quiet appearance on Earth 330 million
years ago as did insects, 20 million years later.

There was another icehouse 300 million years ago. The global icehouse
was a period of cyclical climate change with icehouse cycles of 40 000
to 120 000 years and 235 000 to 400 000 years long. These cycles
resulted from slight wobbles in the Earth's orbit. The fluctuation between
icehouse and greenhouse conditions is recorded in the rocks. During
the greenhouse, seas covered much of the continents and as the sea
level fell during an icehouse, shallow marine sediments were left draped
over the continents. At the same time sediments were sinking due to
compaction and the continents were sinking due to the weight of ice.
Once the ice sheets melted, the continents rose.

In the Northern Hemisphere 300 million years ago, massive amounts
of vegetation accumulated in swamps to be compressed into peat which,
upon further compression and heating, resulted in the large coal deposits
of Europe. Because of the great accumulation of carbon-rich material
in the Northern Hemisphere, this time period was named the Carbon-

iferous. Although these forests were cool and moist, there were forest fires. There have been bushfires ever since there were plants on land.

Lightning strikes commonly start forest fires and they can extend from forest lowlands and peat beds which, once set alight, can smoulder for years. Fires only occur when the atmosphere has more than 14 per cent oxygen. Today it has 21 per cent. The fossil record shows there were catastrophic forest fires 300 million years ago when the oxygen content was 35 per cent. These fires were similar to those of south-east Asia in 1982-1983 and 1996-1997 which occurred during a short-term climatic change when tropical areas were unseasonably dry.

Sandstones in Nova Scotia contain fossilised charcoal logs and charcoal stumps. Many of the charcoal logs contain the charred remains of reptiles and amphibians. It appears that the fauna hid in logs to escape the forest fires and perished by asphyxiation or burning. What we see in the fossil record is little different from modern areas which have been ravaged by bushfires.

Immediately before and during Carboniferous times, Australia was considerably different from the peat-rich cool moist swamps of the Northern Hemisphere. Eastern Australia was blessed with massive explosive volcanoes, earthquakes and deep ocean trenches and Australia continued to grow eastwards. At this time most of the action was in the New England district and far north Queensland. Some of the largest volcanoes in the history of Earth exploded in far north Queensland and hundreds of square kilometres were blanketed by superheated ash flows. Large bodies of molten rock became solid beneath the surface to form granites. Others reached the surface to form explosive volcanoes. Landslides, ash falls and heavy rains left unconsolidated sediment in deltas and on the narrow continental shelf. Submarine debris flows, probably triggered by earthquakes, poured sediment into the deep trenches which sank and buckled as they filled. Volcanic ash was thrown high into the atmosphere and blanketed the land and oceans. Large blocks of the continental shelf, including pieces of coral reefs kilometres long, slipped off the shelf into the ocean deeps.

The oceans were being pulled apart and seamounts, mid-ocean ridges and hot springs were part of the ever changing ocean floor in the Carboniferous. While this intense volcanic activity was taking place, protected shallow water ecosystems had thriving communities of brachiopods, molluscs, crinoids, trilobites and corals. These shallow marine communities were commonly inundated by thick layers of volcanic ash and are preserved as excellent fossil beds in eastern Australia. Isolated lakes and swamps started to accumulate thin peat layers and many times these layers were covered with volcanic ash, sand and mud before the whole peat-forming process started again.

Then the centre of volcanic activity moved to far north Queensland. The twisting, pushing and pulling of the continent resulted in down-warping of the crust and large basins developed. These basins flanked the sea and were filled by debris from the land and the occasional ash fall. Although volcanism had waned in eastern Australia, planet Earth was in the grip of a severe icehouse peaking around 250 million years ago. Glaciers scraped over the land surface, picked up soil and rocks and dropped icebergs into the ocean. As the icebergs melted, the soil and rocks were dropped on the sea floor. This was another period of fluctuating icehouse and greenhouse. With each greenhouse, the ice melted, glaciers retreated, meltwaters were dammed and debris was left in the valleys. The seasonal cycle of sand (summer) and silt (winter) was deposited in the glacial lakes and dropstones show that there were small icebergs in many of the lakes. These glacial rocks are common in

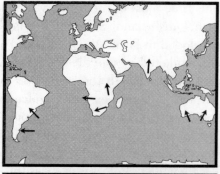

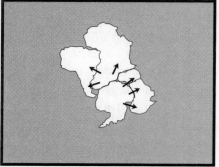

Moving ice 300 to 250 million years ago left debris and scratched bedrocks. When the continents are reunited into Gondwana, the direction of ice flow can be computed.

the Hunter Valley and occur in many other areas of Australia. In parts of Victoria remnant sheets of debris record extensive continental ice sheets that, at times, extended from adjoining Antarctica to central Queensland.

Biodiversity is a crude measurement of climate. In tropical areas today such as the Great Barrier Reef, there is a great diversity in the warm, shallow, sunny water. The shallow marine communities during the icehouse 250 million years ago are characterised by only a few species, suggesting conditions were frigid and life was struggling.

Although it was cool and moist, plants thrived in the Southern Hemisphere. The climate would have been somewhat like that of Ireland. Peat accumulated in swamps, lowlands, deltas and upland bogs. These blankets of peat were covered by sediments such as silt, sand and gravel. Over time, peat was compressed, lost water and was heated to form the massive coal deposits of South Africa, India and Australia. In Australia, the forested upland swamps, the lowland reedy swamps and back dune lagoons all produced a different type of peat. For example, the peaty mud formed in quiet back dune lagoons commonly contains a high proportion of spores and pollen. This kind of sediment consolidates into oil shale. Upon heating, the pollen and spores explode and release petroleum.

The coals of NSW and Queensland formed during the Permian, a name that derives from the Perm Basin of Russia. Permian rocks show that the peat swamps were commonly inundated with sand and gravel, mats of peat were ripped from the floor of swamps and transported to deltas and bays, and the swamp was covered with sediments from flooding. Flood waters flowed down rivers to deltas and, in many places, river channels clogged with flood debris such as branches and logs are preserved. The sediments contain fragments from mountains in the hinterland. After inundation of the peat swamp, the vegetation regenerated and the whole process took place again. Many of the peat swamps were dusted with thin layers of ash from distant volcanoes. Some of the peat swamps were very close to active volcanoes and, in a number of places in eastern Australia, tree stumps and roots of what was a peat swamp are preserved, the trees flattened by a lateral blast from a volcano. Coal is now covered by a thick layer of volcanic ash.

A global icehouse killed off much of the vegetation in the Northern Hemisphere which then became a dry windy place in the Permian. Large areas of salty arid deserts formed, warm oceans teemed with many tropical species and seas evaporated to form thick layers of salt. The desert sediments are now the Permian red sandstones in the UK, France, Germany, Poland and Russia. The salt layers formed at this time are mined for everyday use, Siberia being a good example.

The icehouse conditions came to a sudden end. A mass extinction resulted in the loss of many species, possibly over 95 per cent of all multicellular species. This extinction defines the Permian-Triassic boundary which is dated at 248.2 ± 4.8 million years ago. This boundary is frustratingly difficult to accurately define because of land surface, biological and climate changes. Various texts place the boundary at 245,248,250 and 251 million years ago with 251 million years ago being the most probable date. This was the greatest crisis in the history of life on Earth. Forget the wipe out of the dinosaurs 65 million years ago. This was a far more spectacular mass extinction and it took less than a million years, a blink of the geological eye. The planet had been pushed to almost total extinction of all but bacterial life and we don't really know why. If there had been a 100 per cent kill of advanced life, bacteria would have had to start the whole process again and life on Earth would probably have been completely different from today.

The greatest casualties were shallow marine, floating and terrestrial animals. A near-fatal blow was delivered to mammal-like reptiles that had ruled life on land for 80 million years. Dinosaurs soon stepped into their shoes and took over. Again, the most common survivors lived in specialised niches such as the deep oceans and burrows but there were some surprises. Little squat stubby-legged terrestrial carnivores called cynodonts somehow survived. And a good thing too! The cynodonts were the ancestors of all modern mammals, including us. The extinction almost halted the long and triumphal march of the insects. Insects are abundant on our warm wet vegetated planet. There are more than 10 000 species of beetle.

The extinction can be recognised in plants by a change in the isotopes of carbon, a profound change in fossilised soils, and a change from Permian cold temperate broadleaf deciduous swamp woodlands (which gave the peat for the NSW and Queensland coals) to warmer climate Triassic vegetation. The Triassic coals at Leigh Creek, South Australia, give us a good picture of the vegetation which existed immediately after the mass extinction.

Stream patterns in South Africa changed from a meandering shape, typical in well-vegetated areas, to a braided pattern, typical of areas lacking deep-rooted vegetation. In Antarctica the ancient soils at the Permian-Triassic boundary show that peat suddenly disappeared, there was a high-latitude greenhouse and volcanic ashes ceased to blanket the cold temperate swamps of the Permian.

Old soils, fossil plants, fossil reptiles and carbon isotopes all confirm that, at the end of the Permian, there was a sudden change to low-productivity ecosystems dominated by opportunistic and stress-tolerant organisms. Life was difficult immediately after the Permian-Triassic extinction and we can only wonder how the animal survivors eked out an existence immediately after the mass extinction. In the marine environment the extinction had an even greater effect than on land. The trilobites were gone forever, as were two lines of sea urchins and 2 metre-sized reptiles known as gorgonopsids.

There are no smoking guns that tell about the cause of this mass extinction but circumstantial evidence does exist. The most likely possibility is an asteroid more than 20 kilometres in diameter that impacted Earth. However, evidence is not strong. There is the possibility that this mass extinction is related to the 247-million-year-old 40-kilometre–wide impact crater at Araguainha in Brazil. This Brazilian impact site might indicate that there was an extraterrestrial cluster which hit Earth around about 245 to 250 million years ago.

Calculations of lunar impacting rates, Earth impacting rates and astronomical measurements show that in the last 250 million years of Earth history, there should be 30 craters of more than 100 kilometres diameter and three craters of more than 300 kilometres diameter. Over the history of time on Earth, there should have been half a dozen impact craters greater than 500 kilometres diameter and a few craters more than 1000 kilometres diameter. Ghostly images of circular structures in Western Australia may be the remnants of such enormous impacts. New craters are being found all the time but only a fraction of these large impact sites have been recognised, especially in older rocks, because of constant reworking of the crust on our dynamic planet.

If the Araguainha crater was the impact site of an extraterrestrial body that almost wiped out life on Earth, evidence should be widespread and more convincing. The crater should be far bigger: an impact to produce a solitary crater 40 kilometres in diameter is hardly big enough to produce a great mass extinction. Small amounts of shocked quartz blasted out of an impact crater some 248 million years ago have been found in Antarctica and Australia but the source is unknown. But, if the Araguianha crater formed from a *cluster* of extraterrestrial bodies which hit Earth, then there is the tantalising possibility that there are many other craters of this age. Because quartz is found on the continents and not the ocean floor, shocked quartz can only derive from continental impacts. An impact into the ocean hundreds of millions of years ago is far more difficult to detect and, because the oceans occupy 70 per cent of the surface of Earth then 70 per cent of impacts are expected in them. An oceanic impact would produce tsunamis and volcanic outpourings.

The coincidence of massive rapid outpourings of 1 million cubic kilometres of lava in Siberia, 248.3 million years old, suggests a tantalising relationship between impacting, outpourings of huge volumes of lava over a very short period of time, and mass extinctions. The Siberian traps were not just some little volcanic eruption somewhere in Russia. The lavas would cover Australia to a depth of 4 kilometres. Now that was a volcanic eruption! Forget pathetic little modern eruptions such as Mt St Helens which only belched out just over 1 cubic kilometre of material. The Siberian eruptions ejected monstrous quantities of gas into the atmosphere. The carbon dioxide and methane led to global warming whereas the sulphuric acid aerosols led to global cooling and, with the Siberian eruptions, the end result was global cooling. In the Sydney area, 245-million-year-old soil horizons show structures resulting from permafrost. Although a short-lived climate change might not be the reason for the mass extinction, the volcanism in Siberia could have poisoned the atmosphere with sulphurous gases. The jury is still out as to whether this volcanism was a result of impacting.

The fossils show that land animals became extinct more slowly at higher latitudes. The big kill was in the tropical and temperate areas. After an initial quick cold snap with lowered sea level and acid rain, there was probably global warming. The environmental stress of these extremes in quick succession may have caused the extinction. Plant fossils have an unusual carbon 13 to carbon 12 signature, suggesting they used carbon 12-rich gas spewed out of Siberian volcanoes, that there was sudden death of plants, possibly by volcanic-induced forest fires.

Another type of extraterrestrial cause for this crisis in life is gaining support. Every few hundreds of millions of years, a star explodes within a few tens of light years from Earth. At that distance, high-energy particles and radiation from the explosion would strip away the Earth's ozone layer for hundreds of years. With no ozone layer, ultraviolet light from the Sun and the supernovae would penetrate the atmosphere, changing its chemistry and killing surface life. Hot gas plasma from the explosion might also have disrupted the Earth's magnetic field and allowed cosmic rays to reach the Earth's surface, causing more damage. In Japan, China, India, Armenia, Iran and Hungary what could be the debris of an exploded star has been recognised in rocks 250 million years old and, in these rocks, extraterrestrial gas is trapped in carbon cages, buckyballs.

Sediments dredged up from the sea floor in 1300 metres of water near Mona Pihoa in the South Pacific are clues that exploding stars affect Earth. Although they only represent the last 13 million years of sediment formation, they contain traces of iron 60. This unusual form of iron can only be formed by a flood of high-energy particles from a supernoval explosion a few hundred light years away. The short half–life of iron 60 (1.5 million years) and other supernoval relics such as plutonium 244 are such that they can not be detected in material 250 million years old. Nevertheless, there is a distinct possibility that the biggest mass extinction of all time was related to a supernoval explosion or comet impact.

There could have been widespread depletion of oxygen. Others suggest that the mass extinction could have had a biological origin such as an algal bloom, similar to the modern-day red tides, or a trans-species disease, like influenza, AIDS or Creutzfeld-Jacob disease.

Although there have been enormous advances in science, there are still great unanswered questions. The cause of the greatest mass extinction of all time is this one. The origin of life is a profound question, but it is probably of more importance to understand why most multicellular life periodically disappears, only to appear again. Whatever the cause of mass extinctions, the history of Earth written in stone shows us that species extinction is quite normal. Conservation of species does not occur.

There was a rapid recovery. No new life forms appeared on Earth and the survivors evolved and diversified to fill the vacant ecosystems. The rebound was very rapid indeed and within 5 million years, all ecosystems were again swarming with life. Between 245 and 214 million years ago, most of Australia was a continental land mass. In far eastern Australia (Sydney and Hunter Bowen Basins), far western Australia

(Perth Basin), Erskine Ranges (Kimberleys, Western Australia) and in other small basins (Leigh Creek, South Australia), sediments were dumped from the continent into large basins. There was minor deposition of mud, silt and sand in huge deltas and basins in both marine and lake environments in eastern Australia such as Wollongong, Sydney and Gosford.

Australia was then at low latitudes, probably with a humid temperate climate and marked seasonal rainfall variations. The land was covered with a great variety of plants, mostly ferns, horsetails, conifers and seed ferns. Fish, amphibians and primitive sharks lived in the rivers and lakes. The best known fish fossils are from old brick-clay quarries in the Sydney and Gosford areas and from the Knocklofty Ranges near Hobart. The best amphibian, reptile and mammal-like reptile fossil localities are near Rolleston, Queensland.

At the time the large coal basins were forming in eastern Australia, Antarctica and Australia were one landmass with the mountains in Antarctica shedding sediment into the Sydney and Hunter-Bowen Basins. Much of this sediment derived from continental ice sheets. The Hawkesbury Sandstone in Sydney was once sandy sediment which contained minute quantities of heavy minerals such as zircon. This zircon is dated at 600 million years old. However, there are no 600 million year old rocks in eastern or central Australia and the only 600 million year old rocks which could have been weathered and eroded to form sand are those in the mountains in Antarctica. Weathering and erosion of the Hawkesbury Sandstone has released quartz, zircon and other minerals which have accumulated on the eastern Australian beaches.

A smaller impact in Australia occurred somewhere between 245 and 220 million years ago. The Lorne Basin, 25 kilometres southwest of Port Macquarie, is a circular structure 30 kilometres across and 350 metres deep. Glass with embedded silica spheres contains metallic iron and high-temperature mineral grains. Hills of granite, North Brother, Middle Brother and South Brother, 210 million years old may represent melts which later moved up deep fractures caused by the impact. By calculating the likelihood of extraterrestrial impacts by asteroids greater than 20 kilometres in diameter over the last 120 million years, it has been shown that there should be a few more impact sites in NSW. These have not yet been found.

At about the time when the Lorne Basin was blasted out, the world's first dinosaurs made their appearance. Fossils in Madagascar of a long-necked, small-headed plant eater about the size of a kangaroo are probably the oldest distant relative of dinosaurs known. These are in rocks 230 million years old. In rocks 228 million years old fossils of two-legged predator dinosaurs have been found in Argentina. At that time, the giant supercontinent Pangea was home to these early dinosaur ancestors. It was not long before the giant supercontinent and its dinosaur cargo broke into a number of smaller continents.

It appears that Earth was periodically hit by clusters of meteorites and comets. This process again took place about 214 million years ago. A 220-million-year-old 80-kilometre-wide crater at Puchez-Katunski, Russia, and two impact craters 214 million years ago at Manicouagan and Rochechouart in Quebec left craters 100 kilometres and 25 kilometres in diameter respectively. Other smaller impact craters are known from this time. They are St Martin, Canada, 40 kilometres, 219 million years old; Obolon', Russia, 15 kilometres, 215 million years old; and Red Wing, USA, 9 kilometres, 200 million years old. The dating margins of error are wide, but all overlap at 214 million years ago. By fitting the continents back together, it can be shown that the impacts at Manicouagan, Rochechouart, St Martin, Obolon' and Red Wing were all at the same latitude and within 43.5° of longitude. This strongly suggests that these five impacts formed from the fragmentation of an asteroid or comet some 214 million years ago and calculations of such a fragmentation event show that the impacting over 43.5° would have taken place in a matter of hours.

And again, there was a mass extinction 214 million years ago in which 76 per cent of all multicellular species, predominantly marine, were lost. The mass extinction, a massive volcanic outpouring in the central Atlantic Ocean and the beginning of the fragmentation of the super-continent Pangea are an uncanny coincidence. Did the impact of a cluster of extraterrestrial visitors suddenly jolt Earth into another geo-logical era? The planet was well used to impacts producing earthquakes, volcanism, tsunamis, billowing clouds of dust, glass and fragments which blocked out the Sun and cooled the planet. Both the atmosphere and oceans cooled. Survivors of the mass extinction lived in specialized niches and vacated ecosystems were quickly filled.

The pulling apart of continents and massive outpourings of volcanic rocks are probably due to convective mantle plumes of slightly molten rock and it is well known that mantle rocks partially melt to volcanic rocks by either heating or sudden depressurising. Massive volcanic outpourings of volcanic rock can result from both a mantle plume or depressurising as a result of impact rebound. Impact sites are the loci of numerous very deep fractures. Such sites can be the locus of new mantle plumes and the outpouring of lava.

The massive outpourings of volcanic rocks suddenly degassed the Earth's mantle and added carbon dioxide to the atmosphere. A study of fossilised stomata, the openings in leaves that let in carbon dioxide, show atmospheric carbon dioxide rose from 0.06 to 0.21 per cent. The modern atmosphere has almost 0.04 per cent atmospheric carbon dioxide. This rise in carbon dioxide would have caused a 4 °C temperature rise to a level which was 8 °C higher than the current average global temperature. Some 95 per cent of all plant species and 50 per cent of all land animals perished in this mass extinction. Large-leafed plants were replaced by small or multi-lobed leafed plants. Carbon dioxide-induced overheating of the atmosphere appears to have destroyed land plants and the animals that lived off them. This is the earliest geological clue that extreme global warming can be a killer. Immediately after the mass extinction, mammals first appeared on Earth and filled some vacated ecosystems.

The Earth 200 million years ago had large inhospitable areas. At this time, very large volumes of salt beds formed. These reflect widespread arid warm climates on the supercontinent Pangea. Yet another minor mass extinction of multicellular life took place 190 million years ago. Evidence for the extinction is seen in Siberia, the Andes and the British Isles. It is best recorded by the loss of some bivalves, brachiopods,

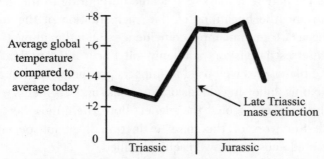

A sudden warming 206 million years ago created a minor mass extinction of plants and land animals.

ostracods, belemnites and dinoflagellates. The reason for the minor mass extinction is unknown. It could have resulted from the spread of oxygen-poor bottom waters associated with a sea level rise, it could be related to a temperature drop or it might result from evolutionary factors, especially the length of time a species lives before becoming extinct.

The study of impacting continues. I suspect that the history of the planet is somewhat like war for a soldier. Long periods of boredom with very little happening (uniformitarianism) punctuated by short periods of abject terror (catastrophism). During these catastrophic periods in the history of Earth, a large proportion of life became extinct and the remaining life evolved very quickly to fill new ecosystems. Climates changed rapidly, continents fragmented and started to drift thereby inducing climate change and major short-term events of volcanism occurred. It is quite probable that all the great changes in the history of Earth over the last 570 million years are the results of extraterrestrial influences. There is an uncomfortable feeling about a great rock in the sky hurtling towards Earth and yet there is nothing we earthlings can do.

6

INLAND SEAS, DIVIDING RANGES, NEW OCEANS AND CHANGED RIVERS

Of Australia:

Well, I say, and repeat, and sustain, that this is the most curious country in
the world . . . In this country the edges rose above the waves before the
centre, like a gigantic ring, and perhaps there still exists a half-evaporated
inland sea in the interior . . .

Jules Verne, *On the Track*

The early explorers in Australia looking for the Inland Sea were
120 million years too late! An inland sea covered most of the
Australian continental land mass during one of the many
prolonged greenhouse events which planet Earth has enjoyed.

There is an uncanny coincidence between a long period of global
warming and the fragmentation of supercontinents. In the period 120
to 80 million years ago, there was an increase in the frequency and size
of plumes of molten rocks in the mantle and an accelerated rate of
production of new ocean crust. Much of the current ocean floor formed
at this time. These processes result in the release of massive quantities
of carbon dioxide from the mantle. The 50 to 75 per cent increase in
ocean-crust production was during a 40-million-year period when there
were no magnetic reversals. In the period 120 to 80 million years ago,
surface sea water was considerably warmer than now. Sea level was far
higher than now, in part due to the large volume of mid ocean ridges
and in part due to the melting of the polar ice caps. A large proportion
of the world's oil and gas formed at this time when the sea floor was

covered with black organic-rich muds. The increased volcanism pumped such large quantities of carbon dioxide into the atmosphere that it could not be removed quickly enough in sediments, hence the atmosphere increased in carbon dioxide which, in turn, enhanced the greenhouse.

This greenhouse was the biggest of them all. Rainfall, temperatures and sea level rose, and life greatly expanded in the additional shallow water ecologies. Much of the land in northern Europe was covered by warm shallow seas that left a chalk—a limey stone—or clay layer draped over what was once land. Chalk was formed from the accumulation of shells on the sea floor from very small organisms that floated in the balmy tropical ocean known as the Tethys. This was one of the greatest episodes of carbonate rock formation in the history of the Earth. Massive amounts of carbon dioxide were extracted from the atmosphere.

At that time, Australia was close to the South Pole yet it was covered by temperate vegetation, some of which accumulated to form dirty coals. There were volcanic eruptions which left ash layers and flattened the forests in parts of southern Victoria and what was the east of Australia. Most of Australia was flat to undulating and was cut by a system of braided streams and rivers which further denuded the continent.

Australia had become a tropical paradise 175 million years ago. Plant species which now thrive in far north Queensland were widespread in southern Australia. The higher rainfall resulted in numerous large inland rivers, lakes and swamps. Australia was blanketed by river sands which formed the basement to the Great Artesian Basin. At this time, the three sub-basins, which constitute the Great Artesian Basin, started to be filled with sediment. Where there were no rivers, muds and clays were deposited in swamps. Although the continents were covered by vegetation, there were no flowering plants and no grass. Fish thrived in small muddy lakes which were often clogged by reeds and mats of rotting vegetation. The river sands were consolidated into highly porous sandstone which now is the host for artesian water, oil and gas in NSW, Queensland, South Australia and the Northern Territory. Some coal formed at this time in bogs, swamps and lakes fed by inland rivers. Minor gravels were left by rivers in flood and some clays were deposited on the floor of inland lakes.

The continents are constantly being pulled apart and stitched back together. The pulling apart of continents initially forms a rift valley such

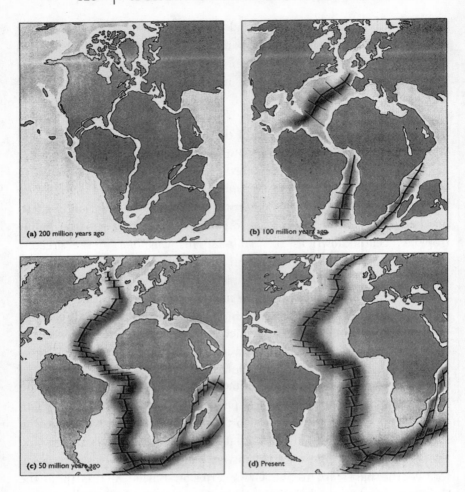

(a) 200 million years ago

(b) 100 million years ago

(c) 50 million years ago

(d) Present

as in East Africa. Further rifting forms a large waterway such as the Red Sea and mature rifting results in the formation of an ocean. Australia had spent far too long joined to Antarctica and was pulling away to drift into a warmer climate. Between 160 and 130 million years ago, Australia and Antarctica started to stretch apart and eight basins developed along the southern seaboard by rifting. The crust between Australia and Antarctica thinned from 40 kilometres thick to 10 kilometres thick and a 400-kilometre-wide rift opened up between them. Basalt volcanoes were active in the rift, lavas were erupted and great quantities of steam and carbon dioxide were released into the atmosphere. Sand and silt from Australia and Antarctica poured into the rift from the elevated Australian and Antarctic continental landmasses. Even though Australia was joined to Antarctica and was close to the South Pole, warm high rainfall conditions existed and conifers, cycads and ferns thrived.

Atmospheric carbon dioxide was about 1 per cent when the world's major coal deposits formed in the period 320 to 250 million years ago. From 300 to 120 million years ago, the global carbon dioxide content varied greatly, increased over time and reached a peak of 6 per cent 120 million years ago. The peak of 6 per cent carbon dioxide was at a time of a protracted greenhouse and maximum sea level. At this time, mean annual surface temperatures were 10 to 15 °C warmer than now. This peak carbon dioxide content also coincides with accelerated sea floor spreading and continental fragmentation. Rifting (sea floor spreading, continental fragmentation) always involves a massive degassing of water vapour, carbon dioxide, helium and methane from the mantle.

During these greenhouse times, some 150 million years ago, the oxygen content rose again to a peak of 26 per cent. Some insects became giant and flighted vertebrates such as birds, bats and dinosaurs evolved to capitalise on the denser oxygen-rich atmosphere. The first bird, *Archaeopteryx*, and pterosaurs appeared during these times of elevated oxygen. As soon as the oxygen content of the atmosphere decreased, the giant insects became extinct as earlier giant insects had done once before, and birds modified their anatomy in order to keep flying. At the peak of these greenhouse times 150 million years ago, flowering plants appeared and filled a warm wet carbon dioxide- and insect-rich terrestrial ecosystems.

This was a time when the carbon dioxide content of the atmosphere rapidly decreased from 5 per cent to 3 per cent before bouncing back to a peak of 6 per cent. Planet Earth then experienced 100 million years with an atmosphere warmer and richer in oxygen and carbon dioxide than at the present time. Carbon dioxide was again extracted from the atmosphere into limey sediments and carbon-rich materials. Since the high atmospheric carbon dioxide levels of 120 million years ago, the carbon dioxide content has decreased from 6 per cent to almost 0.0365 per cent now. This long greenhouse came to an abrupt end with the onset of another icehouse 2 million years ago.

Some 143 million years ago, a minor mass extinction occurred and 42 per cent of all multicellular species disappeared. Again, this mass extinction is probably related to extraterrestrial visitors. A 340-kilometre-wide crater at Morokweng, Kalahari Desert, may be the smoking gun for this mass extinction. This is a huge crater and other smaller craters

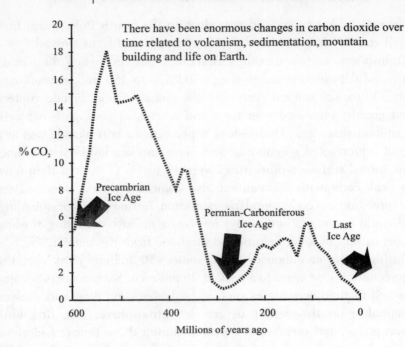

There have been enormous changes in carbon dioxide over time related to volcanism, sedimentation, mountain building and life on Earth.

at this time suggest that Earth was again hit by a cluster of comets or meteorites. The 40-kilometre-wide Mjolnir crater in Russia, formed about 142 million years ago. There are also two impacts in Australia from this time. The 24-kilometre-wide crater at Gosses Bluff, Northern Territory, formed 142.5 million years ago and the 3-kilometre-wide Liverpool Crater in Arnhem Land, Northern Territory, has broken and shocked rock of a similar age. Gosses Bluff has a crater, broken rock, ejected rock, shocked minerals and glass formed from impact melting and is probably one of the best-preserved ancient impact sites in the world. Impacting by a swarm of meteorites or comets may have initiated the break up of continental Africa and the outpouring over a very short period of time of masses of lava in the Sudan.

A later impact occurred, this time in Queensland at Tookoonooka in the Eromanga Basin. A 55-kilometre-wide crater was blasted out 128 million years ago. Although the crater is now covered by a thick sequence of rocks, tell-tale signs of shattered and broken rock and of glass formed from the melting during impact. Elsewhere in the Eromanga Basin at Talundilly, a 30-kilometre-wide subsurface structure of the same age was detected during oil exploration and identified as an impact crater.

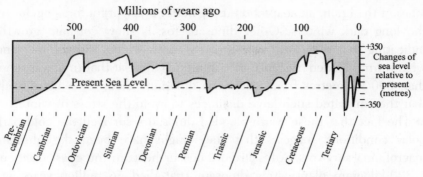

Over time, there have been huge changes in sea level related to continental movement, supercontinents, uplift, subsidence and glaciation.

As greenhouse conditions intensified, sea level rose to a maximum 115 to 110 million years ago. Australia, while still near the South Pole, was covered in a warm shallow inland sea and all that remained of the continental land mass was four low-lying islands. Tropical climates extended above the Arctic and Antarctic Circles. Extinct groups of shellfish, the ammonites and belemnites, lived in profusion in the shallow warm north-south sea throughout central Australia.

During the period of maximum sea level, much of the continent was covered with a blanket of shallow marine sediment, mainly mud, with rare layers of sand and silt. The muds are the opal dirt at Coober Pedy, White Cliffs and Lightning Ridge and they give us a good picture of what Australia was like at that time. At White Cliffs, the opal dirt contains shallow marine fossils of crinoids, lamellibrachs, brachiopods, foraminifera and cephalopods. These fossils are commonly opalised. Fossilised and opalised plesiosaurs and coniferous wood suggest a marine environment close to the shore. Ice-rafted boulders of quartzite occur in the opal dirt and derive from areas which outcrop to the west of White Cliffs. White Cliffs 115 million years ago was at a high latitude adjacent to quartzite mountains within which there were glaciers.

In parts of southern Victoria, the 122- to 113-million-year-old rocks show sedimentary structures which have derived from seasonally frozen ground similar to that which we see today in Siberia. Vegetation was ferny with rare flowering plants. At that time, southern Australia was at a high latitude, probably at 78° South, and the temperature calculated from isotope measurements indicates that the warmest month in southern Victoria was 15.6 to 21.4 °C and the coldest month was −32.3 to −23.9 °C. Dinosaur fossils in the same rock sequence have large optic lobes of the brain, an adaptation using better eyesight for foraging during the long dark winters. Other dinosaur fossils show constant growth, indicating that they were able to eat in both winter and summer and were warm-blooded. Because the Antarctic Circle at that time was more than 600 kilometres from where the dinosaurs died, it seems unlikely that they migrated such large distances to avoid the stress of winter.

The fact that these warm-blooded dinosaurs survived the cold dark polar conditions suggests that they might have been the ultimate macrofauna survivors. A fossilized dinosaur heart in the chest cavity of a 300-kilogram plant-eating dinosaur that died 66 million years ago shows that some dinosaurs were very active and warm-blooded. I wonder if colonies of dinosaurs similar to those that lived at the South Pole in southern Victoria 120 million years ago might have survived the mass extinction 65 million years ago which wiped out all other dinosaurs, only to drift gently into their own extinction a short time later?

Although Earth was in a period of global greenhouse, there were some cold places on Earth where the ground was seasonally frozen, glaciers dropped into the sea and dinosaurs had adapted to live. During this time of maximum sea level, the more northern parts of Australia were a dinosaur paradise. The abundance of lakes and lagoons teeming with life and lush vegetation made survival easy.

At Lark Quarry near Winton in central Queensland, old tidal flats show more than 3300 footprints of dinosaurs. There are footprints of three different species representing some 150 animals. The Winton footprints record 10 seconds of geological time and the drama of a life and death scene in the world of dinosaurs. A herd of small grazing plant-eaters *Wintonopus* and a large number of small coelurosaurs *Skartopus* were cornered on mud flats against a rocky bluff by a large carnivorous dinosaur *Tyrannosauropus*. The small dinosaurs took flight and sprinted at their top speed of 20 kilometres per hour past their predator who, with footprints 0.75 metres long, was probably about 12 metres in length.

Broome is also well known for its dinosaur footprints in the 120 million year old muddy rocks. At least ten different dinosaur species occupied lagoonal and swampy forest areas. Sauropod tracks are the most common but recently a footprint of *Megalosauropus*, a carnivorous 9 metre long beast, was cut out of the rock for sale on the lucrative overseas market. The culprit won himself two years in jail for destruction of a national treasure.

As well as dinosaurs, there were placentals and monotremes on what then was Australia. Asia also had placentals, as did North America where placentals and marsupials coexisted. There is evidence of a migration of placentals at this time and they were dispersed from Australia across the giant supercontinent Gondwana via Antarctica, South America, Africa and Europe. Another group of placentals were transported from eastern Gondwana to Asia on a natural Ark by the northward drifting to Asia of a microcontinent, now part of Myanmar.

Between 60 and 40 million years ago, placentals were extinct in Australia, but were present on all other continental landmasses. Australia had both marsupials and monotremes as did South America and marsupials were also present on Asia, Europe, Africa, North America and Antarctica. By 20 million years ago, the distribution of land animals had again changed. Placentals were extinct on Antarctica and lived on all other continents. Placentals had been re-introduced to Australia. Marsupials also lived on both North and South America. It appears that the drifting of continents played an important part in the distribution of life in the past and the present.

The great inland sea started to retreat and swamps, lagoons and river systems were developed. Some of the muds deposited during the period of maximum sea level 115 to 110 million years ago were eroded by meandering streams, and river sands were deposited on top of the opal dirt. The sea retreated, the continent of Australia was again exposed and weathering and erosion started to reshape the continent. Many of the marine sediments deposited during the high sea levels of the greenhouse times on more ancient rocks in inland Australia were removed.

As the great inland sea was retreating, Australia was still drifting northwards from the South Pole. India, then joined on to Western Australia, started to separate. A rift zone opened up between India and Western Australia some 120 million years ago and, 100 million years ago, India was drifting away from Australia at 5 centimetres per year. The rift zone became the Indian Ocean. In eastern Australia 96 million years ago, rifting between New Zealand and Australia commenced. Some 80 million years ago New Zealand started to drift out into the Pacific Ocean away from Australia. These events had a profound effect on Australia because the stresses and tension from the northward drifting from Antarctica and the westward-drifting of India left their mark on continental Australia.

Another minor mass extinction of multicellular life occurred 90 million years ago. At that time, there was increased melting of the mantle caused by the rise of plumes of buoyant hot rock from very deep. The crust thickened under the Pacific and Indian Oceans, there was a massive outpouring of basalt lava and large quantities of carbon dioxide and other gases were released into the atmosphere as the mantle underwent degassing. The release of sulphur dioxide, rotten egg gas and carbon dioxide into the oceans from the submarine volcanoes made seawater acidic and released more carbon dioxide by dissolving sea shells.

The end result was a run-away greenhouse effect which only stopped when volcanism waned. Greenhouse conditions resulted in increased productivity of ocean surface waters. The atmospheric and ocean temperatures rose, sea level rose and covered low-lying lands, and there was a sudden decrease in oxygen dissolved in ocean waters. Black organic-rich muds formed on the ocean floor became starved of oxygen. Some 26 per cent of multicellular life became extinct, most of it having lived in the deep ocean basins. This runaway greenhouse event provides a sobering message: one volcano can spoil your whole day.

Modern volcanoes lie along mid ocean ridges like Iceland, oceanic hot spots such as Hawaii, continental rift valleys like the East African Rift or continental hot spots like Mt Gambier, South Australia and western Victoria. Carbon dioxide is produced commercially from the Caroline No 1 well 17 kilometres south of Mt Gambier in South Australia. About 4 million cubic metres of carbon dioxide has migrated along faults and accumulated in porous rocks. The carbon dioxide has the chemical signature of the basalt volcanoes in the Mt Gambier area. Extremely large amounts of carbon dioxide forced the volcanoes at Mt Gambier to explode, with the most recent explosion just 4500 years ago.

In many other similar areas, East African Rift, Chile, Alaska and Cameroon, carbon dioxide is also commercially produced from some of the modern volcanoes which exhale massive quantities. There is so much carbon dioxide around the East African Rift that there are specific carbonate volcanoes which have feeder plugs and lavas composed of carbonate minerals. It has long been thought that sporadic and unexplained fish kills in the oceans might be due to a carbon dioxide burp from the rifts in the mid ocean ridges. An old crater lake above an extinct basalt volcano at Lake Nyos in Cameroon burped on 21 August 1986, filled valleys with carbon dioxide and suffocated 1700 villagers and their livestock. A similar burp took place in 1984 at Cameroon's Lake Monoun and 37 people suffocated. Weather conditions may trigger such burps which can pump massive quantities of carbon dioxide into the atmosphere thereby changing climate.

While this runaway greenhouse took place, yet another meteorite hit Australia. The 13-kilometre-wide crater in the Yallalie Basin, Western Australia, is now covered by sediments but broken and shattered rock and subsurface structures might be the smoking gun of an impact cluster which occurred around 90 million years ago. Large numbers of diamond-bearing volcanic rocks in Africa burst from a great depth in the mantle through to the surface 90 million years ago. The landscape of Africa was changed by a major uplift event 90 million years ago.

As New Zealand drifted away, the eastern edge of the Australian continent was warped up and the Great Dividing Range formed. The eastern edge of the Great Dividing Range to the west of Sydney is bounded by the bent rocks of the Lapstone Monocline and broken rocks of the Kurrajong Fault. There were three major warping events of the eastern edge of the Australian continent in response to the opening up of the Tasman Sea. Some rocks did not warp and were broken, and these faults were long active. Stresses were felt inland and faults in inland Australia were re-activated. Some of the eastern Australian faults were very deep and, as a result of decreasing stresses, induced slight melting of the Earth's mantle and basalt lavas moved up them. Each time eastern Australia was warped up, the faults were re-activated and there were basalt volcanoes. These volcanoes were mostly non-explosive and erupted lava flowed down valleys. Huge amounts of carbon dioxide were again released.

Some of these basalt lavas erupted at this time carried material from deep down in the mantle. Bombs of olivine-rich rocks were ejected from some of the more explosive volcanoes and some basalt contained sapphire, ruby, zircon and diamond brought up from the depths. The weathering, erosion and concentration of these gemstones from the rare explosive basalt volcanoes have produced concentrations of sapphire, ruby, zircon and diamond in some of the river systems in eastern Australia.

The rapid rise of the Great Dividing Range changed the course of the major river systems. Before the warping of eastern Australia, many major rivers flowed eastwards into the Pacific Ocean. As a result of warping, some of these rivers were cut in half, some drainage eastwards into the Pacific Ocean and most westwards. For example, the easterly-flowing Condamine River near Brisbane had its course changed by the rise of the Great Dividing Range. The short Clarence River now flows eastwards and the Condamine takes the long inland trip before it finally reaches the ocean. The change from plains to the Great Dividing Range has changed the rainfall pattern, with the high rainfall areas now in the narrow coastal belt and the eastern fall of the Great Dividing Range. The Condamine River carries far less water westwards than it did when it flowed eastwards.

The Great Dividing Range has a gentle slope inland and a steep slope on the coastal side giving the spectacular gorge country along the length of eastern Australia. With the rise of eastern Australia, much water flowed west as underground water. This water filled the pores of the 150-million-year-old sands, and flowed down and westwards into the centre of the Great Artesian Basin. During the passage of the underground water from the eastern highlands, salts dissolved from the minerals in

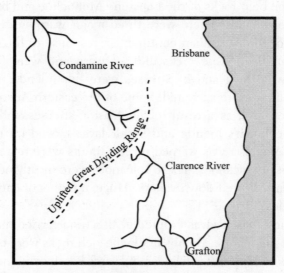

The changing of the course of the Condamine River by the uplift of the Great Dividing Range.

the rocks and the water was heated as it moved to greater depths. As a result, artesian water is now hot, high pressure and saline. In former times, Australia was warm and wet and the Great Artesian Basin was fully charged with water. Today, artesian water at Longreach is 2 million years old. Such fossil water can only be used frugally as we can not sit around for a few million years until the aquifer recharges in the next greenhouse period!

During this time of greenhouse, continental drift and building of the Great Dividing Range, Australia was drenched for millions of years by warm acid tropical rain. This was the beginning of almost 100 million years of tropical leaching of Australia which has left its mark as nutrient-deficient soils, enrichment of iron and other materials in soils, and a characteristic landscape. By contrast, most of Europe and North America were stripped of old leached soils during the last two million years of glaciation and new soils formed from the weathering of rocks over the last 10 000 years.

Deep sea drillings in the North Atlantic Ocean show that there was a rapid change in climate with cool fluctuating temperature 66.8 to 66.5 million years ago followed by an abrupt short warming 65.4 to 65.1 million years ago. This warm pulse could be linked to increased carbon dioxide in the atmosphere but is more probably a result of increased heat transport by ocean currents towards the pole. However, these warm conditions were temporarily interrupted by an extraterrestrial visitor.

Another major mass extinction, called the K-T extinction, occurred 65 million years ago. The Earth then was still a steamy hot tropical planet. The major mass extinction was caused by a random extraterrestrial event and some 75 to 80 per cent of all multicellular species disappeared. This is the most famous mass extinction of all because it signalled the end of the dinosaurs, which had dominated the land for 160 million years. Pterosaurs and plesiosaurs also suffered total extinction. In the seas, the ammonites disappeared. Both floating and deep-water marine animals suffered a catastrophic collapse. Immediately after the impact, some species suddenly spread and thrived (ferns, insects, mammals) and it was only after the K-T extinction that a new plant, grass, filled a new ecosystem on the continental landmasses.

A meteorite 12 kilometres in diameter was heading for Texas. Something went drastically wrong; it missed Texas and hit Chicxulub

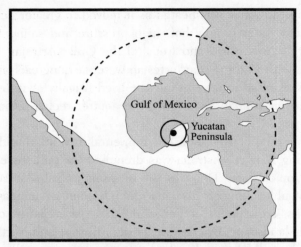

The impact crater (solid line) on Yucatan Peninsula, Mexico and the area which showed extreme impact features (dotted line).

in the Yucatán area of Mexico to form a crater 170 kilometres in size. The impact blasted water, sediment, molten rock and bits of meteorite high into the atmosphere. A tidal wave engulfed most of North America, Central America and adjacent coastal areas. The mass of sediment on the continental shelf collapsed in giant turbidity currents into the ocean deeps to leave a cocktail of debris and shallow water fossils in deep water settings.

In North America, forests were destroyed by huge tsunamis, animals and plants perished and a layer of sand and mud was deposited over the landscape. The backwash killed many of the remaining animals that survived the first tsunami. At Mimbral in Mexico, seven metres of sedimentary rock were laid down in less than a week. With all the dust in the atmosphere, the planet suddenly became dark and cold, plants and planktonic organisms died and the food chain collapsed. Falling debris was heated by friction as it fell to Earth. A shower of boiling hot rocks started global bush fires which have been recorded in places as far apart as Denmark and New Zealand. In fact, much of the methane trapped at low temperatures and high pressures in ocean floor sediments would have been released and lightning bursts in the disturbed atmosphere would have ignited local areas of methane-rich air. In some places, the atmosphere would have been on fire. This fiery apocalyptic end is supported by the abundance of carbon 12 over carbon 13 immediately after the impact, suggesting a lot of methane was burned. This isotopic pattern was not global, supporting the view that methane ignitions were localised. Such catastrophic releases of methane are not unknown. At Black Ridge, off the coast of Florida, a 36 by 22 kilometre area lost a massive amount of methane sometime over the last 2 million years.

The impact filled the atmosphere with choking dust and the planet was blanketed by a debris layer which formed from the falling material ejected from the impact crater. The debris is now exposed as a clay-rich layer with small pieces of glass. The impact vapourised the target rock, which later condensed as small glass spheres. The glass rained down on Earth and formed part of the debris layer. The debris layer also contains charcoal fragments, shocked and high pressure quartz, diamond grains, high temperature nickel-rich minerals, pieces of meteorite, fullerenes (high temperature carbon compounds produced from bushfires) and the chemical signature of extraterrestrial material (iridium, germanium, chromium and helium). Bits of meteorite in sea floor sediments at the K-T boundary have been found in drilling of the floor of the North Pacific Ocean. In the Boticcione Gorge near the medieval city of Gubbio in the Appenine Mountains of Italy, a thin clay horizon is the evidence that the dinosaur world ended. At the boundary, there are fossil traces of earthworms that burrowed into the mud consuming every trace of the biological material which died 65 million years ago. Such is life.

The K-T extinction 65 million years ago might have had an additional deadly factor. The sediments in the Yucatán area were wet and rich in carbonates and calcium sulphate. The impact of a 12 kilometre wide body cruising through the atmosphere at 30 kilometres per second blasted 50 000 tonnes of limestone into the atmosphere. Some 300 billion tonnes of sulphur dioxide, 200 billion tonnes of carbon dioxide and 700 billion tonnes of water would have been released into the atmosphere. In the stratosphere sulphur oxides and water vapour combined to form a sulphurous acid aerosol layer blocking out the Sun, preventing photosynthesis and chilling the planet for a few years. The enhanced greenhouse from the addition of large amounts of carbon dioxide to the atmosphere would have stopped a total freeze. The planet would have been covered in billowing choking sulphurous fumes. Acid rain would have killed much of the life that had survived the initial impact.

Any asteroid ripping through the atmosphere changes the nitrogen and oxygen gases to nitric oxide. Nitric oxide destroys stratospheric ozone, the planet's shield against damaging ultraviolet light. A 12-kilometre-sized asteroid would destroy 85 per cent of the planet's ozone.

Once the dust cloud from the impact settled, survivors would have been exposed to elevated ultraviolet light for one to three years after the impact. Ultraviolet radiation would double with the greatest increase in the shorter wavelengths that would have devastating effects. Stressed plants and animals in the long dark impact winter would have suffered DNA damage. The Earth was lucky that the impact 65 million years ago hit a very rare calcium sulphate rock. Sulphate aerosols absorb ultraviolet light and the lingering of sulphate aerosols in the atmosphere for decades after the impact may have allowed amphibians to survive the event that killed the dinosaurs.

The Chicxulub impact occurred 65 million years ago. Almost at the same time, there was the eruption of 3 million cubic kilometres of lava in India, the Deccan Traps, and millions of cubic kilometres of lava in Pacific submarine settings such as the Carlsberg Ridge and the Emperor-Hawaii Seamount Chain. These eruptions took place over a very short period of time. It is probable that such a massive impact triggered volcanism and mantle convection currents which resulted in terrestrial and submarine volcanism. This volcanism belched out sulphuric acid aerosols which would have induced global cooling and carbon dioxide, which would have induced global warming. The end result of competing cooling and warming processes was an atmospheric cooling of about 1 °C.

The history of impacts on Earth and the observation of the impact of the Shoemaker-Levy-9 impact with Jupiter show isolated impacts are rare. More common are clusters over a period of time. For example, some 100 00 to 200 000 years after the Chicxulub impact in Mexico, there was another impact in Poty in north-eastern Brazil.

The coincidental impacting, rapid and massive outpourings of lava, faulting, rifting, mantle convection currents and mass extinctions of life seem to have happened many times in the geological past and suggest that great changes on our planet may indeed be triggered by extraterrestrial events.

However, there is by no means agreement regarding the extinction of the dinosaurs. The thought of obliterating dinosaurs with one meteorite impact is attractive but things are often not as simple as they seem. Occam's Razor is not always applicable. The K-T extinction was not as sudden as we are led to believe. For 4 million years before the impact, trouble was brewing. The marine environment was stressed, highly specialised animals became extinct, others became rare and evolution of the floating animals virtually came to a standstill. In some places, floating animals show a stepwise or gradual extinction which started before the K-T event. Volcanism could cause such an extinction pattern.

Dinosaurs had been declining in both species and numbers for a few million years too. Separation of Antarctica from southern Australia 67 million years ago might have started the demise of the dinosaurs before the K-T event. Around 65 million years ago, there were many drastic changes to the environment. Immediately before the K-T extinction there were cool fluctuations (66.8 to 66.5 million years ago) and a short warming (65.4 to 65.1 million years ago) induced by a change in ocean currents. There had been a decline in the oxygen content of the atmosphere, flowering plants had flourished and largely replaced the earlier flora, and there were large changes in sea level. All these events stressed dinosaurs. At the K-T extinction, dinosaurs both large and small became extinct, but other reptiles such as lizards, snakes, crocodiles and tortoises together with small mammals and birds continued to the present day. The K-T extinction affected all groups of organisms from the largest to the smallest floating plankton. There are tantalising unanswered questions. For example, why did small dinosaurs die out but not birds or mammals?

Was the asteroid impact at Chicxulub the straw that broke the camel's back?

Australia was recovering from the K-T extinction in warm tropical conditions but it was still under the influence of other global forces. India was still racing away from Australia towards Asia, the New Zealanders were travelling eastwards and Australia was moving at some 7 centimetres a year northwards from Antarctica. While eastern Australia was being warped up, inland Australia was being eroded down to a plain. For example, 60 million years ago inland Australia was a plain which had been deeply leached during the prolonged tropical times to form a laterite soil. These soils are characterised by pebbly ironstones underlaid by leached white clays. Such conditions currently exist in the Amazon Basin and, 60 million years ago, inland Australia was a comparably warm lush paradise. This 60-million-year-old erosion surface, called the Yudnamutana Erosion Surface, can still be seen. For example, in the North Flinders Ranges at Arkaroola at an altitude of 650 metres, the Yudnamutana Erosion Surface dominates the northern skyline. About 60 million years ago, Australia was hit by another meteorite which formed a 9-kilometre-wide crater in the Connolly Basin of the Gibson Desert in Western Australia.

Although most of inland Australia was a plain, the stresses from the continental fragmentation were such that faults became active. Some areas were uplifted or tilted and others subsided as a result of the warping up of the Great Dividing Range. The combined effect of the retreat of the inland sea and the upwarping of the Great Dividing Range left a number of continental depressions which were later filled by sediments.

A minor mass extinction of multicellular life occurred 55 million years ago. Sea temperatures rose as much as 8 °C for up to 100 000 years and may have reached 18 °C off Antarctica. Atmospheric carbon dioxide was 8 to 10 times higher than today and the surface waters of the oceans at pH 7.4 were more acidic than any time since. This was a very rapid process that occurred on both land and sea between 54.93 and 54.98 million years ago. The increased carbon dioxide content of the atmosphere probably resulted from the release of water-bearing methane from the ocean floor. The dramatic greenhouse resulted in many deep-sea animals becoming extinct and many terrestrial animals migrated. In the past there have been large natural disturbances to the global carbon cycle. This particular rapid change can be used to show that the residence time of carbon in the global carbon cycle 55 million years ago was about 120 000 years. This is what would be expected if there was a massive input of methane into the oceans and atmosphere. This residence time of carbon is similar to that induced today by human activity.

One volcanic event can set off a chain reaction resulting in a minor mass extinction.

The eruption of volcanoes in the Caribbean 55 million years ago blasted aerosols of sulphurous gases into the stratosphere which resulted in reflection of sunlight and the cooling of tropical surface waters. The cooler tropical surface waters sank, giving a change in ocean circulation patterns. The resultant low-latitude bottom waters released methane. In the ocean the methane reacts to form carbon dioxide, some of which would rise to the surface and cause greenhouse warming. As warm water holds less dissolved oxygen than cold water, deep-sea animals would have suffocated. Such a process probably would not take place today because the bottom waters of the oceans are far colder than they were 55 million years ago.

Huge growths of plankton formed in the oceans shortly after the mass extinction and absorbed so much of the atmospheric carbon dioxide that temperatures returned to normal within 60 000 years. Although the minor mass extinction 55 million years ago was the end for some organisms, there was a boom in the diversity of life following the mass extinction 10 million years earlier. Bats had evolved from insectivores, primates were rapidly becoming established, rabbit and rodent diversity expanded, toothless mammals and whales started to diversify, and other mammals started to dominate in the absence of dinosaurian predators. The recently evolved new plant, grass, assisted the rapid evolution of terrestrial animals. The world was becoming a real Garden of Eden.

During these greenhouse times 55 million years ago, Australia was hit by another meteorite which formed a 5-kilometre-wide crater at Goat Paddock in the Kimberleys of Western Australia.

After the minor mass extinction 55 million years ago, atmospheric carbon dioxide contents crashed from 3500 to 700 parts per million within a million years. Carbon dioxide levels stayed low until 47 million years ago, bumping up and then coming down again to near the present level of 365 parts per million some 40 million years ago. The fundamental questions are still unanswered: where did the carbon dioxide come from and where did it go to?

After the global greenhouse 55 million years ago, there was a great change to the drainage of south-eastern Australia. In the time period 55 to 40 million years ago, the Murray River flowed in a westerly direction because of the uplift of the Great Dividing Range. At Morgan, South Australia, the river flowed in a west-north-west direction along the present day Burra Creek and the Broughton River, to enter Spencer Gulf at Port Pirie. The old delta of the Murray River is the present day Pirie Plains and the delta extends as a shallow submarine fan towards Whyalla. The large amount of sediment in this delta suggests that, for most of its life, the Murray River entered the sea at Port Pirie. The straight 270-kilometre path of the ancient Murray River from Loxton to Port Pirie suggests that the river was following an ancient fracture in the basement rocks.

India collided with Asia 50 million years ago and, as the Earth buckled, the Himalayas and the Tibetan Plateau were pushed up. The Tibetan Plateau is still being pushed up. Mt Everest rises 2 centimetres per year. Himalayan rocks were bent, broken and melted. Rocks which contain shallow marine fossils occur at the peak of Mt Everest. The new rocks were deeply weathered and eroded material went down the great rivers into the Arabian Sea and the Bay of Bengal as a result of increased weathering and erosion. Weathering extracts carbon dioxide from the atmosphere to form bicarbonates in solution and carbonate minerals on the sea floor. Carbon dioxide may be stored in carbonate minerals for very long periods of geological time before the rocks are recycled and the carbon dioxide is again released.

With an atmosphere considerably poorer in carbon dioxide, solar energy was not retained and global cooling commenced. The atmospheric global carbon dioxide content has been measured over the last 750 million years by measuring the carbon isotopes in limestone, the sea floor spreading rate and the rate of formation of submarine volcanic rocks. From these studies, it appears that global cooling over the last 50 million years is principally a result of the degree of volcanic activity and the uplift of the Himalayas and the Tibetan Plateau. The uplift of the Tibetan Plateau was not a minor local event. The area of land on the Tibetan Plateau above 5 kilometres altitude is almost the area of Australia. Furthermore, high pressure, high temperature rocks are exposed at the surface of the plateau, rocks originally cooked up at a depth of 6 kilometres. Hence a slice of land 5 kilometres thick and a patch of ground almost the area of Australia has been removed by weathering and erosion. This weathering took place when ocean temperatures were 12 to 15 °C warmer than now. Weathering and erosion were far faster than now resulting in the removal of massive amounts of carbon dioxide from the atmosphere and, as a consequence, global cooling.

The carbon dioxide content of the atmosphere is a delicate balance between additions from the outgassing of volcanoes, degassing from deep in mountain belts and biological activity, and subtractions by chemical weathering, carbonate mineral precipitation on the sea floor and biological activity. The long period of global warmth from 120 to 40 million years ago was during a period of high atmospheric carbon dioxide maintained by enhanced carbon degassing from mantle plumes which pulled the sea floor apart.

As the Tibetan Plateau started to rise, the flow of tropical air was changed and a Himalayan mini-climate formed, a feature we still see today with monsoons south and arid conditions north of the plateau.

Australia continued to stretch away from Antarctica and, 45 million years ago, it finally broke away and started to move northwards at a rapid rate of about 12 centimetres per year. The southward flow of warm ocean currents was changed by the northward drift of Australia. This helped refrigerate Antarctica. The northward drift of the Australian continent would have added large amounts of carbon dioxide to the atmosphere, belched out of submarine volcanoes in the Southern Ocean. Antarctic volcanoes such as Big Ben and Mt Erebus still release a deadly cocktail of chlorine- and fluorine-rich gases. This is rather interesting in the light of the Antarctic ozone hole. CFCs were first used in 1959. The ozone hole was discovered in the International Geophysical Year, 1957.

As a result of the collision with Asia, the northward movement of Australia is now 7 centimetres per year. Collision with Asia has caused the volcanoes and earthquake zones of Indonesia and has stressed inland Australia. These stresses are released occasionally as very large earthquakes in inland Australia, the most recent of which was in 1990 in Tennant Creek, Northern Territory. This type of earthquake occurs in areas not recognised as earthquake zones and can be catastrophic. For example, similar earthquakes in China resulted in casualties in Shanxi Province 1556, Richter magnitude 8.0, 1 000 000 casualties; Shandong Province 1668, Richter magnitude 8.5, 50 000 casualties; Haicheng 1975, Richter magnitude 7.5, casualties unknown; and Tangshan 1976, Richter magnitude 8.0, 242 000 casualties. Most of the stress is released in inland Australia as earth tremors resulting from sporadic slight movement along existing faults. Some areas such as Lake Eyre have sunk whereas other areas such as the Flinders Ranges have a long history of uplift or tilting. Some areas such as Arkaroola in the far north Flinders Ranges have a long history of very regular earth tremors, many of which are audible. These tremors are currently centred in the Leigh Creek–Copley area and, on a sunny cloudless day, the tremors sound like a distant peal of thunder.

The time Australia finally escaped from Antarctica was the time that the depressions in inland Australia started to be filled with sediment derived from uplifted blocks. However, Antarctica had a surprise for planet Earth. It grew an ice cap. This can be linked to changes in ocean circulation, volcanoes and possibly meteorite impacting. The oceans were totally different from those of the global greenhouse conditions which peaked 115 to 110 million years ago.

In the Murray Basin to the south of the Barrier Ranges, floodplain and swamp sediments covered the floor of the depression 40 million years ago. Close to the mouth of the Murray Basin, there were minor shallow marine embayments and some lagoons started to evaporate and leave salts behind. The climate then was still warm and moist and rainforest covered Australia. In this Amazonian-type environment, Australia was undergoing intense and deep weathering. To the north-west of Broken Hill, the Lake Torrens area at that time was a sizeable inland lake and sediments filling the lake were derived from the Broken Hill, Olary and Mount Painter Blocks. Elsewhere in inland Australia and near the Gulf of Carpentaria, similar depressions started to be filled with sediments.

Australia was on its northward flight from Antarctica. There was a seaway developed between Australia and Antarctica 35 million years ago. However, the Tasman Rise inhibited cold ocean currents and warm tropical oceans extended to a latitude of 50° South. Today, the tropical oceans extend to about 25° South. The Tasman Rise was breached some 25 million years ago and the change in the flow of ocean water initiated icehouse conditions and a rapid sea level fall.

On the other side of the world the Mediterranean started to close and become a dry basin some 37 million years ago when bits of the crust started to slide in a south-westerly direction. At this time muds formed in shallow marine settings and extensive salt and limestone layers formed as the Mediterranean evaporated.

Another peak of global greenhouse occurred some 36 million years ago. The oceans were warm, their temperature changed little and deep circulation was sluggish. With the onset of polar glaciation 33 million years ago, deep cold polar waters flowed towards the equator and a zoned climate was formed. Some 30 million years ago, there was a slight cooling followed by warming when the Murray Basin was filled with water. There was then a period of profound cooling.

There is an impact crater in North America at Chesapeake Bay, New Jersey of 90 kilometres diameter. Another at Popigai, Siberia is 100 kilometres in diameter. The Chesapeake Bay impact structure is the best known site but it is part of a North American multiple impact

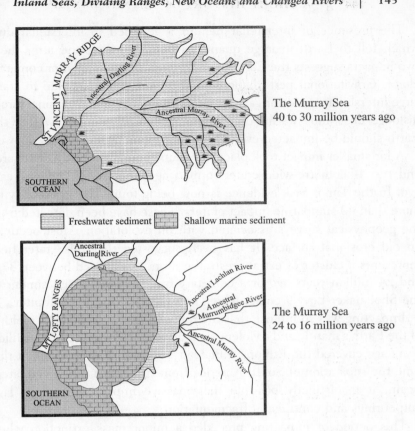

The Murray Sea
40 to 30 million years ago

Freshwater sediment   Shallow marine sediment

The Murray Sea
24 to 16 million years ago

field which sprayed molten rock over a wide area. There is a 10-million-square-kilometre area of eastern North America and the West Indies where impact debris blasted out of impact craters has been found. This impact debris, now glass, was reworked by tsunamis and massive submarine debris flows indicating that impacting was in the ocean. In Italy, a layer 35.7 million years old contains abundant shocked quartz, sand-sized grains of glass and minerals typical of the interaction of meteorites with the Earth's atmosphere.

The very similar ages of Chesapeake Bay and Popigai craters suggests that there was one impacting event in two different places, possibly a large meteorite or comet that exploded into two parts high in the atmosphere around 35.5 million years ago. However, interstellar dust in ocean sediments show two distinct events around 35 million years ago separated by less than 1 million years. There are two distinct horizons of impact glass, both of which are enriched in iridium. Therefore, the planet was impacted twice, probably by comets.

The presence of interstellar helium 3 attached to interstellar dust which fell to Earth in large quantities before, during and after these two impacts suggests the Earth went through an interstellar or cometary cloud. Gravitational perturbations of the Oort cloud are due to stars, large interstellar clouds or galactic tidal forces. These gravitational forces dislodge dust and swarms of comets, and calculations show that the Earth should be impacted every 40 million years by a cometary shower.

A far smaller impact took place at Mount Toondina, Oodnadatta area and the 4-kilometre-wide crater formed at or before 35 million years ago. In the Timor Sea, evidence is now being found that there may be more than 40 submarine impact craters. These have been detected from the geophysical surveys associated with oil exploration. Most occur at an old erosional surface. It has been suggested that this crater field represents a cluster of extraterrestrial visitors that arrived between 37.5 and 24 million years ago or a cometary fragmentation event similar to the Shoemaker-Levy 9 comet which spectacularly impacted Jupiter.

Impacting was so intense that the rebound shock caused the melting of the Earth's mantle and a violent short-lived volcanic episode 35 million years ago covered the Ethiopian Plateau with lava. Furthermore, at this time the separation of South America from Antarctica was accelerated. Again, it is distinctly possible that massive impacting initiates lava outpourings and continental fragmentation.

This period of impacting preceded a minor mass extinction when some 30 per cent of multicellular life became extinct 33.7 million years ago. Although the planet was still getting dusted by a larger than normal amount of helium-enriched interstellar particles, it is hard to see how such a small amount of dust could induce a minor mass extinction. The minor mass extinction was due to the sudden onset of a cold climate, probably related to the opening of the Drake Passage between South America and Antarctica.

The mountainous dunes of the great sand sea in the Egyptian Sahara hide many secrets. A few thousand tonnes of a greenish-yellow glass lie scattered in the dunes. The glass contains bubbles, very high temperature mineral grains and wispy white and black layers. It contains more than 98 per cent silica, unlike any known volcanic rock and has been dated at 28.5 million years old. The glass contains the tell-tale chemical signature of extraterrestrial material. Despite an extensive search, no impact crater has been found.

Two sites of oval to circular shaped areas of glass have been located and it has been suggested that a meteorite about the size of a house formed the glass from the vapourisation and melting of the sandstone bedrock in the Egyptian Sahara. The friction and massive shock wave in front of a falling meteorite compressed and heated the atmosphere, the meteorite shattered in midair 10 to 12 kilometres above the desert and the heat from the explosion toasted the sand and rock beneath. The heat was so great that the glass was probably molten for a few weeks. There is a growing consensus that impacts caused by extraterrestrial bodies 30 to 50 metres across, such as the Tunguska cometary impact, happen every two or three centuries. Prehistoric tools 100 000 years old made of this impact glass have been found in the Sahara Desert and the centre stone from a scarab found in Tutankhaman's tomb is composed of the impact glass. Ancient Egyptians obtained this cosmic gem in the desert some 700 kilometres from the centre of their civilisation.

The Murray Sea started to move inland and covered much of what is now the Murray Basin. The surging growth and recession of Antarctic ice resulted in variable sea level, changes to oceanic and atmospheric currents and such changes are seen in the Murray Basin. The planet was coming out of a long period of greenhouse and lurching towards a very changeable climate. When the Murray Sea retreated, tropical soils formed on sea floor muds, silts, sands and limey rocks left behind by the shallow warm sea.

During warmer wetter times, the Murray Sea advanced again about 30 million years ago and reached a maximum some 15 million years ago. What were meandering river systems were inundated, and shallow marine and lagoonal conditions dominated. This 15-million-year northward growth of the ancient Murray Sea left behind sediments deposited in deep water, on the then continental shelf, in lagoons and in deltas. Heavy mineral-bearing sands were deposited on what was the continental shelf at Horsham, Victoria. During this period of the northward expansion of the Murray Sea, global temperatures were warmer than today and, although fluctuating, sea level was higher. Australia was still moving northwards and blocks of inland Australia were still subsiding or being uplifted.

Concurrent with tropical weathering and erosion forming plains, there was sporadic fault-controlled uplift from 30 million years ago to the present which would have accelerated weathering. Blocks were uplifted and tilted west (Mt Painter Block) or east (Broken Hill Block) shedding sediment into what were large river systems and basins.

Continent-wide events such as the Grenvillian (1200 million years ago), Pan African (500 million years ago) and Alice Springs (400 to 280 million years ago) were responsible for cooling and reheating of the rocks in much of inland Australia. Episodes of cooling of the rocks occurred during major events in the ancient supercontinent of Gondwana and were caused by the reactivation of faults and the consequent uplift of blocks of ancient rocks to form mountains. The present day increase in temperature with depth of 20 °C per kilometre in the Broken Hill area indicates that some 20 kilometres of rocks have been removed by weathering and erosion over the last 1700 million years.

7

THE DAY BEFORE YESTERDAY

They already had a long history, though they had no memory or record of it. We talk today of the vast span of time since the building of the pyramids in Egypt, but that span was merely a wink compared to the long history which the human race had already experienced. One early record has been uncovered in Tanzania. Two adults and a child were walking on top of volcanic ash softened by recent rain. Their footprints then were baked by the sun and slowly covered by layers of earth. The footprints, definitely human, are at least 3 600 000 years old . . . young in the history of the living world.

Geoffrey Blainey, *A Short History of the World*

Elsewhere in the world, there was a profound change to life on Earth as a result of the extinctions of competitors 65 and 55 million years ago and the prolonged greenhouse conditions. While the Murray Basin was expanding northwards 30 million years ago, anthropoid primates lived in what is now the Faiyum Desert of Egypt. Their fossils show that an ape-like animal lived in a tropical paradise with swamplands bordered by forests or savanna. Fossils of birds, which are distant relatives of modern tropical birds, are found together with anthropoid fossils, which are distant relatives of modern primates such as ourselves.

During that period of time when the Murray Basin slowly advanced northwards over a 15-million-year period, the anthropoids from Faiyum had rapidly diversified into the various primate groups which ultimately led to the modern chimpanzees, gorillas, humans, gibbons, old world monkeys and new world monkeys.

Back through the generations, we humans have deep evolutionary roots in the primates. The brain is one such link. Fossil evidence indicates that monkeys living 20 million years ago had bigger brains

million
years
ago

7

6.5

6

5.5

5

4.5

4

3.5

3

2.5

2

1.5

1

0.5

present

149

than the primates of 50 million years ago. Even today, the old world monkeys, apes and humans have larger brains than new world monkeys such as tamarins and capuchins. In the hominids, brain size has increasingly outstripped body size in relative proportion. Pregnancy is another link. Chimps, gorillas and humans have the longest gestation periods of primates.

Over time, there has been a gradual change in the skeleton, brain and external features such as body hair. There has been almost no change in internal organs. In the eighteenth century Peter Camper dissected an orang-utan and was greatly alarmed at the very close similarity between the internal organs of an orang-utan and humans. How could a primitive beast have an internal anatomy so similar to that of we superior humans?

The common ancestor of humans, gorillas and chimps lived 8 million years ago. Our common ancestor gave rise to the chimpanzee family *Pan* and us. Some 7 million years ago, the gorilla line split off and 4.4 million years ago we see the first hominids.

Some 2 million years ago we see the first chimps in the fossil record. The genetic make up of chimps is 98.5 per cent identical to humans but the 1.5 per cent difference counts for a lot and could affect up to 1500 genes. What really is the significance of this 1.5 per cent difference? It makes us human. It does not mean that chimps are 98.5 per cent human. Similarly, nearly 75 per cent of genes in humans are also found in nematodes (minute soil-dwelling worms) and it is hard to argue that worms are 75 per cent human. There are others that argue that, on the basis of faith, humans are far too special to only have a slight genetic difference from chimps. The evidence from science is a far more exciting story than that from dogma.

While sediments were forming in the Murray Basin and anthropoids were diversifying, the Drake Passage between South America and Antarctica enlarged. There were three events of enlarging the Drake Passage, 40, 23 and 18 million years ago. The first and largest event, 40 million years ago, led to very rapid cooling in Antarctica over a period of 500 000 years. With the earlier separation of Australia from Antarctica and the separation of South America from Antarctica, the giant circum-Antarctica current was established. More and more water became cool and more and more of it was deflected to the equator as a deep cold

승차권 (승객용) No. 00309111

광주 Gwangju	요금 16,100 원 (부가가치세포함)	인천 Incheon	고속

911.4 인천

출발 Date of departure	시간 Time	좌석 Seat NO.	운송회사 Express co.	승차홈 Platform
09.14 일	07:25	09	삼화	6

승인번호 9467109
승일 16,100

911.4 인천

요약
운송약관

1. 승차권 기재사항을 임의로 변조한 것은 무효입니다.
2. 본 승차권의 환불은 지정차 출발시간으로부터 출발 시간전까지 10% 공제 후 승차 이용권터 이름까지 20%를 공제하며 열차 출발이후 지정차 출발 +운전시간 공제하며 환불이 됩니다.
3. 환급 및 수수료 게시 이후 100분 단위로 산정되었습니다.
4. 다음 경우에는 환급을 거절할 수 있습니다.
 가. 인쇄 물질과 승차권 분실물을 주는 물품소지자,
 나. 판매 또는 선매 물질된 것,
 다. 증행시의 단독권 또는 전매원것,
 라. 인터넷을 이용하여 승차 지세에 출력된 것,
 마. 동물·지세(모인 기관에서 영수를 발행한 매 [인은 것은 제외됨).
5. 승차 후에는 미소, 분실 및 도난 등의 경우 책임없습니다.
6. 사용하지 않은 승차권은 출발 이름이 지나면 사용할 수 없습니다.

*탑승방송 자전통특보 http://한글명수록 등

current. Over time this led to the onset of the refrigeration of Antarctica which, only 20 million years earlier, had been a lush moist warm green paradise. By 33.7 million years ago, the planet had become so refrigerated that there was a minor mass extinction of multicellular life on Earth. The creation of the Drake Passage initiated the striking variation in climates we now have from the poles to the equator. In earlier greenhouses there was little variation in climate across the planet.

While the planet was cooling it had a short burst of very warm weather, the warmest climate for 35 million years. In southern Australia and the Murray Basin, there were shallow tropical seas. Warm water was carried from northern Australia to south-eastern Australia and currents from the Indian Ocean in the Great Australian Bight would have given Melbourne a tropical climate. Between 17 and 14.5 million years ago, the mid-latitude oceans were 6 °C warmer than today and yet the atmospheric carbon dioxide was between 180 and 290 parts per million. This greenhouse event occurred when atmospheric carbon dioxide was 30 to 50 per cent lower than at present.

By 14 million years ago, the huge East Antarctic ice sheet had formed. By 6 million years ago, the smaller West Antarctic Ice Sheet covering offshore islands and intervening basin areas had formed. This sequence of events led to a long period of global cooling from 11 to 6 million years ago. There was a rapid global fall in sea temperature and sea level. Water retreated from the Murray Basin and the Australian continent underwent renewed weathering in a cooler drier environment. Many of the uplifted blocks in inland Australia underwent renewed weathering which shed large volumes of sand, silt and clay into the river systems and inland basins. The products of tropical weathering and erosion were replaced by those derived from a more temperate climate.

The Mediterranean Sea again dried up between 7 and 6 million years ago in what is called the Messinian Salinity Crisis. Land level changes closed the Strait of Gibraltar, isolating the Mediterranean from the Atlantic. Some 5.8 million years ago, continental drift pinned Morocco to Spain and the Mediterranean Sea dried up and died. Layers of soils with plants sandwiched between beds of salt occur more than 2 kilometres below today's sea level. The great thickness of salt, some 2 kilometres, suggests that the Mediterranean must have dried up and refilled many times. The evaporated water fell back to Earth as rain and made the oceans less saline. With less salt to act as anti-freeze in the oceans, parts of the ocean that would not normally freeze became sea ice. The ice reflected sunlight and the planet cooled. Eventually, after 400 000 years, the dam was breached at Gibraltar and a torrent ripped into the Mediterranean, and cut out the Strait of Gibraltar. A waterfall one thousand times bigger than the Niagara Falls filled the Mediterranean, reheated the oceans and the planet.

This was one of the most dramatic sea level changes in the geological record. The Mediterranean coastline shifted 70 kilometres and sea floor dropped as much as 2 kilometres over a period of 2 million years. The Mediterranean Sea was at its lowest level 5.8 to 5.5 million years ago and thick sequences of salt were left on the old sea floor. A rapid sea level rise over a 200 000-year period covered the salt layers with sand, silt and mud. These salt layers were discovered in the early 1970s as part of the Deep Sea Drilling Project and have been found in many Mediterranean islands such as Sicily. The Messinian Salinity Crisis carries a near-continuous record of aridity, evaporation, faunal dispersion and extinction. It has happened before, and will happen again.

The River Nile has a 6-million-year history. During the Messinian Salinity Crisis when the Mediterranean Sea was far lower than its present level, the river cut deep into bedrock. A canyon the size of the Grand Canyon of Arizona formed reaching from Aswan to the Mediterranean. The canyon varied between 10 and 20 kilometres wide, had a depth of 170 metres at Aswan, 800 metres at Assuit and 2500 metres north of Cairo. Cutting such a substantial canyon requires high rainfall. The climate then was wet and very variable. The rain water could have derived from the evaporating Mediterranean or, more probably, from monsoonal rains from the south. The ancient Nile carried huge volumes of sediment into the sea and left some 70 000 cubic kilometres of sediment in the Nile Delta. When the Mediterranean Sea rose after the Messinian salinity crisis, the canyon was filled with sediment washed down the Nile River.

The uplift of Australia's Great Dividing Range had changed the course and the sediment load of the big river systems. The Darling, Lachlan, Murrumbidgee and Murray Rivers brought sediment into the Murray Basin from the uplifted Great Dividing Range which had been stripped of some 5 to 8 kilometres of rock. The Sydney Basin, Hunter-Bowen

Basin and Great Artesian Basin were also uplifted and underwent weathering and erosion with much of the sediment being carried down the Darling River.

There was a temporary return to a virtually ice-free world some 5 million years ago. At the same time, stresses in inland Australia caused the Murray Basin to subside. The combination of these two events resulted in the inundation of 320 000 square kilometres to form the shallow warm Murray Sea. The collapse of the Antarctic ice sheets was accompanied by a sea level rise of some 65 metres above the present day level and much of the planet was inundated. The very rapid rise in sea level allowed the constant reworking of sediment brought into the Murray Basin by a long period of tropical weathering. The sediment was sorted into sand, silt and clay, depending upon the strength of the currents and wave action. This sorted sediment was left on the floor of the Murray Sea as the invading sea pushed beaches further and further inland. Eventually, the Murray Sea stopped growing 5 million years ago.

There were surf beaches along the eastern edge of the Mt Lofty Ranges in South Australia and also at Menindee, Ivanhoe, Griffith, Wagga Wagga, Albury, Benalla, Bendigo and Horsham. The surf 5 million years ago in the Murray Sea was far bigger and better than the surf in coastal Australia today. Massive offshore sandbanks, a westerly longshore drift, big swells reflecting the rapidly-changing climate and beaches formed by storm activity would have produced big sets of waves breaking to the right and giving a long ride. Furthermore, the water would have been warm with familiar marine life such as sharks and dolphins, fossils of which are found in the Murray Basin. The beach of my choice would

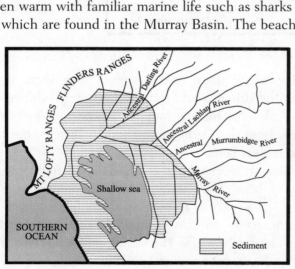

The Murray Sea
5 million years ago

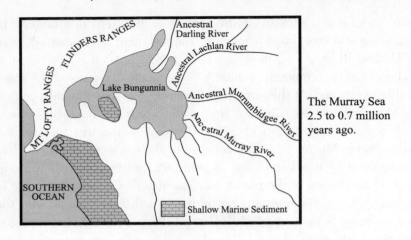

The Murray Sea 2.5 to 0.7 million years ago.

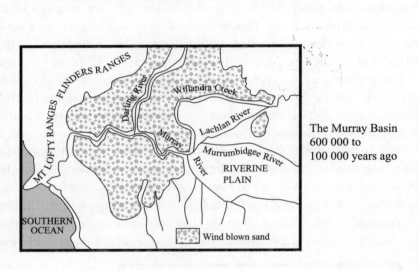

The Murray Basin 600 000 to 100 000 years ago

have been at Ivanhoe where there was maximum long shore drift, maximum exposure to the strong westerlies and the stormy southerlies, numerous headlands with a flat rock bottom and a good supply of sand for offshore sandbanks from the Darling and Lachlan Rivers. One can only dream of such a perfect surf.

The quartz-rich sediments dumped in the Murray Sea 5 million years ago contained traces of heavy minerals such as ilmenite, zircon and rutile. During storms, sediment was thrown up on beaches and, with later wave activity, the quartz was winnowed out of the sand concentrating heavy minerals in the ancient beaches. The same process has occurred on coastal beaches in more recent times and on almost any sandy beach south of latitude 25° South, these black heavy minerals can be seen.

Between 5 and 1 million years ago, the Murray Sea retreated in a stepwise fashion. A small retreat was followed by an even smaller advance and the end result is that there are more than 250 old beaches left in the Murray Basin, many of them rich in heavy minerals. At that time there were strong westerly winds blowing across the sea with the result that longshore drift shifted sand from the west to the east. The present coast line at the Coorong is parallel to these old beaches. As the Murray Sea retreated, the old beaches and sea floor were weathered to form a soil and then covered with alluvial sediments, swamps and lagoons. In places, these old soils contain roots and burrows.

The retreat of the Murray Sea was due to a global climate change. A profound cooling locked up water in Antarctic ice and lowered sea level. By 3.5 million years ago, the Antarctic ice cap had recovered to half its present volume. This renewed cooling was strengthened by the closure of the seaway between the Americas.

Western Victoria was and still is sited over a hot spot, volcanic activity was common and the land level rose as a result of pumping large amounts of molten rock into the crust beneath western Victoria. However, as the Murray Sea retreated, the Murray River was in for a surprise.

When the Murray Sea had covered the Basin, the Mt Lofty and Flinders Ranges were uplifted and the Murray River entered the Murray Sea at the eastern edge of the Murray Basin. When the Murray Sea retreated, the Mt Lofty Ranges were now blocking the flow of the Murray River to its original delta at Port Pirie. The Murray River was now forced to take a different course and it flowed south from Morgan, the North West Bend was formed and the Murray River entered the sea at its present site. The delta at Port Pirie is far greater than the delta at the Coorong, which only represents the last 2 to 3 million years of sediment deposition at the new mouth.

Every time the climate cooled or the planet lurched into an icehouse, there were one of two changes to the anthropoids: extinction or rapid evolution. In the East African Rift, the onset of a cold climate 5 million years ago was such that tropical forests became grasslands with residual copses of trees. The habitat for primates contracted, competition and mortality increased. Mobility meant survival and one branch of primates became upright and walked. The hip and neck structure show this as

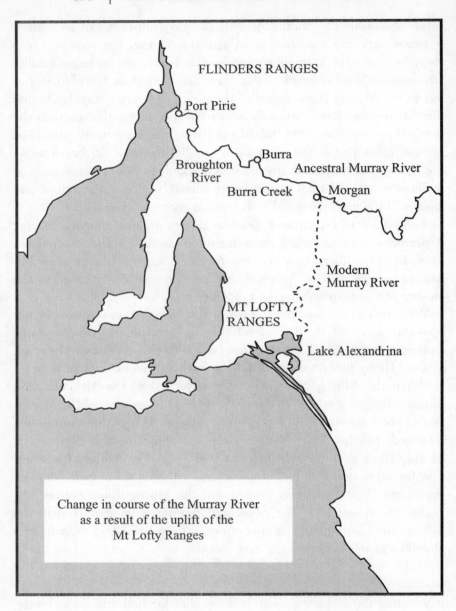

FLINDERS RANGES

Port Pirie

Burra

Broughton
River

Ancestral Murray River

Burra Creek

Morgan

Modern
Murray River

MT LOFTY
RANGES

Lake Alexandrina

Change in course of the Murray River
as a result of the uplift of the
Mt Lofty Ranges

do footprints in volcanic ash. These early hominids, the australopithe-
cenes, were not as tall as modern humans and had a far smaller brain.
They came in robust and gracile varieties, lived a fairly short life span,
were hunted by big cats, were mostly vegetarian but ate what meat they
could scavenge.

Our oldest known potential hominid is *Ardipithicus ramidus*, represented by some fragmentary fossils from the 4.4-million-year-old site at Aramis, Ethiopia. *Ardipithicus ramidus* may have walked upright but was quite ape-like. The better known and slightly younger *Australopithecus aramensis* fossils in northern Kenya are 4.2 million years old. This hominid is very similar to the 3.8- to 3.0-million-year-old *Australopithecus afarensis*, a small-brained big-faced species which walked. The best known example is Lucy. *Australopithecus afarensis* has been found in many sites in the East African Rift and it has been suggested that the fossil sites of *Australopithecus afarensis* might contain more than one hominid species. *Australopithecus afarensis* was not alone in Africa at that time; another hominid *Australopithecus bahrelghazali* has been discovered in 3.5- to 3.0-million-year-old rocks in Chad. This hominid species lived at the same time as Lucy. A yet unnamed and undescribed primitive hominid which walked upright has been found in 3.3-million-year-old rocks in Africa. At least three species of hominids co-existed in Africa. *Australopithecus africanus*, as the name suggests, is a southern primate which dwelled in Africa. This was the first australopith to be found and fossils have been found in 3-million-year-old rocks in South Africa. This species may have lived in Africa from 3 to 2 million years ago. Which australopith was our precursor? Did global cooling drive speciation in the australopiths?

Around 2.67 million years ago, there was another period of profound cooling of the planet. This contributed to the retreat of the Murray Sea as did the uplift of the Murray Basin. Climates are greatly affected by the transfer of warm and cold waters by ocean currents. Before 3.5 million years ago, North America was separated from South America and equatorial currents moved great volumes of water between the Pacific and Atlantic Oceans stimulating a warm global climate, especially in the Northern Hemisphere. The eruption of central American volcanoes 3.5 million years ago resulted in the formation of the Isthmus of Panama which eventually closed the seaway between North and South America. The connection of the Americas shifted ocean currents, stopped the transfer of water from the Pacific to the Atlantic Ocean and the changed oceanic circulation had a dramatic effect on global climate. If the Panama Canal was opened to a passage many kilometres wide, the climate may again quickly revert to greenhouse conditions.

The formation of the Isthmus of Panama by volcanism coincided with another large volcanic event, this time in the North Pacific Ocean.

Drilling of sea floor sediments shows that in the North Pacific Ocean, there was a sudden change from marine sediment to ice-rafted sediment. Icebergs were melting and dropping sediment 2.67 million years ago. The change to a glacial climate took place over 2000 years, far too rapid to have formed from changes to the Earth's orbit. Such a rapid change in climate is probably related to the widespread episode of explosive volcanism that began at that time in Kamchatka and the Aleutian Islands. Ocean waters cooled by at least 5 °C, marine life died or rapidly evolved to cope, atmospheric temperatures dropped markedly and, by 2.5 million years ago, ice developed around the North Pole, northern Canada, Greenland and Scandinavia.

This global cooling event 2.5 million years ago also greatly affected the hominids in the East African Rift. The forest habitat contracted and grasslands dominated. The australopiths diversified and a 2.5-million-year-old species, *Australopithecus garhi*, falls in an intermediate position between *Australopithecus africanus* and a larger group that includes *Homo*. That is, us. By 2.5 million years ago, another australopith called *Paranthropus aethiopicus* made an appearance, the best known of which is the 2.5-million-year-old Black Skull of Kenya. *Paranthropus aethiopicus* was the first known of a group of very robust hominids which appeared all over Africa between 2 to 1.4 million years ago. The robusts occurred in east Africa as *Paranthropus boisei* and in South Africa as *Paranthropus robustus* and the closely related species *Paranthropus crassidens*. This rapid speciation of hominids again took place at a time of global refrigeration, the number of hominid species is probably an underestimate and we don't know how long each species lasted. What we do know is that Africa was the home to numerous kinds of hominid.

Homo first appeared in the Rift Valley of East Africa. This genus of mammal is only indigenous to the Rift Valley and southern Africa and has invaded most terrestrial ecosystems on Earth. To talk of indigenous humans outside Africa is nonsense. We made our first appearance 2.5 to 1.8 million years ago in the Rift Valley and southern Africa as an oddly assorted and diverse lot. Over the last 5 million years, new hominid species have regularly emerged, competed, co-existed, colonised new environments, and succeeded or failed. There have been some big leaps in the evolution of humans. The first stone tools were manufactured some 2.5 million years ago. This required a cognitive leap and a mental template to be remembered. It took another million years of technology before the hand axe used by *Homo ergaster* was invented.

The two conventionally assigned species *Homo rudolfensis* (eastern Africa) and *Homo habilis* (sub-Saharan Africa) are the tip of the iceberg and numerous other *Homo* species might have co-existed at that time. Handy man, *Homo habilis*, had a far bigger brain than his competitors, the australopiths. Furthermore, the fossils show that *Homo habilis* had the neck and cranial structure for primitive speech and campsites show that handy man had an arsenal of crude hunting tools, fire and cared for those who did not hunt. *Homo habilis* survived because of being able to communicate, especially while hunting, and had tools, fire and a non-vegetarian diet.

In Kenya's east Turkana in 1.9- to 1.8-million-year-old sediments, fossils of both *Paranthropus boisei* and *Homo ergaster* occur. Different types of hominids shared the continent and the landscape at the same time. With the freezing of Earth, there would have been intense competition for resources. During this very cold period, the australopiths became extinct. A nagging suspicion lingers that fellow hominids hunted them to extinction. Whatever competitive forces were on the hominids, there was massive migration around 2 to 1.8 million years ago. Hominids reached China and Java. Was migration climate-driven?

The Earth 2 million years ago was an exciting place: rapid global cooling, profound changes to the flora and fauna, a sudden diversity in the genus and species of hominids on Earth and an extraterrestrial visitor. An asteroid some 3 kilometres across travelling at 12 kilometres per second hit the east Pacific Ocean 2 million years ago and sent a water spout nearly 20 kilometres into the air and sprayed 250 cubic kilometres of water vapour high into the atmosphere. The water vapour formed ice clouds that shaded the planet. The planet was in a cooling phase and this impact just accelerated it. The big splash created waves hundreds of metres high in the open ocean but when these waves reached the shore, they could have been 25 times higher.

This might explain the mixture of bones of marine and terrestrial animals in the mountains at Pisco, Peru. They look as if they have been thrown together in a washing machine. Trace remains of microscopic fossils from the deep sea floor are present in the Transantarctic Mountains more than 2500 kilometres from the shore. These might have been thrown up from the ocean floor together with all the water that flew into the sky and dropped on Antarctica. Such an impact today in the Pacific would kill more than half of the planet's humans.

The eruption of Mt St Helens in 1980 showed how volcanoes fall apart. Following the explosion, the entire northern flank of Mt St Helens fell into the river valley below.

The same has occurred on Hawaii. Massive earthquakes and eruptions at the Koolau volcano on the Hawaiian island of Oahu have split a mountain right down the middle. Thousands of blocks of rock the size of a football field rumbled down the slope, followed by pieces as big as towns and, finally, one chunk the size of London tumbled and came to rest 100 kilometres from the shore. This all took place only 1 million years ago. The slide of one tenth of Oahu into the Pacific Ocean started a massive tsunami. The Pacific rim was hit by the biggest tsunamis ever to strike its shores. The Hawaiian islands are girdled by landslide debris. To date, 17 different landslides covering more than 100 square kilometres of the sea floor have been recognised.

The effect of a landslide as big as London hitting the ocean produced tsunamis more than 200 metres high. Boulders of coral reef material which fringed the islands were washed high up on the volcanic rocks of Hawaiian islands. These boulders have been found 375 metres above sea level which gives some idea of the power of the tsunamis. If such a landslide occurred again, about 40 per cent of the world's human population would be destroyed. Will it happen again?

A large earthquake in 1868 moved half of the side of the Hawaiian Kilauea Volcano and this piece slipped down slope. Satellite measurements show that the entire southern side of Kilauea is slipping towards the sea at 10 centimetres a year. In 1975, a Richter magnitude earthquake of 7.2 pushed Kilauea volcano outwards by 10 metres and downwards by 3 metres. The piece of Kilauea on the move is far bigger than the chunk the size of London which slipped into the sea 1 million years ago. When it ultimately drops into the Pacific, I don't want to be around. The only place to be is well above sea level in the centre of a continent, such as Europe or Africa.

The Canary Islands are also unstable. When 500 billion tonnes of rock slid into the Atlantic from the El Hierro volcano in the Canary Islands 120 000 years ago, a tsunami raced 6000 kilometres across the Atlantic at the speed of a jet aeroplane. A wall of water 50 metres high

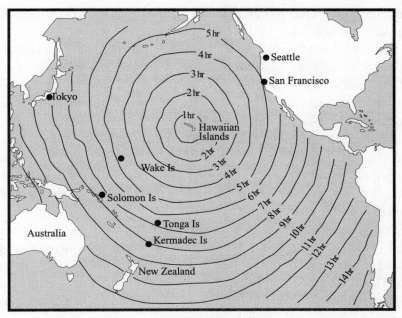

Map showing the speed of a tsunami if a large landslide occurs in Hawaii.

hit the Caribbean islands, Florida and the rest of the eastern seaboard of USA surging up to 20 kilometres inland and engulfing everything in its path. La Palma, the most volcanically active island in the Canaries is unstable. If the flank of the volcano slides into the Atlantic, a tsunami between 50 and 250 metres high will swamp all coastal areas in North America around the North Atlantic.

There might have been another cluster of extraterrestrial visitors between 1.1 million years and 700 000 years ago. If so, these impacts did not cause a significant extinction on Earth. In West Africa 1.1 million years ago, glass was blasted out of a 10.5-kilometre-diameter impact crater. Most of the glass fell into the ocean. At Tonle Sap in Cambodia a 100-kilometre-wide crater formed as a result of an impact 770 000 years ago and fragments of black glass were sprayed all over the Indian Ocean, Australia and south-east Asia. These are the tektites of inland Australia, commonly called australites. Their shapes show that on entry back to Earth, they were spinning and, as a result of the frictional heat of re-entry, melting. Button, disc and dumb bell shaped tektites are the most common types. The button shape of tektites was copied by NASA as the perfect shape for a lunar re-entry module.

Tektites have a fascinating history. By using some of the radioactive dating techniques, we can show that they derived from 1100-million-year-old material at Tonle Sap that was melted by the impact 770 000 years ago. This material went for a trip in the upper atmosphere where it was bombarded by cosmic radiation. When the material fell through the atmosphere, the frictional heat was so intense at the edge of the tektite that the temperature of the glass reached 2000 °C, it remelted and sprayed off bits of molten glass during its flight back through the atmosphere. We can calculate the entry time as the remelting of the flanges of tektites reset the clocks in the rocks.

A meteorite hit Mt Darwin near Queenstown, Tasmania, 740 000 years ago to form a 1-kilometre-wide crater. This might have been part of a swarm of extraterrestrials that hit Earth around 770 000 to 740 000 years ago. The ancient rocks in western Tasmania were melted by this small impact, solidified to form glass and are locally known as Darwin glass.

Hominids were still in the East African Rift 1.6 million years ago when the Murray Sea was draining from the Murray Basin. By then, some hominids had migrated out of Africa into China and Java and it is quite possible that there was a wide dispersal of hominids at the warmer latitudes. Unlike earlier hominid species which appear to have hugged the cover of Africa's Great Rift Valley, *Homo erectus* moved out into the more open highlands in search of big game. In popular literature *Homo erectus* has been painted as a smart ape but recent work shows that *Homo erectus* used fire, constructed hearths consisting of rings of stone, and was a skilled hunter and toolmaker. During the glacial climate, *Homo erectus* would have needed fire for warmth and protection. *Homo erectus* had significantly smaller teeth and jaws than its predecessors, thought to be a result of their switch from a diet of tough plant material to one containing more meat. But it was not until modern *Homo sapiens* appeared that there was a second dramatic drop in tooth size, as our species started eating more chewable food.

Certainly by 1 million years ago, *Homo erectus* was well established in China and Java and it is possible that there was also a more robust species present in Java. *Homo erectus* was a larger, stronger hominid with a bigger brain. Habitats had again shrunk, competition for food was intense and, with more efficient hunting tools and a larger brain, *Homo erectus* migrated to other low latitude areas. Fossils of *Homo erectus* have been found in North Africa, Mediterranean Europe, India, China and South East Asia ('Java Man'). In icehouse times, *Homo erectus* existed at latitudes less than about 35 degrees whereas in greenhouse times, *Homo erectus* was more widespread. As *Homo erectus* became a more efficient hunter in rapidly changing climatic regimes, there were sufficient time and resources to care for the sick and elderly in well-established and protected cave sites and camps.

Climate was changing rapidly. This opened up new areas in greenhouse times and pushed hominids into competitive stress in icehouses. By 800 000 years ago, another hominid was living in Europe. The oldest-known European hominid fragments, called *Homo antecessor*, were found in Spain. It is intriguing that another hominid, *Homo heidelbergensis*, appeared in Africa 600 000 years ago and was well established in Europe and possibly China from 500 000 to 200 000 years ago. The European and western Asian *Homo heidelbergensis* gave rise to *Homo neanderthalensis* who flourished between 200 000 and 30 000 years ago. Contrary to popular myth, Neanderthal man had a larger brain capacity than modern humans. *Homo neanderthalensis* and *Homo erectus* probably coexisted for about 50 000 years some 300 000 years ago. Neanderthal man had efficient hunting tools which enabled survival in the difficult ice age times and they buried their dead. Grave sites show no evidence of symbolic objects and burial might have been for pragmatic reasons.

Modern humans, *Homo sapiens*, first appeared in Africa 200 000 to 150 000 years ago. The fossil records indicate that independent developments were taking place in Africa, Europe and Asia. *Homo sapiens* appeared in Europe, Asia and Africa but the presence of *Homo erectus* fossils from Ngandong, Java, dated at 40 000 years and well after the appearance of *Homo sapiens* elsewhere suggest that many areas had their own separate evolutionary history. Neanderthal man lived in the climatic extremes of Europe and the northward migration of modern humans from Africa led to a meeting of Neanderthals and modern humans in what is now Israel. Neanderthal man and modern humans probably coexisted for about 20 000 years. A sample of DNA from a Neanderthal differs from that of modern humans but suggests we share genes through a common ancestor, possibly *Homo heidelbergensis*, in Africa 600 000 years ago and also suggests Neanderthal man did not evolve into *Homo sapiens*. *Homo sapiens* was well established in Europe

40 000 years ago and, by 30 000 years ago, Neanderthal man had vanished. There is no convincing evidence to demonstrate how Neanderthal man and modern man interacted. However, the behaviour of modern man towards his fellow beings over the last few thousand years suggests that modern man was a formidable competitor who drove Neanderthals to extinction.

The spread of *Homo sapiens* brought art in the form of carvings, engravings and cave paintings. Records were kept on stone, bone and wood plaques, musical instruments were crafted and personal jewelry was prized. The dead were given elaborate burials with grave goods which suggested social strata and a belief in an afterlife. The evolutionary appearance of symbolic thought was the start of religion. The living sites of *Homo sapiens* were highly organised, a social pecking order developed, the young and elderly were looked after by those who were fitter, and there was sophisticated hunting and fishing. Technological innovation advanced at a rapid rate with a constant refinement of tools. We modern humans are an anomaly. For the last 5 million years, various species of hominids have co-existed in the same place at the same time. We don't.

At the time when Neanderthal struggled for survival in Europe 300 000 years ago, another meteorite hit Australia. The Wolfe Creek Crater in the Kimberleys of Western Australia was blasted out and the 880-metre-wide crater still contains bits of the meteorite which did the damage. At the impact site, the basement rock was melted and rapidly solidified to glass which is still abundant on the floor of the crater at Wolfe Creek.

For the last few hundred million years, ours was a warm wet greenhouse world. The change from that 50 million years ago to glaciation appears to be primarily due to plate tectonic processes such as the collision of India with Asia, the opening of the Drake Passage, and exacerbated by the closure of the seaway between the Americas. Normal geological processes changed climate.

Over the last 5 million years at least 23 periods of glaciation waxed and waned and, as a result, sea level rapidly rose and fell many times. Once an ice sheet starts to grow, it almost becomes a self-fulfilling process. Ice reflects solar energy and, as a result, the atmosphere does not heat sufficiently, cooling takes place and the ice sheet grows. These rapid climate changes, unrelated to atmospheric carbon dioxide content,

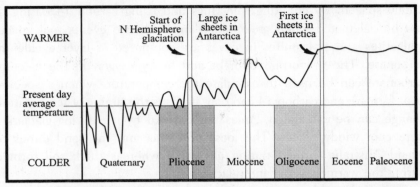

The present glaciation was 50 million years in the making. Large ice sheets started to grow in the last 35 million years and temperatures fluctuated wildly. The previous times such ice sheets existed was 250 million years ago.

suggest climate change is far more complicated than we are led to believe in the popular press. There are clearly other factors during the last 5 million years of Earth history which have driven rapid change producing alternating icehouses and greenhouses. Over the last 2 million years, only some 10 per cent of time has encompassed greenhouses like the one we now enjoy. Whatever the origin of climate change, it is a normal natural phenomenon. It would be unusual if the Earth's climate did not change.

The piecing together of the history of climate over the last 2 million years involves an arsenal of scientific techniques. Drill holes give us a trip through time and the deeper the hole, the longer we can look back. Ice sheets and sediments in lakes, seas and oceans are a goldmine of information. The ratio of oxygen 18 to oxygen 16 is a measure of temperature: in warmer times, more heavy oxygen is evaporated. The ratio of heavy to light oxygen is preserved in snow and retained when snow becomes ice. By measuring the proportion of heavy oxygen to light oxygen in ice, shells and fossils, the history of water temperature on Earth can be calculated. Ice and sediments contain ash and aerosols from past volcanic eruptions, cosmic fingerprints from solar flaring and supernoval explosions, and the products of human pollution.

Lake sediments also contain fossils of pollen grains which chronicle the climate-driven changes in vegetation. Minute fossils in lakes and oceans are very sensitive monitors of climate change. So are tree rings. In times of stress such as glaciation, many organisms die and tree growth is slow, showing closely spaced rings. In greenhouses, tree rings are widely spaced. By counting tree rings and using carbon 14 dating, it can be calculated when greenhouse and icehouse events took place. Stalactites and stalagmites in caves are composed of layered calcium carbonate. The proportion of light and heavy oxygen in the calcium carbonate can be used to calculate the temperature when a specific layer formed, and carbon 14 can date it. Thus the timing of temperature change can be calculated. Areas not covered by ice during glaciation were cool windy places. The loess of China and the sand dunes of inland Australia formed during glaciation whereas thick soil formed during the warmer wetter interglacial times.

The weathered horizons in inland Australia, formed in tropical times, were probably overprinted numerous times by minerals formed in cold, windy, arid conditions when the water table was low and saline (glacial) and by minerals formed in warm wet conditions when an acid water table was high (interglacial). The legacy of these events is preserved in a wide range of landscapes, old beaches in the Murray Basin, heavy mineral sand deposits, ancient soils, salt lakes, dunes of wind-blown sands, fossils and marine, lake and river sediments.

The clues regarding the driving forces for climate changes in recent geological times are in drill cores from Greenland and Antarctic ice, sea floor sediments and lake sediments. The records from ice and sediment cores are especially good from 700 000 years ago to the present. Drilling of sediments on the floor of oceans can give an even longer look into past climates. For example, 43 million years ago the world was 5 °C warmer than today. Yet the pH of the surface water was 8.05 suggesting that atmospheric carbon dioxide levels were not substantially higher than today. The connection between atmospheric carbon dioxide and temperature is far too simplistic.

We know bacteria are the largest biomass on Earth and that bacteria thrive in all sorts of habitats. There are some faint clues that the role of bacteria in processes involving carbon dioxide is far more important that we once thought. For example, a copper sulphide ore will weather at the surface to green copper carbonate, malachite, and blue copper carbonate, azurite. It was always thought that the carbon dioxide for these coloured copper minerals came from the air. Recent carbon and oxygen isotope studies show that the carbon is of bacterial origin. Bacteria rule the Earth but we don't know how many of them there are and how big their empire might be. We do not know how the bacterial biomass has changed with time. If the bacterial biomass changed with

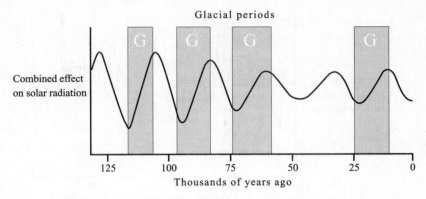

Milankovitch cycles result from changes in the earth's orbit over time.

time, so would atmospheric carbon dioxide. We do not know how much biomass is represented by recently-discovered types of life such as thermophilic bacteria and nanobes. Until we understand the bacterial empire, we can not comprehend atmospheric carbon dioxide and climate change.

Today, the Earth's equatorial plane is tilted at 23.4° to the ecliptic, but this angle varies from 21.5° to 24.5° every 41 000 years. Decreasing the inclination results in a cooler summer in the Northern Hemisphere and favours ice accumulation. The Earth's orbit also changes shape from a circle to an ellipse. The ellipsoidal orbit results in a warmer than average winter. This is orbital eccentricity. The Earth also wobbles as it rotates with a wobble period of 19 000 to 23 000 years and the intensity of the seasons varies with the wobble. These three orbital features are known as Milankovitch periods.

Over the last 700 000 years, Northern Hemisphere sediments show that there has been a modern climate regime with pronounced temperature fluctuations over a 100 000-year cycle, especially at the higher latitudes. Orbital variations can be correlated with changes in radiation received from the Sun. Over the last 700 000 years, it appears that the cyclical changes in climate on a 100 000-year periodicity appear to be related to the 100 000 year variation in the Earth's orbital eccentricity. However, at shorter periods than 100 000 years, the impact of orbital features is unclear. There are leads, lags and harmonics in the climatic response to the cycles of radiation.

During the latest glacial event, there were ice-rafting events about every 7000 years. Huge volumes of ice broke off from the Northern

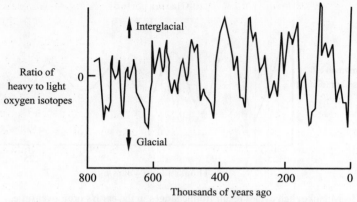

Changes in heavy and light oxygen in the shells of floating animals are an accurate measure of temperature changes over time.

Hemisphere glaciers, floated south and melted. Ice-rafting events are not due to climate change, but they are probably a force that drives significant climate change. Even smaller cycles of climate change occur every 1100 to 1500 years and, over the last 350 years of astronomical measurements, there is a very suspicious correlation between sunspot activity and very slight changes in global climate every few decades. We are currently in Sunspot Cycle 23. Millennial scale periodicity of ice rafting events and lesser climate variations have taken place in the North Atlantic Basin for more than a million years. For the last 10 000 years, there has been cyclical climate every 1500 to 1800 years. These cycles, Bond Cycles, are correlated with the strength of the tides resulting from the changing alignment of the Earth, Moon and Sun. There is clearly much more to climate change than can be explained by current knowledge.

There is a good global record of alternating icehouses and greenhouses over the last 500 000 years with greenhouse periods peaking around 410 000, 330 000, 240 000, 123 000 and 6000 to 4000 years ago. Some of the greenhouse or interglacial periods are characterised by thick piles of sediments on the floor of the eastern Mediterranean. For example, a 3000-year monsoonal period from 528 000 years ago left a plant-rich layer on the sea floor showing that North Africa was thickly vegetated and massive monsoons eroded North Africa. Sandy deserts now dominate North Africa. During some of the icehouses, the level of the Mediterranean dropped. The load on the floor of the Mediterranean Sea decreased and the sea floor rose producing numerous earth tremors. The sea level drop associated with the cooler drier times resulted in an increase in the salinity of the sea. These conditions produced submarine debris flows and currents that carried sediments from shallow water and dumped them in deep waters on the floor of the Mediterranean. We see the same features in arid Australia. In greenhouse or interglacial conditions, inland waterways flowed and lakes were full of water which supported a great diversity of animals and lush vegetation. When the inevitable icehouse conditions followed, the water evaporated and the plants and animals perished. Good examples exist in the Willandra Lakes area of NSW.

Australia was a far more hospitable place in the greenhouse times of around 500 000 years ago. This greenhouse lasted for at least 60 000 years and was actually three intense greenhouse events. During the three greenhouse events, sea level was 2.5, 7.5 and 20 metres above the current level. Sea level remained at the 7.5 metre level for most of the greenhouse, then rose quickly 400 000 years ago to the 20 metre level where it stayed for a few thousand years, before dropping to the today's levels for another few thousand years. During glacial times, there are rapid climate fluctuations. Changes in air temperatures have been recorded from the Greenland ice cores and these are consistent with shifts in the magnitude of heat carried north by North Atlantic surface ocean water. Cold water was generated more or less continuously in the Nordic Seas and this sank to the ocean deeps.

The Earth was enjoying optimum conditions during the peak interglacial some 123 000 years ago. Sea level was 4 to 6 metres higher than at present. Many beaches formed at this time are still present around Australia. Again, the surf would have been better than now. As ice melted, the melt waters were added to the ocean. The increased weight of water in the oceans pushed on the ocean floor, which sank a little deeper into the Earth's mantle, accompanied by thousands of minor earth tremors. The sea level was initially lowered and, as the temperature of the seawater increased, the additional volume of the water and the expansion of the water made the sea level rise. The addition of a large volume of melt water slightly decreased the salinity of the oceans.

The previous greenhouse conditions were at their zenith 129 000 to 118 000 years ago. Climate then began to cool at an increasing rate and sea level fell as ice accumulated at high latitudes and at altitude. There was an abrupt cooling event over a period of only about 400 years some 118 000 years ago, leading on to the return of a harsher and more variable climate and, some 40 000 years later, to full Ice Age conditions.

The latest segment of geological time shows extreme climate variability is normal. Sediment cores from the Pacific Ocean and the West Indes show that, over the last 80 000 years, there have been at least 40 significant sea level rises and falls. The beginning of the end of the last interglacial was a change in the flow of heat to the North Atlantic Ocean caused by large alterations in ocean circulation. When the warm Gulf Stream penetrates between Iceland and Scotland into the Arctic Ocean, a warm climate prevails. When the current is slightly displaced towards the east, it misses the opening, and returns to the south thereby warming the coast of Portugal. The climate of northern Europe is then much colder. The onset of ice growth at the end of the last interglacial was accompanied by a sudden change in circulation in the North Atlantic Ocean.

We can get a good picture of the latest climate changes from ice cores in Greenland and Antarctica, North Atlantic marine sediment cores and Northern Hemisphere lake sediment cores. The heavy and light oxygen isotopes in the ice from Greenland ice cores show that over the last 100 000 years there have been numerous rapid climate fluctuations. North Atlantic marine sediment cores show a comparable variability in sea surface temperature and deposition of ice-rafted debris. Lake studies show that the coupled ocean-atmosphere system of the Northern Hemisphere extended its influence to the Mediterranean and major vegetation changes on the land were very rapid and commonly took place in less than 200 years.

During the transition from an icehouse to a greenhouse, the ice sheets and glaciers on the continents retreat and leave a blanket of debris. The melting of ice sheets and glaciers in continental Europe, Asia and North America dumped gravels over a very large area. The melt waters later reworked some of these glacial gravels. During the transition from icehouse to greenhouse, the planet warmed, rainfall increased and cold winds decreased.

Although most of inland Australia was not ice-covered like upland southern Australia, the effects of glaciation were very strong cold anti-cyclonic winds. These winds blanketed inland Australia with the fine grained red dirt typical of outback Australia and the winds were so strong that they brought salt spray from the oceans inland. During interglacials, the warmer higher rainfall conditions leached the salts down creeks and they accumulated in inwardly draining basins such as

Lake Eyre and Lake Torrens. When the interglacial changed back to glacial conditions, the waters in the inland lakes evaporated, salt crusts formed and the strong westerly winds blew the salt and clay into dunes on the eastern side of inland lakes. These dunes, lunettes, are very common in the beds of the old Darling and Lachlan Rivers and in lake systems such as at Willandra Lakes and Lake Mungo. This salt is still trapped in inland Australia as salt lakes, salt crusts, saline groundwaters and salinised soil. Some of this inland salt may be a relic from when Australia was covered by an inland sea 120 million years ago. As the inland sea retreated, it left isolated saline lakes such as Lake Winton, the precursor to Lake Eyre.

Another icehouse was on the way and sea level started to rapidly fall after the interglacial maximum 123 000 years ago. Sea levels lowered, shallow water ecosystems became less common, and life adapted as quickly as possible to the new colder conditions. The transition into the latest icehouse event was complete 74 000 years ago.

The northward movement of the Australian plate beneath Indonesia produces volcanoes and the earthquakes in Indonesia. There was a massive eruption of the volcano Toba, Sumatra, 74 000 years ago. The explosion sent 2000 cubic kilometres of ash and gas high into the atmosphere, one of the biggest in the last million years. Within a few months, this ash blanketed the globe. The very fine-grained ash and sulphur-rich aerosols throughout the Earth's atmosphere reflected radiation from the Sun. Less solar radiation reached the Earth and the planet started to cool.

The explosion of Toba triggered a major climate change. In the Northern Hemisphere, there was rapid ice accumulation and the first significant peak in ice rafting in the Northern Hemisphere during the last glacial cycle. There was a drop in seasonal sea surface temperatures in the North Atlantic of 10 °C in less than 5000 years and a drop in sea level of 40 metres in less than 7000 years. This was a significant climate change which, in palaeoclimatology parlance, is the 5a-4 Stage climate boundary.

It is quite possible that the northward drift of the Australian plate to produce the eruption of Toba and the consequent lowering of sea level aided the southward migration of humans into Australia.

One volcano in Sumatra triggered global cooling with its greatest effects in the high latitudes of the Northern Hemisphere. Toba shows that planet Earth's climate is dynamic and that there are a great diversity of reasons for rapid climate changes.

With the lowering of sea levels, humans migrated as resources shrank. A coastal Negroid population in the Andamans moved in waves across the equator and ended up in Australia, possibly as far back as 80 000 to 100 000 years ago. The end result was the population of Australia by *Homo sapiens*. Or was it? With the knowledge that *Homo erectus* survived in Java until 40 000 years ago, were the original colonisers of Australia *Homo sapiens* or another hominid species?

With the immigrants from the north came their stone tools, fire sticks, Neolithic culture and, much later some 4000 years ago, their domestic dog, the dingo. Another Negroid population colonised Australia and the two Negroid populations intermingled. Further waves of immigrants from the north colonised Australia and the mixed population continued to interbreed. An early population was isolated in Tasmania as the sea level rose in post-glacial times and their continental relatives either interbred or were extinguished by the new wave of immigrants. The oldest cave paintings in the world, painted 38 000 years ago, record family history, hunting and the geographic maps of the Australian aborigine. Their entry onto the Australian continent was accompanied by a mass extinction of macrofauna. As the grip of the icehouse on the world tightened, the European cousins of the Australian aboriginals recorded cave painting scenes of great bravery during hunting and recorded the macrofauna that existed in Europe 28 000 years ago.

The last icehouse was at its peak only 18 000 years ago. In geological terms, that was only this morning. Ice covered one third of the planet's landmasses. Much of the sea at high latitudes would have been covered in ice and there would have been changes in the ocean currents that have a great effect on climate. The Mediterranean Sea was 6 °C cooler than now, sea level had dropped to 120 metres lower than the present level, many plants and animals became extinct and the remaining flora and fauna had to adapt to the new climate or die. The temperature on land at higher latitudes was up to 10 °C cooler than now. Despite this severe climate, many large European animals like elephants and mammoths survived, only to become extinct after the icehouse times as a result of over-hunting by the ever-expanding population in the warmer times.

The epicentre of North American ice formation was Hudson Bay. Ice was more than 3 kilometres thick. Detroit was covered by 1 kilometre of ice. There were substantial centres of ice deposition in Scandinavia and European Russia. The Scandinavian sheet covered the North Sea and Scotland and the Kara ice sheet of European Russia stretched across the Barents Sea to the islands at the edge of the deep Arctic Ocean. The Kara ice sheet was 6 million square kilometres in area and would have blocked north-flowing rivers. European ice sheets started to melt 14 700 years ago but the Kara ice sheet formed a dam until 13 000 years ago. The ice sheet expanded 11 000 to 10 000 years ago and 8500 to 8000 years ago, and these expansion and contractions of the Kara ice sheet allowed large scale damming and release of water from the north-flowing Russian rivers.

As the continental ice sheets began their great meltdown, large portions of the Northern Hemisphere ice sheets became grounded below sea level in areas that now are the shallow seas of Hudson Bay, the Baltic and the Kara Sea. As sea level continued to rise, the ice sheets calved into the oceans and continued to force a sea level rise.

The peaks of the Great Dividing Range, most of Tasmania, upland South Africa, the Andes, Canada, the northern US, northern China, Russia and Europe north of the Alps were covered by ice which, when it retreated, left large areas of glacial gravels. This gravel dammed up meltwaters to form lakes. Some of the glacial lakes burst as they were filled with meltwaters, great floods and destruction took place and much of the landscape was covered with flood debris. Glacial gravel was reworked by running water and a blanket of glacial debris was left behind. Much of Europe is still covered by this blanket.

During the last icehouse, Australia was a cold windswept continent. Strong anticyclonic winds carried sand and draped much of Australia in red dunes. The area which is now Bass Strait was a cold windswept plain covered with red dunes, now about 100 metres beneath sea level.

Northern Europe sank under the weight of ice during the last icehouse and this was accompanied by myriads of earth tremors. The equator of the Earth bulged slightly in response to the massive amount of polar ice. Raised and tilted shorelines around the Gulf of Bothnia show that the land rose 395 metres since the Scandinavian ice sheet melted. Hudson Bay rose 300 metres and Scotland rose 35 metres. Scandinavia is still rising in response to the melting of the ice sheet and, to counterbalance this rise, Holland is sinking. For example, some

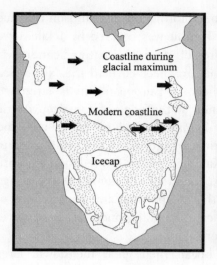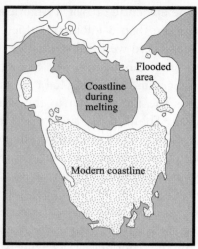

During the peak of the last ice age 18 000 years ago, Bass Strait and northern Tasmania were covered by sand dunes and the highlands of Tasmania were covered by ice. Melting of ice sheets flooded Bass Strait 14 500 years ago.

parts of Finland have risen 5 metres over the last 800 years. The castle at Turku was built on an isolated island in the Gulf of Bothnia in the thirteenth century. One can now walk to the castle on land more than 4 metres above sea level. The eighteenth-century port at Turku has been uplifted so much you have to climb down a ladder to board a boat!

The Earth's equator started to shrink a little once the ice melted resulting in a change of the speed of the rotation of the Earth and, as a consequence, a change in the ocean currents. As a result of such changes in elevation to large areas of land, predictions about human-influenced sea-level changes must be viewed with healthy scepticism.

During the last icehouse, surges in the continental ice sheets rafted trillions of tonnes of ice armadas into the North Atlantic Ocean every 7000 years. These are called Heinrich Events. The periodicity of Heinrich events is such that they are not related to orbital variation. There must be another cause. The oldest detected Heinrich event in North Atlantic sea floor sediments is 260 000 years old. The ice armadas, derived from glaciers, carried boulders, sand and rock flour out into the ocean. When the ice melted, dropstones and finer grained sediment rained on to the

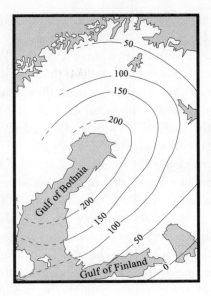

Scandinavia was pushed down by the weight of kilometres of ice. Since the melting of the ice sheets, the land has been rising more than 1 cm per year. The contours are metres of uplift over the last 8000 years.

sea floor. For example, such layered dropstone sediments have been deposited for the last 130 000 years on the Dreizack submarine sea-mount in the eastern North Atlantic Ocean. These dropstone sediments contain the shells of what were floating fauna and the ratio of heavy to light oxygen isotopes in these shells indicates very cold sea surface temperatures.

The proportion of heavy and light oxygen in sea floor sediments and in Greenland ice cores, and the pollen distribution in lake sediments in France show the ice armadas correlate with periods of Northern Hemisphere cooling. The periods of cooling were very quickly followed by rapid warming, up to 7 °C over several decades or less. The cool times were some 10 to 12 °C colder than present temperatures.

Fast and dramatic climate variations during the last glacial event, called Dansgaard-Oeschger cycles, produce rapid warmings of several degrees centigrade over a few decades followed by a slower cooling and return to full glacial conditions. Smaller ice armadas associated with the Dansgaard-Oeschger cycles occur with a frequency of 2000 to 3000 years. For example, between 30 000 and 10 000 years ago, there were 13 Heinrich and Dansgaard-Oeschger ice-rafting events.

During the last 500 000 years, there have been very rapid changes to global temperature. Numerous events at some point show that immediately after a period of Northern Hemisphere cooling, there is a collapse of Northern Hemisphere ice sheets to form an ice armada and the temperature of the North Atlantic Ocean then increased rapidly.

It's counter-intuitive, but true that ice armadas warm the planet. We know that a great deal more heat is stored in oceans than in the atmosphere. By cooling the upper 50 metres of the seas they travel through, the dense cold water sinks, and is replaced by the slightly warmer water below. This warms the surface, creates surface currents and encourages rainfall—all three greenhouse contributors.

Instead of global temperature increasing the melting of ice sheets, the collapse of ice sheets was probably a major driving mechanism for rapid climate change. Ice armadas occurred 45 000, 37 000, 27 000 and 22 500 years ago with the last great ice armada between 17 600 to 17 200 years ago. However, the Irish Sea became covered again with ice 16 400 years ago and this ice joined the British ice sheet. The 800-year lag between an ice armada and the growth of ice sheets suggests that the combination of ice armadas and ocean currents might be the key to understanding rapid climate changes. The Antarctic ice is surrounded by great oceans which promote long-term climate stability, whereas the Arctic ice is almost surrounded by continents which greatly influence the Northern Hemisphere response to global climate change. Surges of continental ice sheets, mostly originating from the Baffin Island region of North America, and the consequent launching of iceberg armadas into the Atlantic Ocean via the Labrador Sea have had a dramatic effect on climate in the North Atlantic Basin.

The weight of ice forces continents to sink. The ice descends into the lower warmer layers of the atmosphere, reflection of sunlight from ice is decreased, ice melts, sea level rises, the sea invades continents and percolates under ice. Ice sheets which were grounded on continents are sheared off and launched into the sea as ice armadas. This raises sea level further. Slower spinning of the Earth and a greater opportunity for the warm North Atlantic current to penetrate the Arctic Ocean follow as a result. Warm Northern Hemisphere climates occurred when warm northerly-flowing water passed between Scotland and Iceland. If warm water passed further to the east, far northern climates were substantially cooler.

Ice armadas correlate with periods of Northern Hemisphere cooling followed by very rapid periods of warming of up to 7 °C in less than a century. Between ice armada events, there were plentiful short duration episodes of abrupt warming. Ice armadas transported trillions of tonnes of ice into the North Atlantic Ocean in less than 1000 years. Each armada would have produced a rise in sea level thereby causing our spinning planet to slow down in order to preserve angular momentum. Transfer of angular momentum into the oceans would result in adjustments to the movement of oceanic waters with resultant changes in the quantity and path of heat transfer away from the equator. The end result: climate change around the North Atlantic Basin.

Ice surges resulting in the disintegration of an ice sheet could be related to a lubricating water layer at the base of the ice. This water can be injected or formed by geothermal heating. There is another possible explanation for ice surges. When rocks are under pressure, the mineral grains align and the rock slides along the aligned layers. The same process occurs in ice. The pressure of the overlying ice in a thick glacier can align ice crystals. When the aligned crystals shear along the plane of alignment, large masses of ice suddenly move along shear planes in the glacier and huge volumes of ice surge into the ocean. Ice surges producing ice armadas can be internally triggered. This is expected because ice is an exceptionally good insulator.

By contrast, the much simpler geometry of the Southern Hemisphere supports the theory that ice armadas in the Northern Hemisphere would have produced far greater climate variations in the Northern Hemisphere than in the Southern Hemisphere. The evidence shows that melting of ice sheets forces climate change, not the inverse.

The melting of ice from the zenith of the last icehouse 18 000 years ago was almost complete 6000 years ago. Residual ice remains at the poles, especially Antarctica. The end of the last glacial event is well recorded in polar ice cores, sea floor sediments and lake sediments. The transition from an icy world to a greenhouse was a global event but its advent was not contemporaneous everywhere. Ice melting commenced 16 000 years ago in Australia, 14 700 years ago in Europe and 13 000 years ago in Asia. The process of ice melting was irregular, rapid and at times the temperature rose and at other times it fell. For example, in Scandinavia there was sudden warming about 13 000 years ago, a sudden cooling at the onset of the Younger Dryas 12 800 years ago and an intense warming 11 600 years ago at the end of the Younger Dryas. These have been determined by carbon dating. The corresponding sea level changes were a rising, a falling and a rising trend respectively.

Studies of more than 50 mountain glaciers in Alaska and Swedish Lapland show that glacial advances and retreats occur at the same time on both continents. The rising and falling spruce line in North America mirrors it.

There was a glacial advance 8000 years ago and a renewed advance between 5800 and 4900 years ago. Since then, North America and Western Europe have experienced two further glacial advancing episodes at 1300-400 BC and 1300-1920 AD. Most of the twentieth century was dominated by rebound from the cold period after 1920.

Throughout geological history, our planet only very rarely has had polar ice caps. The presence of polar ice in Antarctica and Greenland is geologically unusual and tells us that we are still within an extended icehouse period within which extreme icehouse and temperate greenhouse conditions fluctuate.

The ice sheets have an evocative story to tell. Currently some 90 per cent of the planet's continental ice is in Antarctica, of which 10 per cent is in the West Antarctic Ice Sheet. Drilling of the ice sheets has been used to try to understand the past climates by measuring volcanic fallout, carbon dioxide, methane and past temperatures. Unconsolidated snow was consolidated into ice and bubbles of air at the time it snowed were trapped. Heavy and light oxygen isotopes and nitrogen 15 and nitrogen 14 in trapped air can be used to calculate the temperature at the time of the snowfall. This trapped air is a sample of a past atmosphere: carbon dioxide and methane content of the ancient atmosphere can be directly measured. Such measurements allow a correlation between temperature and the past carbon dioxide and methane contents of the atmosphere. There is a correlation between the Dansgaard-Oeschger temperature fluctuations recorded in Greenland ice cores and parallel variations in methane concentration of contained air bubbles. Furthermore, there is also a correlation between the methane contents of Greenland and Antarctic ice cores, but no similar correlation between the Northern and Southern Hemisphere carbon dioxide fluctuations.

By using the proportion of heavy to light nitrogen isotopes in trapped air bubbles in ice, the average surface temperature can be calculated. Melting of ice and global warming after the zenith of the last ice age was punctuated by some very cold snaps. One of them, called the Younger Dryas, was 12 800 to 11 600 years ago. The surface temperature in Greenland then was −46 °C compared to −31 °C today. At the end of the Younger Dryas, a rise of 5 to 10 °C occurred in several decades or perhaps in even less than a decade and the change from icehouse to greenhouse conditions was completed over the next 1500 years. The very abrupt warming at the end of the Younger Dryas was in response to an extreme climate event. Methane concentration started to rise 30 years after the increase in temperature at the end of the Younger Dryas and it appears that methane additions to the atmosphere are an outcome, not a cause, of warming.

In the Antarctic ice cores, the atmospheric carbon dioxide tracks variations in climate which can be correlated with orbital changes to Earth. These orbital changes drive climate change which, in turn, results in changes in carbon dioxide. However, a correlation between Greenland and Antarctic ice core shows that natural methane fluctuations can be correlated but there is no correlation with carbon dioxide. Rather than carbon dioxide driving global climate change, it appears that changes in atmospheric carbon dioxide are a result of global climate change driven by another mechanism.

Large volcanic eruptions such as Towada, Japan (6722 BC), Hekla, Iceland (4988 BC, 1103 BC, 1971 AD), Kizimin (5279 BC) and Sheveluch (54 BC) in Kamchatka, Santorini, Greece (1470 BC), Krakatoa, Indonesia (535 AD), El Chichón, Mexico (1259 AD), Laki, Iceland (1781 AD) and Tambora, Indonesia (1815 AD) blasted out massive quantities of sulphuric acid which, in the upper atmosphere, reflected sunlight and resulted in atmospheric cooling. Acid precipitates are preserved in ice cores within volcanic ash layers from huge explosive volcanoes such as the Indonesian volcanoes of Toba (74 000 years ago; 2000 cubic kilometres of ash), Tambora (1815 AD, 100 cubic kilometres of ash) and Krakatoa (535 AD, 100 cubic kilometres of ash; 1883 AD, 18 cubic kilometres of ash). Upper atmosphere ash also reflects sunlight and there are good historical records of years of cooler climates after a volcanic eruption.

The West Antarctic Ice Sheet has been changing rapidly over the last 6000 years and is disintegrating. Most of the base of the sheet is below sea level. Since the glacial maximum, it has lost two thirds of its ice, contributing 11 metres to the 120 metres of post-glacial sea-level rise. If it collapsed today, sea level would rise 6 metres and what was the West Antarctic Ice Sheet would be a combination of open water, sea ice, fringing ice shelves, coastal tide-water glaciation and ice tongues.

After remaining dormant or in retreat for many years, there are rapid advances and surges in the West Antarctic Ice Sheet. Some glaciers in the West Antarctic Ice Sheet are currently moving at ½ to 2 kilometres a year. West Antarctica is the most prominent ice-filled basin on Earth. It is currently drained by fast moving ice streams that extend far into the ice sheet interior. The West Antarctic Ice Sheet is unstable. If there was a large ice surge, the equivalent of another Heinrich event, sea level would rise significantly, and the Antarctic Ocean would cool and the climate of Europe and the adjacent North Atlantic Basin would suddenly change. Ice surging is also currently taking place in the south-eastern Greenland glaciers. Between 1993 and 1998, the ice thinned by as much as 10 metres due to ice creeping and stretching seawards.

The low sea levels during the last icehouse enabled waves of migration on foot across land bridges from Russia into Alaska and the southward migration through the whole of the Americas before, during and after the latest icehouse until high sea levels prevented migration. Although humans and many animals were migrating south, there was also minor migration of animals to the north and eventually to Russia. The horse migrated from its ancestral home in North America to Eurasia.

As the sea levels rose, the human population in the Americas became isolated, the population increased and continued to migrate southwards. A mass extinction of the macrofauna of the Americas took place as soon as humans set foot. It appears that negroids from Australia were in South America for up to 30 000 years before the southward migration of Europeans. The australoids quickly became extinct but interbred genetic remnants may still exist in Patagonia.

Icehouse conditions had a profound effect on the flora and fauna of Earth, and planet Earth is on the rebound from the most recent icehouse conditions. For example, at the peak of icehouse conditions only 18 000 years ago, the Amazon rainforests were nearly destroyed: grasslands dominated the Amazon Basin, a different fauna existed and the residual forests were only 10 per cent of the current area of forests. During the last 2 million years, coral reefs appeared and disappeared with monotonous regularity.

On a global scale, during the latest maximum greenhouse 123 000 years ago when sea level was 6 metres higher than at present, vegetation was 155 per cent that of today and atmospheric carbon dioxide was 78 per cent that of today. At the glacial maximum 18 000 years ago, vegetation was 27 per cent that of today and

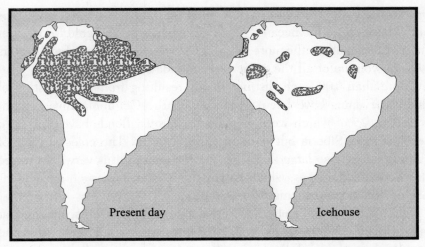

At the peak of the last icehouse 18 000 years ago, Amazonian rainforests were far smaller than today.

atmospheric carbon dioxide was 54 per cent. During the climate optimum 6000 years ago, vegetation was 120 per cent that of today and atmospheric carbon dioxide 76 per cent. Carbon dioxide can not cause Milankovitch orbital variations and atmospheric carbon dioxide levels are an outcome of climate change, not the cause. Ocean sediments record the extraordinary rate of climate changes over the last 15 000 years. The Barra Fan, located at the continental margin of north-west Scotland, shows clays deposited in cold periods, sand in warm ones. Radiochemical tracers such as thorium 230 show that there were great shifts in sediment supply over time spans of less than a century related to rapidly fluctuating climate.

In some places the last icehouse ended with a bang. Large lakes of meltwater were held back by debris left by retreating glaciers. One such lake in what is now Missoula, Idaho, contained a mere 2500 cubic kilometres of meltwater: more than the combined amount of water in the modern Lake Superior and Lake Erie. Ancient shorelines 600 metres above the floor of the valley still exist. When meltwaters filled to about 90 per cent of the height of the dam wall, the ice barrier in the dam wall became slightly buoyant and rose a little. Water trickled underneath the ice, drilled holes in the ice and enlarged a tunnel in the dam wall. Eventually, the dam caved in and the lake emptied in a matter of days 15 000 years ago. This flood of all floods scoured the land to form the scablands, still an unhealed wound on the Earth's surface. Water dug out plunge pools in river systems, piled up debris as big as battleships and emptied into the oceans. Sea level rapidly rose and cold fresh water formed a layer above the more saline ocean water. The flood of meltwaters was the volume of all the planet's rivers today.

More than 100 such distinct floods resulting from the bursting of meltwater dams have been recognised in the Columbia River, north-west US, 25 of which were megafloods. Similar floods have now been recognised in Siberia but none in Europe so far. The colossal scale of such flooding is so large that when on the ground, it is very hard to see the wood for the trees, which is why the evidence for such megafloods has not yet been recognised in Europe.

During the latest icehouse, periodic ice-rafting events occurred at approximately 7000-year intervals, tree lines advanced and retreated and sea level rose and fell. The last great icehouse ended in Europe 14 700 years ago and the planet lurched towards another inevitable greenhouse. The cycle reversed when the Northern Hemisphere retreated into near glacial conditions, possibly as a result of the breaching of the large Kara ice dam in European Russia. Massive volumes of cold fresh water suddenly entered the North Atlantic, the sea surface temperature plummeted and near glacial conditions would have quickly appeared. This event, the Younger Dryas, is unrelated to orbital, Heinrich or Dansgaard-Oeschger events and appears to be a one-off event. Some 11 600 years ago, there was an abrupt re-instatement of warmer conditions with a temperature rise of 7 °C in 50 years! This reversal and rebound to greenhouse conditions was a Northern Hemisphere event. 'Global' climate change is not global.

By 11 000 years ago, the Beringia land bridge was flooded, the Bering Strait formed and European migration into the Americas slowed to a trickle. Up to about 9000 years ago, during the last greenhouse, there was continuous habitation in Mediterranean Europe, Asia Minor and much of the ancient world. The high rainfall made the Persian Gulf and other adjacent areas attractive places for human habitation. The Sahara was a lush green meadow with annual grasses and shrubs. Then, the Northern Hemisphere received more summer sunlight, amplifying the African and Indian summer monsoons. For example, in the Thar Desert of India, lake levels fluctuated rapidly and show that there was a prolonged wet period from 9000 to 7500 BC. Since then, the area has become and remained arid. Changes in the Earth's orbit and the tilt of its axis gradually cooled the Northern Hemisphere, starting about

9000 years ago. The Earth's axial tilt was 24.14°, as compared with the current 23.45°. Some 9000 years ago the Earth's orbit that was closest to the Sun occurred at the end of July. Now the orbit closest to the Sun is in early January.

By 5000 BC, Europe enjoyed a climate optimum and was 2 to 3 °C warmer than at present. The melting of continental ice was raising sea level and the floating Arctic ice shrank. Heavy rainfall in this period swamped many forests and turned them into peat bogs; remnants can still be seen in the bogs of Ireland. In the climate optimum, vigorous winds brought regular summer rains to the Sahara which became vegetated. However, the climate again changed. Warm periods of lessening intensity alternated with cool periods of deepening chill.

In the Sahara transition to today's arid climate occurred in two stages. Each of these periods of great drought was separated by warm moist periods. The first, and less severe, drought occurred between 4700 and 3500 BC. There was an abrupt change over 300 years from grasslands to desert about 3400 BC. The water table was lowered to the same or lower levels than today. This dry period was at the same time as a period of global cooling which coincided with the rise of the first cities in Mesopotamia. The second stage, which was brutal, lasted only 400 years—from 3000 to 2600 BC. Fresh water lakes and streams dried, ancient Saharan civilisations were devastated and their socio-economic systems collapsed. The population moved eastwards from the cool dry conditions of the Sahara to settle in the Nile Valley. After this period, the climate again warmed.

There are some novel ways of monitoring climate change during the last icehouse. For example, the fossil larvae of flies and midges have been used to monitor the most recent changes. Each species of these insects 'lives within a very narrow temperature range and by counting the relative abundance of different species in the mud from old lakes, past temperatures to within 1 °C can be calculated. Although the ice age ended 14 700 years ago, the insect population shows that there were rapid fluctuations in temperature for the next 5000 years. There were some 20 cold snaps between 14 000 and 9500 years ago. The most intense started 12 800 years ago when summer temperatures in northern Europe plummeted by 11.5 °C over a 150-year period. That's enough to freeze any fly.

The melting of ice profoundly affected humans. As the planet warmed and the human population increased, agriculture was established in Asia

Minor 10 000 years ago. The climate stress of the Younger Dryas forced hunter-gatherers to become agriculturalists. The first agriculturalists worked far harder than hunter-gatherers: they had a shorter life span, were more diseased and were shorter in height. Much of the agriculture took place on the fertile coastal plains of the Levant utilising the rich alluvial fans deposited by the glacial meltwaters. Villages were established and fortified as a result of disputes between populations competing for the same resources. The European macrofauna became extinct and smaller docile animals such as goats, sheep, cattle and camels were domesticated rather than hunted.

In North America, the sudden disappearance of mammoths, mastadons and other macrofauna soon after the arrival of humans presents an enigma. Stress from hunting, forced migration and depletion of habitats probably drove extinction. However, there had been a very rapid climate change during the preceding 18 000 years and this may have changed the vegetation thereby resulting in nutritional stress. This idea was tested by measuring the chemistry of teeth of macrofauna from glacial to late glacial times because teeth reflect diet and water composition. Teeth chemistry shows that macrofauna had specialised diets but nutritional stress was not the cause of extinction. The macrofauna species extinction was due to humans.

On the scale of tens of millions of years, plate tectonic processes or impact-driven plate tectonic processes appear to drive major climate trends.

On the scale of hundreds of thousands of years, orbital variations appear to drive it. Orbital changes are miniscule but very small fluctuations in solar radiation appear to have a significant effect on climate.

As the volume of water in the ocean changes with icehouses and greenhouses, so does the planet's rotation. During the peak of the last glaciation, ice was at the poles and sea level was low. In order to preserve angular momentum, the planet was required to spin more rapidly. As a consequence, the east-west equatorial ocean currents were faster and the returning currents such as the Gulf Stream and the Kuroshiro Current deflected more sharply towards the equator.

As a result, the track of the Gulf Stream-North Atlantic Current changed, warm water failed to reach northern Europe, but points south were warmed. The Gulf Stream is like a huge conveyor belt. It carries light warm water from the tropics to the Arctic where it cools, gains salinity, sinks and moves south as the North Atlantic Current. These currents drive large and local climate variations in the North Atlantic Basin. Because the oceans have nearly 2000 times the heat-storing capacity of the atmosphere and preserve angular momentum far better, any changes in the movement of water masses relative to the land masses will have a great effect on the distribution of global temperature. The top few metres of the ocean have the same heat capacity as the entire atmosphere and the upper parts of the ocean can easily absorb and drive atmospheric heat changes.

During the glacial maximum 18 000 years ago, the Gulf Stream only reached Portugal. When the European ice sheets started to melt 14 700 years ago, the Gulf Stream terminated between Scotland and Iceland but, during a warmer phase from 13 000 to 12 800 years ago, it reached northern Norway. During a very cold snap in the Northern Hemisphere between 12 800 and 11 600 years ago, the Gulf Stream was again offshore from Iberia. There was a northward movement of the Gulf Stream and, in the Little Climate Optimum from 1000 to 1200 AD, the Gulf Stream encircled Iceland and warmed Greenland such that the south-eastern coast of Greenland was ice free. During that time the Vikings were able to circumnavigate and settle Greenland. Even more intriguing relationships have been found. The accumulation of continental ice sheets appears to be related to the locational change in the Earth's magnetic pole whereas the collapse of the ice sheets appears to be related to locational changes in the Earth's rotational axis.

8

THE GEOLOGY OF HISTORY

And the flood was forty days upon the earth; and the waters increased, and bear up the ark, and it was lift up above the earth. And the waters prevailed, and were increased greatly upon the earth; and the ark went upon the face of the waters. And the waters prevailed exceedingly upon the earth; and all the high hills, that were under the whole heaven, were covered. Fifteen cubits upwards did the waters prevail; and the mountains were covered. And all flesh died that moved upon the earth, both of fowl, and of cattle, and of beast, and of every creeping thing that creepth upon the earth, and every man: All in whose nostrils was the breath of life, of all that was in the dry land, died.

Genesis 7:17–22

Many great catastrophic events in our history were normal geological events. Some of these events are recorded as legends and myths. Others have entered the diverse scriptural writings with moral overtones. These catastrophic geological events had a profound effect on humans and many times resulted in greatly decreased population.

In the post-icehouse, the cold arid climate was once more changing rapidly to a warmer wetter climate. Global climate warmed between 9000 and 6000 years ago (although, in the Northern Hemisphere, there were events of alpine glaciation 8000 and 5000 years ago). Optimum greenhouse conditions 6000 years ago in the Northern Hemisphere saw temperatures 2 to 4 °C warmer than those that exist now, 20 per cent more rainfall and sea level was 1 to 3 metres higher. In the Southern

Hemisphere, tree ring measurements in Tasmania show that the greenhouse zenith was 4000 years ago and in Queensland 5000 and 3500 years ago, the temperature was 3.5 °C warmer. The latest event of 'global' warming was not global!

Villages, fields and livestock of post-glacial human populations were on the continental shelf, then a coastal plain, climatically protected low-lying areas and river valleys. Neolithic populations probably would have lived in river valleys or on the former continental shelf close to the glacial meltwater streams, rich alluvial soils, grasslands, fields and fishing grounds. One such low-lying place is part of the 160 000 square kilometre area now occupied by the Black Sea. This area was the breadbasket of the ancient world. There was probably much cross fertilisation of ideas and languages in these protected basins that were the cradles of modern civilisation.

After the icehouse, the melting of glaciers and polar ice caps resulted in a very rapid rise in sea level. The Neolithic populations had to pack up and move rather quickly to higher ground. Global sea level has risen 120 metres since the last icehouse and the remains of Neolithic villages and fireplaces are recorded in many places currently 100 to 120 metres below sea level. With the rising sea level, islands formed trapping humans and animals who perished as the islands became covered with water. Islands not covered by water isolated communities which may or may not have survived.

Before and during the last icehouse, there were two large freshwater lakes in what is now the Black Sea. Almost 25 per cent of the Black Sea is flat lying and less than 100 metres beneath sea level. It was once the rich coastal plain at the delta of the Danube, Dnieper and Don Rivers. At the end of the last icehouse, the outlet connecting the freshwater lakes to the Mediterranean was probably a channel through the Sakarya River to the Gulf of Izmit, an eastern arm of the Marmara Sea. The Anatolian Fault has been active for hundreds of millions of years and renewed slipping along the Anatolian Fault changed the course of the Sakarya River, the outlet was closed and the water in the freshwater lakes started to evaporate. At that time, there was no Bosphorus, just a low valley with a rock outcrop at its headwaters. This kept the Mediterranean Sea out of the Black Sea Basin.

But as the Mediterranean rose in greenhouse times, the pressure on the natural dam increased. Eventually, 7600 years ago, when the dam was 150 metres higher than the floor of the Black Sea, it broke and the sea cascaded into the basin. The torrent of Mediterranean seawater carved out a deep narrow strait, the Bosphorus.

The Bosphorus and the Black Sea Basin filled with saline water in one or two years. Seawater poured into the Black Sea Basin with a force equivalent to 200 Niagara Falls. The heavy salt water sank to the bottom of the Black Sea. On average, the water level rose 15 centimetres a day. In some places, the shoreline advanced a few kilometres each day and the roar of water entering the Black Sea Basin could be heard hundreds of kilometres away. There was enormous turbulence as seen in the earliest marine sediments on the floor of the Black Sea. Marine sediment was deposited on the fertile soils. Today, the Black Sea bottom waters are heavy and salty water capped by fresher surface waters. The bottom water of the Black Sea has no deep water currents and no oxygen allowing the preservation of most materials on its floor.

People and animals perished. A few terrified survivors were dispersed around the rim of the new sea. The survivors carried with them their culture, language, agricultural and animal husbandry skills, and horrific stories about a year-long flood, death and destruction. The flood led to rapid dispersal of farming techniques, metallurgy, language and culture.

It is no surprise that many cultures have myths and legends about a great flood. This period of huge floods on many parts of the globe was the most tumultuous event humans ever experienced. Attempts to interpret the meaning of this catastrophic geological flooding of the Black Sea Basin were passed down from generation to generation. These culturally and linguistically transposed stories appeared as a fragmentary Sumerian story dated at 3400 BC, the Mesopotamian myth of Atrahasis, the Babylonian tale of Ut-napishtim in the Epic of Gilgamesh, the Greek stories of Deucalion and Pyrrha, the geologically intriguing story of Dardanus and the Biblical Great Flood of Noah. The post-glacial sea level change was so rapid and incomprehensible to the ancients the Great Flood was interpreted as the action of a god who flooded the known world in order to rid it of evil.

During the thaw after the icehouse, many lakes dammed by glacial debris burst, there was widespread flooding and lakes were completely emptied. For example, the breaching of an icehouse lake allowed the enlargement of Big Stone Lake on the South Dakota-Minnesota border and much of the good farmland in North America is on what were the floors of lakes during icehouse. Spectacular examples of post-icehouse bursting of lakes and flooding occur in Scandinavia. The Jutulhogget, the Giant's Cut, in central Norway was eroded during a catastrophic drainage of ice-dammed Lake Glomsjö about 8800 years ago. Today, Jutulhogget is a dry canyon that cuts through a mountain range. According to legend the giant of Glomdal made the canyon in an attempt to divert a river in order to drown his rival, another giant. In the highlands of south-eastern Australia and Tasmania, both dammed and breached glacial lakes occur. However, because Australia was at lower latitudes than the heavily glaciated areas of the Northern Hemisphere, the effects of glaciation are not nearly as widespread.

The fossil outer reefs in Florida show sea level change after the last glaciation too. Dating of the coral *Acropora palmata* by uranium-thorium methods has shown that the Great Flood was not global. This coral lives in Caribbean waters less than 5 metres deep and is very sensitive to environmental changes. *Acropora palmata* can grow up to 14 mm per year and so is a good tracer of sea level rise, but its death can be used to show a catastrophic sea level rise. But at no point in the 12 000 year Florida-Bahamas record does sea level rise approach rates at which *Acropora palmata* could not keep pace.

Drilling of the coral reefs and dating of the corals shows a 20-metre rise in sea level between 17 000 and 12 500 years ago, a rapid rise of 24 metres from 12 000 to 11 000 and a decreased rate of sea level rise from 11 000 to 10 500 years ago. Sea level rose 17 metres between 8500 and 6500 years ago. At the time of the flooding of the Black Sea 7600 years ago, the coral record in the Florida-Bahamas area shows no great or catastrophic sea level rise, supporting the view that the Great Flood was a local event. The coral record does show that there was a huge sea level rise.

Between 7600 and 7200 years ago, there was a very rapid 6.5 metre rise and this has been attributed to instability, the surging of the West Antarctic Ice Sheet and to changes in marine ice extent between 8000 and 7000 years ago. Between 6500 and 5000 years ago sea level rose 3.7 metres and another 7.5 metres over the last 5000 years.

The rate of sea level rise is highly variable. Throughout post-glacial times sea level rose at 9.5 mm per year and, about 9000 years ago, slowed to 1.25 mm per year. The maximum rate of sea level rise was 45 mm per year between 7600 to 7200 years ago. The numerous sea level rises and very rapid rates of sea level rise did not kill coral reefs.

The most dramatic prediction about anthropomorphic global green-house predicts a 3 °C rise in temperature in Greenland, triggering an irreversible melting of the ice sheets. This would produce a rise in sea level of 7 metres over the next thousand years, far less catastrophic than the 6.5 metre sea level rise measured over the 400 years between 7600 and 7200 years ago.

After the last Ice Age, there was climatic stability and temperatures were a little warmer than now 9000 to 6000 years ago. What are now arid zones were much wetter, summer rains brought life to the Sahara and inland Australian lakes contained water.

Cultures changed slowly during that warm era. There was a peak in cultural development 5800 years ago, a time when global temperature rose by 2 °C. This date coincides with emergence of the El Niño/Southern Oscillation Cycle when strong climatic fluctuations started about 6000 to 3000 years ago as civilisations emerged from the Stone Age. There was a change in agriculture, pottery and tools coinciding with the appearance of El Niño and people ate more seafood, reflecting the post-glacial rise in sea level. The climate change brought the cattle-grazing community from the Saharan grasslands into what became ancient Egypt. Climate then deteriorated and glaciers expanded in the period from 5800 to 4900 years ago.

Pollen records from Greek lakes show evidence of massive deforestation in the Early Bronze Age, 3500 to 2100 BC. Grazing and farming on steep slopes resulted in repeated episodes of catastrophic erosion that gave rise to the barren landscapes seen in many areas of Greece today. Greek mythology makes reference to environmental damage in ancient Mesopotamia that resulted in deforestation, flooding, silting of irrigation channels, salinisation and the collapse of Sumerian city states. Written records dating back to almost 3000 BC describe declining crop yields, decreasing production of wheat relative to more salt tolerant barley, and patches of soil which turned white suggesting massive salinisation of agricultural lands. Climate change exacerbated salinisation as the warmer drier conditions reduced the flow of the Euphrates and made it impossible for the Sumerians to flush the salts from their fields.

Some 4200 years ago there was a 300-year El Niño-induced drought. The effects of this were felt in the Middle East, the Americas and the rest of the populated world. For example, the former northern Mesopotamian city of Tell Leilan had been a thriving agricultural civilisation dependent upon rain. When the rains did not come, the civilisation collapsed. The remnant inhabitants fled to southern Mesopotamia, where irrigation with river water allowed farmers to grow crops in drier conditions.

Communities thrived in the Indus Valley between 2500 and 1500 BC in cities such as Harappa and Mohenjo-dar, cultivating grain, cotton, melons and dates in what is now Pakistan and north-west India. The sudden collapse of the Harappan civilisation shows no evidence of warfare or rebellion and there was a total abandonment of settlement sites, which invites a climatic explanation. Eventually the remaining Harappans succumbed to Aryan invaders from the north.

Although the area once occupied by the Harappans is now arid, it was once a land of rich vegetation. Fossils, pollen and lake sediments show there were bulrushes, sedge, grass, mimosa, jamun trees and many other species. Jamun trees need a rainfall of at least 50 centimetres a year, more than twice the current rainfall. Dating these fossils shows that there was a very wet period from 3000 until 1800 BC. Rainfall decreased appreciably between 1800 and 500 BC associated with the El Niño-induced drought, and communities in the Middle East and the Indian subcontinent were greatly stressed.

At the same time, there was another period of global cooling. Between 1300 to 500 BC, glaciers in Alaska, Utah, Scandinavia and Patagonia advanced again. The widespread effects of climate change may well have had a lot to do with the human upheavals of that time, which saw great migrations and invasions. The civilisations of the Hittites and Mycenae fell, as the Assyrians, the Phoenicians and Greeks rose. There were, of course, other factors such as the destruction of the Minoan Empire by the 1470 BC eruption of Santorini and a technological transition from bronze to iron.

Rapid geological changes such as volcanoes, El Niño, climate change and sea level changes have had a profound effect on us and have triggered or been instrumental in shaping the course of history.

Planet Earth has been peppered by meteorites and comets throughout its history. Because comets leave only very small amounts of extraterrestrial debris which is later incorporated in rocks, it is hard to piece together the blow by blow history of cometary impacting. Meteorite impacting leaves its mark, principally as craters. Craters are far easier to identify in young rock sequences and parts of Australia which have been flat and stable for 1600 million years give us a good sample of the history of impacting on Earth. Australia has no more impacts than other places on Earth, but the record is better preserved.

During the last 5 million years when hominids have been evolving on the planet, three impacts blasted out craters greater than 10 kilometres wide in size. These are at Bosumtwi, Ghana, Zamanshin, Russia and Elgygytyn, Russia. Since humans appeared, between 200 and 500 extraterrestrial bodies several hundred metres in size impacted. About two thirds of these fell into oceans producing huge tsunamis. Those that penetrated the sea floor produced even greater tsunamis yet records of tsunamis several hundred metres high are poor. Historically, few population centres existed around the Indian Ocean, Atlantic Ocean and Pacific Ocean shores. The cradles of civilisation were the sheltered valleys around the smaller seas like the Mediterranean and Red Sea, or mountain areas like the Andes or the south Indian highlands. The growth of civilisation around the shores of oceans may well have been interrupted by numerous tsunamis caused by extraterrestrial visitors. Common threads exist in ancient lores such as falling stars, sky fire and floods, and the myths and legends of the ancients may not have been just fiction.

Those living on the south-east coast of Australia might not be comforted to know that giant tsunamis have thrown huge boulders many kilometres inland. This is best seen inland from Nowra, NSW. These tsunamis occur approximately every 300 years and may be related to sediments perched on the continental shelf collapsing into the ocean deeps, not impacts. Such submarine debris flows are triggered by earthquakes and numerous earthquakes occur in south-east Australia associated with compression and the uplift of the Great Dividing Range.

But numerous impacts took place during human occupation of Australia. There is no doubt that some of these would have been seen and heard as they occurred in areas where there had been partial habitation for thousands of years. The Boxhole Crater in the Northern Territory is 170 metres wide and formed 30 000 years ago. Fragments of the original meteorite have been found. The age of the Veevers Crater in the Canning Basin of Western Australia is not exactly known but it is less than 20 000 years old. The exact age of the 29-metre-wide Snelling Crater in the Kimberleys is also not known but it is probably less than 5000 years old. The 24-metre-wide Dalgaranga Crater near Yalgoo in Western Australia also contains bits of meteorite and the crater was blasted out by impacting less than 3000 years ago. At Henbury in the Northern Territory, there are 14 craters from 6 to 180 metres in size from impacts 4200 years ago. A meteorite exploded just before impact, sprayed Henbury with high-velocity meteorite fragments which blasted out craters, melted rock and left behind smaller pieces of meteorite fragments to pollute the area with material from space.

Scientists have recognised consistent patterns in ancient writings suggesting cometary impacting. Over the last 5000 years, it appears that comets may have been responsible for famine and massive social disruption. In fact, cometary impacting might have had a profound effect on the human population of the Earth over the last 5000 years. A cometary impact can trigger earthquakes, volcanic eruptions, tsunamis and the release of poisonous gas from the sea floor. Nevertheless, we happen to live on the only planet in our solar system that can support multicellular life as we know it and, because of the infrequency of large extraterrestrial visitors, it is a very safe planet.

Historically comets have been interpreted as portents and signs of difficult times in the future, which may not be myth. There is a correlation between increased cometary impacting and global environ-mental shocks that lead to the onset of dark ages for society, producing famine and the destruction of cities and populations.

The period of impacts from comets 2354 to 2345 BC was one of untold misery, mass famine, destruction of cities and populations, earthquakes, tsunamis, volcanic eruptions and poisoning by gases released from the oceans. It is interesting that the disasters, including the falling of red hot stones from the heavens, led to the collapse of Egypt and the Exodus at this time. Cometary activity was high around 1600 BC and recorded in the Bible and contemporary Chinese writings. Cometary impacting from 1159 to 1141 BC may have triggered the famine in the Biblical account of King David's reign.

In 372 BC, the Greek historian Ephorus observed the fragmentation of a giant comet. Fragments pass some 700 000 kilometres from the Sun every 800 years and each time the strong gravitational field of the Sun pulls them apart. Most of the icy fragments evaporate as they get close to the Sun but there are still about 90 fragments in the orbit of the original giant comet.

Cometary impacting also took place 208 to 204 BC and it appears

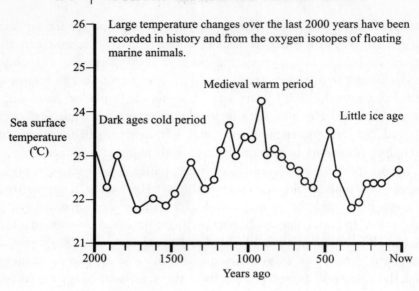

26 — Large temperature changes over the last 2000 years have been recorded in history and from the oxygen isotopes of floating marine animals.

Sea surface temperature (°C)

Dark ages cold period

Medieval warm period

Little ice age

Years ago

that the aftermath of this event led to the downfall of the Ch'in Dynasty in China, suggesting most of the comets hit Asia. Another cometary impacting period from 536 to 545 AD was at the beginning of a period of global cooling and may have led to famine. This period of impacting was immediately after the massive eruption of Krakatoa, Indonesia in 535 AD. There was so much dust in the atmosphere that there were years of darkness, hence the term the Dark Ages. Crop failure, bitterly cold weather, famine and disease followed. Massive depopulation occurred, farmers became hunter-gatherers and warfare was constant. Another large eruption, Rabaul in New Guinea in 536 AD, added to the misery. Concurrent were the deaths of King Arthur and Merlin. We can only wait for the next cometary impact. It will not be long.

Nomadic clans of hunters and gatherers could have better adapted to the sudden global changes resulting from a small impact than an agricultural civilisation which depended upon optimal sunshine, temperature and rain. Urban populations today are even more fragile because they depend not only upon agriculture and transport, but a complex infrastructure vulnerable to tsunamis, earthquakes, fire and flood.

In 1490 AD in Shanxi Province, China, an estimated 10 000 people were killed by what was described in contemporary Chinese literature as falling stones, obviously a fragmented asteroid. Such stones fall after the atmospheric explosion of a meteorite less than 1 kilometre in diameter.

The effects of natural phenomena on human history are probably underestimated. Alternating icehouse and greenhouse conditions forced migration, creativity and rapid human evolution. Earthquakes, volcanoes, extraterrestrial impacts, tsunamis and gas releases have weakened and destroyed whole civilisations thereby opening the door for the next phase of history. The same has happened to all life forms on Earth with mass extinctions of multicellular life and the sudden filling of new vacated ecologies. Storytellers passed on the fact and interpretation of such natural events to the next human generation. By the time such stories had been written down, they had been embellished and modified many times as they crossed cultures. Moral overtones were added. Such stories may be the badly coded messages of great real events.

A 1.6 kilometre wide asteroid 1997XF11 has a calculated near-Earth pass in the year 2028. Swarms of smaller near-Earth and Earth-crossing asteroids are known and the probability of Earth being hit by one of these smaller bodies is between 1 in 10 000 to 1 in 20 000. Civilisation-destroying impacts occur every 300 000 to 1 million years. During the time humans have been on Earth and assuming that the average human lives to 75 years old, humans have the same chance of dying in a jet aeroplane crash as by a cometary impact. It is still infinitely more unsafe to smoke, drink alcohol or cross the road so I can live with the odds of being wiped out by an extraterrestrial visitor. Perception and reality are two different things. The perceptions of risk from impacts is smaller than being killed in a plane crash because planes crash at a steady rate with relatively few deaths per event whereas lethal impacts are rare and kill a large number of people.

The Swift-Tuttle Comet crossed the Earth's orbit in 1737, 1862 and 1992 and in 2126 will only be 14 days flight from Earth. This comet is twice the size of the extraterrestrial mass which struck Earth 65 million years ago and resulted in a dinosaur-killing mass extinction.

Only 5 per cent of the asteroids which cross the Earth's orbit have been recorded. For example, the kilometre-sized asteroid, 1989FC missed the Earth by 650 000 kilometres, only 6 hours flight away. This asteroid was only spotted after it had passed through the Earth's orbit and, if it had struck Earth in 1989, it had the potential to destroy civilisation. If 1989FC had hit the land a 10 kilometre wide crater would have formed from the impact, the energy released would be equivalent to detonation of the total global nuclear arsenal and massive earthquakes of Richter magnitude greater than 10 would be triggered. (The most intense earthquake recorded in the history of measurement was on 22 May 1960: a Richter magnitude 9.5 earthquake hit Chile as bits of the Pacific Ocean were pushed under the Andes.) If 1989FC impacted a terrestrial landmass, tens of thousands of square kilometres around the crater would be burned and billions of tonnes of rocks and dust thrown into the atmosphere would cloud the stratosphere, block sunlight, lower air temperature, stop photosynthesis for several years, create acid rain and destroy the ozone layer. Impact of 1989FC into an ocean basin would trigger tsunamis which would destroy civilisation around the ocean.

A fly-by of the asteroid 1992KD took place on 29 July 1999. NASA's Deep Space 1 flew within 15 kilometres of the asteroid, otherwise known as Braille. This was the closest ever approach to a planetary body without actually landing on it. Deep Space 1 was primarily used to demonstrate new technology, its ion engine and autonomous navigation system, and the Braille fly-by was a minor diversion. That's the good news. The bad news is that the Deep Space's camera was pointing in the wrong direction at the time!

The possibility that some of the larger asteroids might have moons has been debated long and hard. The unusual light curves, slow rotation rates and double impact craters were some of the strongest lines of evidence before the Galileo spacecraft 1993 fly-by of Ita's moon, Dactyl. By using a ground-based telescope, a moon to the asteroid 45 Eugenia was discovered. The moon has a diameter of 13 kilometres, an orbital period of 4.7 days and is 1190 kilometres from Eugenia. The discovery of Eugenia's moon enabled calculation of the density of the asteroid. With a density slightly higher than ice, Eugenia is probably composed of primitive dirty ice, rather like a comet.

On St Valentine's Day, 2000, the NASA satellite NEAR (Near Earth Asteroid Rendezvous) arrived at the asteroid Eros and slipped into orbit in preparation for what was to be a successful landing. The potato-shaped Eros is 33 kilometres long and 13 kilometres wide with an orbit tilted at 10° to that of Earth. Rather than a rubble pile, Eros is a solid rocky asteroid pitted with impact craters. If Eros impacted with Earth, there would be a mass extinction of life on Earth.

A volcano can ruin your day. Volcanoes derived from the pulling apart of the Earth's crust in mid-ocean regions like Iceland or from hot spots like Hawaii erupt large volumes of lava and rarely have minor explosive eruptions. By contrast, volcanoes that derive from the pushing of the wet ocean crust deep into the mantle beneath a continent produce massive earthquakes and violent explosive volcanic eruptions that erupt almost no lava. These eruptions are explosive because of the large quantity of gas, mainly steam. Such eruptions occurred in modern times in the Mediterranean, the Indonesian island arc and the Pacific rim of fire which extends from Mt Erebus (Antarctica) to Chile, Peru, Ecuador, central America, western USA, the Aleutian island arc, far east Russia, Japan, the Philippines, Papua New Guinea, Fiji and New Zealand. Some of the largest volcanic explosions on Earth have occurred in Papua New Guinea, especially New Britain. Not only have eruptions such as those at Lamington and Rabaul thrown massive quantities of ash into the atmosphere and created tsunamis, they have wiped out populations.

There is a long history of destruction of populations by volcanic eruptions in Central America, the Mediterranean, Indonesia and the Pacific rim of fire. The most common eruption product is called ash or tuff. Volcanic ash is composed of billions of very fine-grained particles, needles and razor-sharp shards of volcanic glass. Volcanic ash forms when steam streams through molten rock and creates a froth which is blown high into the atmosphere. The molten rock cools so quickly it forms a glass. Slower cooling produces crystals. The ash is not hot and a blanket of ash covers thousands of square kilometres around the volcano.

Twice in recent years passenger jet aircraft stalled all engines in high-altitude volcanic-ash clouds in south-east Asia only to restart their engines at a lower altitude following a few minutes of a hair-raising death-defying dive. These ash clouds were hundreds of kilometres away from the eruption and 12 kilometres above the ground.

Most fatalities during volcanism result from asphyxiation due to ash. Ash also accumulates on buildings which collapse under the weight. The particles of ash high in the atmosphere act as nuclei for water vapour and heavy rain and lightning normally follow a large eruption. Ash particles high in the atmosphere reflect sunlight, the atmosphere cools, a period of cooler weather follows a volcanic eruption and, if the eruption was large, there may be a total collapse of the climate. The runoff from the heavy rain results in the damming of watercourses, flooding, landslides and mudflows. More energetic ash eruptions blast out fragments of rock. The destruction of buildings and killing of inhabitants by volcanic bombs is common. History shows far more deaths are from famine following natural disasters than from the disaster itself. Repeated crop failures follow large eruptions. So does cool dark wet weather. So do disease, warfare and massive social disruption. With some larger eruptions, the geological record shows us that the planet collapses into an ice age.

The recent tracking of high-altitude ash clouds and the correlation of past climate changes with volcanicity show that some eruptions have a profound effect on global climate.

Cool winters followed the 1883 eruption of Krakatoa because the ash particles reflected sunlight and acted as nuclei for clouds. The ozone layer probably vanished for a few years. The Tambora eruption of 1815 produced a severe year without a summer and a bitter winter. Other times of climatic misery can be correlated with very large volcanic eruptions. For example, the permanent fog in the 1783 Northern Hemisphere summer and the cruel winter in the Northern Hemisphere of 1783-4 followed the 1781 eruption of Laki in Iceland. The fatal summer in Scotland in 1695 followed four substantial eruptions in Indonesia in 1693 and 1694. Other substantial eruptions which cooled global climate were Mayon, Philippines, in 1766, Coseguina, Nicaragua, in 1835 and Krakatoa, Indonesia in 535 AD.

Large volcanic eruptions that eject sulphur compounds leave their record as thin sulphate deposits in the polar ice sheets. This record of volcanic eruptions extends back for thousands of years in the Greenland ice sheet. Sulphates act as nuclei for the formation of rain droplets and promote cloud formation. Clouds reflect more sunlight and so keep the Earth's surface cooler, and radiate heat thereby cooling the atmosphere.

Laki, Tambora and Krakatoa each discharged more than 50 million tonnes of sulphuric acid into the air. Toba probably ejected 3 billion tonnes of hydrogen sulphide and sulphur dioxide, 500 billion tonnes of water vapour and 2 billion tonnes of dust. This cooled the atmosphere by 3 to 5 °C. This raises the possibility that extreme volcanism, such as Toba 74 000 years ago, can trigger an ice age.

The geological record of the Mediterranean shows that superheated ash flows were not uncommon. One raced across the surface of the Aegean Sea for 35 kilometres and then deposited ash on the island of Kos. About 35 000 years ago an ash flow covered 32 000 square kilometres in and around the Bay of Naples to a depth of up to 100 metres with a total volume of 500 cubic kilometres. At Yellowstone in the US, an eruption 600 000 years ago spewed out 1000 cubic kilometres of ash and pumice, and 2 million years ago 2500 cubic kilometres were erupted. If such a large eruption occurred today, the devastation would be unthinkable.

The eruption of Santorini (Thira or Thera), probably in 1470 BC, changed the course of human history. This eruption, called the Minoan eruption, blasted out 18 cubic kilometres of ash into the atmosphere. The eruption occurred in four major phases spanning days or weeks, producing ash flows and an ash column over 30 kilometres high. Eruption deposits on Santorini are over 50 metres thick, a layer of 10 centimetres of fine ash has been found in the Nile Delta and vast rafts of floating pumice in the eastern Mediterranean suggest repeated tsunamis. On Santorini, the Bronze Age town of Akrotiti was buried in ash. Greek mythology, recorded in *Theogony*, describes the account of the battle between Zeus and the Titans. This has been interpreted as a contemporary account of the eruption and, like many descriptions of catastrophic geological events, has settled in mythology.

By investigating modern catastrophic volcanic eruptions elsewhere on Earth, we can understand the impact of the Santorini eruption on the Minoan culture, based in Crete. Many scholars believe that the Minoan eruption and the destruction of Santorini led to the myth of Atlantis. A strong case can be made that Plato invented the whole story or used a garbled historical account of the eruption of Santorini, perhaps to warn his fellow Atheneans of the risks he saw in their corruption. Like most myths, they are neither right nor wrong.

Fossil beaches in Hawaii show that at about the time of the Santorini eruption 3500 years ago, sea level was some 2 metres higher than at present. The Santorini eruption of 1470 BC weakened the dominant Minoans such that they were overthrown by the Myceneans a few years later. If history is any guide, then most of the fatalities would have occurred from famine. The Myceneans then rose to power, classical Greece became a dominant force and the rise of western culture was initiated. If it was not for the Santorini eruption, the path of human history would have taken a vastly different course. The remaining Minoans interbred in Asia Minor with the Philistines who were the precursors to the Carthaginians and Phoenicians. Santorini is still active and last erupted in 1950. Santorini and other nearby Greek islands are populated and attract a huge number of tourists in summer, another catastrophe waiting to happen.

Massive eruptions in 535 AD at Krakatoa in Indonesia and 536 AD at Rabaul in New Guinea had a world wide effect. Chroniclers from Rome and China record the Sun dimmed dramatically for 18 months and there were widespread crop failures. Tree ring measurements from north-western Europe show that the dust veil in the upper atmosphere had produced a significant deterioration in the climate. It is not possible to draw direct conclusions but immediately following the Rabaul eruption, there were signs of great social stress in the Byzantine Empire.

Immediately before the eruption of Rabaul, Constantinople had a population of 500 000 but, by the mid-eighth century, the population was 25 000 to 50 000. Trade and economic activity almost ceased and Byzantine society drifted back into subsistence agriculture. This whole sequence of events may have been triggered by Krakatoa and Rabaul. Crop failures probably stressed the Byzantine community and, when bubonic plague arrived from Ethiopia in 542, a third of the population of Constantinople died. Bubonic plague then returned with terrifying regularity, every 15 years or so, to most major cities. There was massive depopulation and some cities that had survived since antiquity ceased to exist. The Byzantine Empire entered a dark age. Both the Byzantine Empire and the Persians were exhausted after the Byzantine victory at Nineveh in 628. Arabia had been spared of the effects of bubonic plague and expanded to fill the vacuum. Constantinople was blockaded by the Arabs from 674 to 678 and put under siege in 717 and 718.

The eruption of Mount Pinatubo, Philippines, in 1991 was one of the biggest in that century. In just five hours the volcano spewed out 9 cubic kilometres of ash, incinerated vast tracts of forest, buried some areas by up to 200 metres and released massive quantities of CFCs. There was a period of global cooling and colourful sunsets in the two years following the eruption. In some parts of the Southern Hemisphere, the average temperatures dropped by 1 to 2 °C. If Pinatubo or any other equatorial volcano ejected 5 or 10 times as much ash, then there would have been profound social effects on the planet. Such volcanoes are common. If 100 cubic kilometres were blasted out of Pinatubo, then crop failures, famine, economic collapse, mass social stress, a drift from an urban to a rural subsistence lifestyle and possibly war would have preceded the collapse into another icehouse. We humans live right at the edge of survival.

Another deadly eruption product from volcanoes is a mixture of superheated lava, gas and crystals. These travel at hundreds of kilometres per hour, can flow uphill and actually heat up when they start to become solid. At 7.50 am on Ascension Day, Thursday, 8 May

1902, the volcano Mount Pelée on the Caribbean island of Martinique erupted. The town of Saint-Pierre was flattened and 28 600 people died. There were two survivors: one was Augustus Ciparis, a murderer imprisoned in a windowless dungeon, who received a free pardon, joined a travelling circus and earned his living recounting his horrific tale. Sometimes crime does pay.

Romans and Vikings spread their influence and range in a greenhouse. The last 4000 years of climate records preserved in ice, lakes, tree rings, fossils and deep sea sediments show that there are cycles of climate change, the strongest being about 1500-year cycles with several weaker century to millennial scale cycles. The current natural warming trend is projected to continue until about 2300-2500.

After the eruption of Santorini and the destruction of the Minoan culture, there was a period of global cooling from 1300 to 500 BC. High latitude and alpine glaciers expanded. Global warming commenced again about 500 BC. The Empires of Ashoka in India, the Ch'hin Dynasty in China and the Romans in Europe, North Africa and the Middle East all grew during this warmer period. In Roman times, the global climate was considerably different and the planet was in another one of its numerous greenhouses. The very clothing worn by Romans shows the climate was far warmer than now. A great period of cultural growth took place. The planet was warmer and wetter. Grapes and citrus fruit grew in north England. What was the Roman port of London, now underwater, shows the normal geological process of subsidence. The Romans left England at the start of a period of global cooling and the Dark Ages began.

In North America there was endemic warfare in the Early Period, 0 to 900 AD, during a period of global cooling with the resultant great competition for resources. Glaciers expanded, especially in Alaska, from 700 to 900. During the Dark Ages in Europe, there was extreme drought on the Great Plains of North America. This, and other drought periods from 200 to 370 AD and 700 to 850 AD, were far greater than anything modern farmers in North America have experienced. Warfare declined in the Middle Period, 900 to 1200, during a period of warmer climate and forests grew much further north in North America than they do today. The American mid-west was warm and dry whereas China and Japan were cool. Slight climate changes might not be global or may well have long lag times. In North America's Late Period, there again was widespread war.

The Roman Empire left its mark on Europe. Tourists see the aqueducts, arches, theatres and memorials but the greatest legacy is from mining and smelting. Although gold, silver, copper and tin were prized, the Romans needed huge amounts of lead as a corrosion-resistant metal for plumbing, shipbuilding and storage of foods and wines. The smelting of lead ores quadrupled the lead content of the atmosphere and contaminated Europe. Unusually high quantities of lead occur in the part of the Greenland ice sheet which formed between 600 BC and 300 AD. The isotope fingerprint of the lead in the Greenland ice show that the lead derived from the mines in the Iberian Pyrite Belt of southern Spain and Portugal. The Iberian lead-silver-copper-gold mines were initially exploited by the Celts and, in the Bible in I Kings 10, are mentioned as one of the mining centres of King Solomon. Carthaginian and Phoenician mining was substituted by Roman activities which ceased about 400 AD. There was no mining by the Moors. In the late eighteenth century the Iberian mines were rediscovered. They are still being exploited.

A study of shells in the Mediterranean show humans have been redistributing lead in the environment since the Bronze Age. Shells formed in Roman times contain a similar lead content to those formed today and modern shells derive their lead from port and harbour traffic. Fresh snow in Greenland contains minute amounts of lead which in autumn-winter derives lead from North America and in spring-summer, from Eurasia. Like the Romans, we continue to add the products of our industry to the atmosphere, water and soils.

The sediments of the Tinto River at Huelva in Spain record 4500 years of pollution. Copper, lead, zinc, silver and gold orebodies have been mined from the third millennium BC to the present. Sediments are enriched in lead, barium, arsenic, copper, zinc, tin, thallium, cadmium, silver, mercury and gold. A 4500-year-old metal contamination has been spread 100 kilometres down the Rio Tinto. It appears that ancient mining pollution may be a far more serious problem than the impact of much larger modern day operations. Notwithstanding, the anthropo-morphic input of metals may remain immobilised in estuarine sediments for millennia. Humans have left our geological mark.

Between 1000 and 1200 AD there was another greenhouse event known as the Little Climate Optimum or the Medieval Warm Period.

In England, France and Germany the warmer wetter climates produced more crops and an excess of wealth. This resulted in the building of castles, cathedrals and monasteries which are now significant tourist attractions in Europe. Again, there seems to be an increase in cultural development during greenhouses.

The Vikings were the first to be affected by the sudden change into the warmer conditions of the Little Climate Optimum. They erupted into colonisation and expanded from their newly-warmed Scandinavian bases into France, England, Russia, Iceland, Greenland and North America. A Viking village is well preserved in Newfoundland. Sea crossings were no longer hampered by ice, storms and variable weather. The climate in the Northern Hemisphere was so pleasant Vikings colonised Iceland in 874 and Greenland in 982. They grew grain crops on Greenland, which is why the island was called Greenland, and farmed livestock.

Such balmy conditions allowed a great expansion of the area of Viking influence in the eighth to tenth centuries. In his *Risala* of 922, the Arabic scribe Ahmed ibn Fadlan gives an eye-witness account of the Vikings and their trade of furs, amber and swords in return for silver coins. The Viking traders navigated the complex river and lake systems of what is now Russia, often portaging between waterways, to reach the Arab world and Persia. Silver coins, dirhams, from Baghdad, Cairo, Damascus, Isfahan and Tashkent, have been found in Viking burial sites in upland Sweden and north Germany. This coin helped fund the Viking Age but the dirhams started to become rare in the late tenth century as the Samanid silver state had collapsed, its mines exhausted. The Vikings did not use the dirhams as coinage; they melted the coins to make decorative armbands and ornaments.

This warm period came to an abrupt end with another climate change. The change from the Little Climate Optimum to the Little Ice Age may have taken place in less than 50 years and possibly over 20. Grain production on Greenland and Iceland stopped and was severely reduced in Scandinavia. Communication with the Vikings in Greenland was gradually lost. In 1492 the Pope complained no bishop had been able to visit Greenland for 80 years because of the ice. What the Pope did not know was that a visit was not necessary. By 1450 his flock had all frozen to death or starved. Vikings elsewhere interbred in the areas where they conducted trade such as Russia, France, Sicily, al-Andalus in Islamic Spain, the British Isles, Russia and Asia Minor.

In Northern Europe the Baltic Sea froze over twice, in 1303 and 1306-7 and this was followed by unseasonable storms and rains. The rapid plunge into the Little Ice Age with repeated crop failures and shorter growing seasons led to a massive famine in Europe in 1315.

For the last 30 000 years there have been little icehouses at about every 1100 to 1500 years, the most recent of which was the Little Ice Age from the early fourteenth to the early twentieth centuries. The Little Ice Age was not an isolated event and was only the most recent cold phase in a series of millennial-scale events. Following an initial glacial advance from 1270 to 1385 there was a slight respite. The period 1643 to 1653 had very severe European winters. Villages near Chamonix, France, were overwhelmed by advancing glaciers. There was another massive glacial advance from 1710 to 1720 with less severe re-advances from 1750-60, 1810-20 and 1840-50. Glacial recession began about 1860 and was especially rapid in the decades following 1920. The mid 1800s brought the return of a more 'normal' climate but it was not until the 1920s that it could be said the Little Ice Age was over. The twentieth and the early twenty-first century are times of natural rebound. There was a period of warming of 0.37 °C from 1920-45 and another of 0.32 °C which commenced in 1975.

The maximum cold period coincided with reduced sunspot activity from our irregular Sun and it is quite possible that small-scale climate change may well be driven by changes in solar activity. There were three sunspot minima which produced reduced solar radiation and planetary warming during the Little Ice Age at 1440-60, 1687-1703 (Maunder Sunspot Minimum) and 1808-21 (Dalton Sunspot Minimum). Gold was mined in the Austrian alps in the Middle Ages. The mine workings were covered by glaciers which are now retreating to expose mines and associated settlements. Furthermore, the Greenland ice cores show that there was a major unidentified volcanic eruption in 1259 and, thereafter volcanic eruptions were at a much higher rate than in the following few hundred years, especially between 1285 and 1295 and in 1340-50. Such eruptions would have contributed to global cooling.

The Little Ice Age resulted in untold misery in continental Europe, although the climate extremes would have been less in Mediterranean areas that were tempered by the sea and lower latitudes. Russia must have been especially bleak. The fourteenth century in Europe was ravaged by apocalyptic events such as famine, war and the plague. Such events were not confined to Europe and were probably global. China lost 40 per cent of its population in the fourteenth century and in North America the northern limit of maize cultivation receded southwards by 320 kilometres. Exceptionally severe winters gripped northern Europe in 1303 and 1306 and between 1314 and 1317, there was a run of extraordinarily wet cold summers. Crop harvests were disastrous. In 1315 the fertile land in the Bishopric of Winchester in England produced a mere 2½ grains of wheat for every grain sown. In London by the early summer of 1316, the price of grain had risen eightfold.

North American trees remember the Little Ice Age. Tree ring counts and isotopes show that an exceptionally dry period began in 1271. At that time the farming civilisation of the Anasazi was at its peak. Prayers and rainmaking ceremonies failed. Although it was warm at the start of this dry period, it then became very cold. Soon after, the Anasazi had to abandon their sacred mountains and cultural centres at Mesa Verde in Colorado, Chaco Canyon in New Mexico and Kayenta in Arizona. Among the buildings they deserted were three great newly-completed cliff dwellings in what is now the Navajo National Monument. When the Little Ice Age really took grip 200 years later, mountain populations moved and settled at lower altitude close to more permanent water.

A military campaign by King Louis X of France to bring Count Robert of Flanders to heel failed. In the waterlogged Flemish countryside, horses sank up to their saddle girths and wagons became so bogged that even seven horses could not move a wagon. Louis gave up after a week. The constant rain, low temperatures and cloudy skies prevented salt production by evaporation in western France, and salt was worth more than gold at one time. France produced a tiny harvest of sour late wine. Grain prices rose and many sheep and cattle died of diverse diseases. Throughout Europe starving peasants ate frogs and dogs. There were reports of cannibalism, graves were robbed for meat and the bodies of executed criminals were eaten. Mouldy grain resulted in outbreaks of ergotism and erysipelas. Much of the weakened population died of ill-defined fevers or simply starved. In Ypres, detailed records show the city lost 10 per cent of its population in the summer of 1316.

Horrendous floods devastated China in 1332. Several million were killed and there was a substantial movement of wildlife, including rats in which bubonic plague is endemic. The mixing of different populations of rats probably initiated new outbreaks of the black plague in China and its spread across Europe appeared to be unrelated to weather and climate change. But humans in the Northern Hemisphere were already greatly stressed, a disease pandemic waiting to happen. The heat of the summer in 1348 has been invoked to explain the spread of the plague in England. More than half of the remaining human population in Europe was killed by the plague. It took hundreds of years for the European population to be restored to the pre-Little Ice Age level as a result of the lethal coincidence of the Little Ice Age with the black plague. We still carry memories of the black plague with the children's nursery rhyme 'Ring-a-ring-a-rosy'. The words 'We all fall down' refer to the plague.

The fifteenth century did not carry the horrors of the fourteenth although there were bitterly cold years and crop failures in 1439 and 1482. The Little Ice Age is well recorded by contemporary reports. Although there are no accurate meteorological reports in Medieval Europe, the date of French wine harvests, the Beveridge European wheat sales 1500-1869 and the Hoskins grain sales for England 1480-1759 are all accurately recorded and indicate the weather. It appears that there was great variation in European weather until 1556 when extreme cold wet weather again hit. There were poor harvests in 1555 and grain prices rose sharply. Famine and epidemics of disease again sent the death rate up in 1556. By 1560 clear evidence of severe climate deterioration in north-western Europe exists. Cold weather between 1591 and 1597 again stressed the community and the English parliament enacted panic legislation rezoning land and attempting experiments on poverty relief.

The seventeenth century started with crop failures and many late wine harvests. The English mortality statistics show that there was a marked peak in 1625 but this has more to do with it being a plague year in London than cold wet weather. England had hot summers in 1636, 1637 and 1638 which led to a rise in mortality rates due to dysentery. The 1640s were characterised by poor harvests whereas harvests in the early 1650s were abundant, before the variable weather plunged into another cold period. Poor harvests in 1661, 1673, 1676, 1678 and 1684 were interspersed with good grain yields. The last decade of the century was one of cold wet summers and long bitter winters and, following the second consecutive bad harvest in 1693, Europe was hit by one of the worst famines since the early Middle Ages. In Finland, the famine of 1697 killed a third of the population, as the Scandinavian glaciers expanded and marginal land was abandoned. The same story emerges from records in Scotland, where between 1693 and 1700, seven out of the eight harvests failed in the upland parishes. Up to 66 per cent of the population in some parishes died, exceeding the figures recorded for the black death.

The harsh Little Ice Age years forced political change. The economic consequences of the catastrophic years in Scotland between 1693 and 1700 made the union with England in 1707 inevitable. The cold climates had other cultural effects. The Dutch masters painted scenes reflecting far colder conditions than are currently enjoyed in The Netherlands. In London the Thames froze over many times. King Henry VIII was able to cook an ox over a fire on the frozen river. War diaries of General Washington chronicle the incredibly cold periods in North America.

In France from January to March 1709 the Seine and other rivers flowing into the Atlantic were frozen and winter wheat was destroyed by unseasonal frosts. Fruit, olive and some 70 per cent of the walnut trees died in south-eastern France. The French supply of walnut for English furniture was destroyed and manufacturers have used North American walnut and Central American mahogany ever since. Vines perished, rabbits froze in their burrows and there was a great loss of livestock. Even the Sun King, Louis XIV, was cold in his palace at Versailles. Intense cold again struck in 1725 and, in England, there was high mortality from 1726 to 1729, probably due to whooping cough. Every month in 1740 in Europe, England and Ireland was below average temperature, wheat prices rose sharply and the wine harvest was late. The Irish potato crop failed. There was a mortality crisis in 1741, possibly due to infectious diseases in the weakened population, rather than famine resulting from a poor harvest. Variable climate dominated the remainder of the eighteenth century with poor harvests in 1770 and 1771.

Catastrophic natural events occurred in the late seventeenth and eighteenth centuries. At 9 pm on 26 January 1700, a piece of the Juan de Fuca plate beneath the Pacific Ocean plunged beneath North America. The 1000-kilometre-long Cascadia Fault catastrophically lurched producing a Richter magnitude 9 earthquake. Japanese scribes described an orphan tsunami, one with no observed associated earthquake or volcanic origin, on 27 January. Such tsunamis are real killers as there is no warning.

One of the best-recorded earthquakes happened at 11 am on All

Saints Day in Lisbon in 1755. The breaking of rocks on the floor of the Atlantic Ocean gave rise to two shocks 40 minutes apart followed by a third shock with an epicentre near Fez, Morocco. The first shock brought down most of the buildings of Lisbon in avalanches of masonry and the accompanying fires and 10-metre-high tsunamis killed many of the survivors from the initial seismic shock. It seemed incomprehensible that such a devastating earthquake should have occurred on a Holy Day. Most deaths were from collapsing masonry at the time when the city churches were crowded with worshippers at Mass.

The earthquake shocked Western civilisation and led to an unprecedented outburst of public discussion. The earthquake was variously attributed to the Devil and evil spirits, God's anger against the dreadful behaviour of His worshippers in the Lisbon churches, the need for frightening sinners into repentance, the need to punish Portugal for the undue severity of the Inquisition, and the need to remind humanity of the fiery Hell within the Earth. There was a view that earthquakes were punishments for sin. Do those who live at plate boundaries sin more than those who live on the middle of them?

European philosophers differed from the fire-and-brimstone moralistic clergy. The Lisbon earthquake was the stimulus for Voltaire's *Candide*, a chronicle of logic and scepticism. Kant suggested earthquakes were natural and unrelated to the Almighty, and that citizens should try to understand where earthquakes were likely to happen and then take care not to build cities in such places. Rousseau suggested humans might not be able to prevent earthquakes and noted that the building of a large number of churches in active earthquake zones did not seem to prevent them.

In the Northern Hemisphere, the Little Ice Age was at its maximum with the last severe cold period from 1810 to 1820. In the Southern Hemisphere a 3700-year tree ring record from Tasmania shows that the coolest time in Tasmania in the Little Ice Age was in the late nineteenth century. Again, what appeared global was not global.

The Arctic has warmed twice as much as the rest of the planet over the last 150 years. Half of the warming took place over the last 60 years, probably due to natural causes. In the Arctic, the seventeenth century was cold and the eighteenth was warm. The nineteenth started cold, which prevented explorers finding the Northwest Passage. This cold period is probably related to numerous major volcanic eruptions in the early 1800s. There has been a sustained period of warming in the Arctic since the early nineteenth century, except for a brief cooling period in the 1960s.

On 10 April 1815 Indonesia's Tambora volcano exploded. The explosion was heard 850 kilometres away, and the top 1400 metres of the volcano was blasted into the air leaving a crater 6 kilometres across and a kilometre deep. The explosive force was equivalent to 60 000 Hiroshima-sized bombs. The blast had a devastating effect on the local population. Tambora threw out more than seven times the number of ash particles into the atmosphere than the more famous Krakatoa eruption of 1883. Ash from the eruption was even trapped in the ice sheet in Greenland. The Indonesian islands were plunged into darkness for two days. Most crops were destroyed by the ash fall and tsunamis.

Nearly 10 000 islanders on Tambora were engulfed by ash, all vegetation on Lombok and Bali died and the epidemics and famine in the months following killed more than 80 000 islanders. Contemporary Chinese records show that at Hainan Island, 2000 kilometres north of Tambora, the Sun disappeared. The combination of low temperatures, excessive rainfall and unseasonal frosts played havoc with agriculture. China experienced exceptionally cold and stormy weather in 1816-17 with disastrous crop failures. In Europe and North America 1816 was called 'the year without a summer'. Three long cold periods ravaged Canada and New England. The first, in June, killed most crops. The second, in July, killed replanted crops and the third, in August, killed corn, potatoes, beans and vines. In the US, 1816 was the coldest year for 200 years. There was rain and snow every month, crops repeatedly failed and bankrupted farmers migrated from the east to the mid-west.

Europe was still recovering from the disruption brought on by the Napoleonic Wars which took place during a period of cool wet years. The cold years of 1816-17 created a food crisis and widespread social unrest, especially in France. The cold years drove immigration from Europe to the US and US farmers from northern to more benign latitudes. Average temperatures in the UK were 2 °C lower and it rained or snowed almost every day. Prices on the London Grain Exchange went through the roof.

Crop failures in Bengal in 1816 resulted in famine which triggered a major outbreak of cholera. This spread outwards from Bengal created the world's first cholera pandemic. It reached north-western Europe, Russia and the eastern US in the summer of 1832. One wonders whether there is a relationship between major volcanic eruptions, bad weather, harvest failures and global pandemics such as in the sixth, fourteenth and nineteenth centuries.

William Turner, the English landscape painter, became famous in the art world for his sunsets. He was actually painting English skies full of Tambora dust. At Lake Geneva the poet Lord Byron and his guests Mary and Percy Bysshe Shelley used the gloomy summer of 1816 to write. Mary Shelley wrote *Frankenstein* and Byron wrote a poem called *Darkness*.

> I had a dream, which was not all a dream.
> The bright star was extinguish'd, and the stars
> Did wander darkling in the eternal space,
> Rayless, and pathless, and the icy earth
> Swung blind and blackening in the moonless air;
> Morn came and went—and came, and brought no day,
> And men forgot their passions in the dread
> Of this their desolation; and all hearts
> Were chill'd into a selfish prayer for light.

What a bleak, cold, gloomy summer. Tambora gave the world a window into the aftermath of one volcanic eruption with a global effect. At home, Tambora gave Sumbawa and its neighbours a long-term gift. Fertile soil. Ash from Tambora increased fertility, Bali became a rice exporter and the Tambora ash is still used to sustain a large Indonesian population on a very small area.

Periods when the grip of the Little Ice Age heightened were dreadful times to be *Homo sapiens*. Today, infrastructure, immunisation and a more diverse diet are such that human longevity is the highest it has ever been. If I was King of the World, I would make icehouse events illegal and decree that Earth would always be a balmy greenhouse with high sea levels and high rainfall.

We are currently in a climatic rebound period from that Little Ice Age. Modern temperature measurements are normally made near cities or towns and mostly in wealthy countries, predominantly in the Northern Hemisphere. Most measuring stations are on land and there is poor coverage in oceanic and ice cap areas. Cities pump out huge amounts of heat and modern cities are far warmer than they were a few hundred years ago. This urban heat island effect renders temperature measurements in populated areas unreliable. The measured temperature at Northern Hemisphere sites has been increasing since the Little Ice Age ended. There are some measuring stations such as Cape Grim which have been carefully selected to minimise the urban heat island effect. Warm periods measured by satellites correspond with the El Niño events of 1983, 1987, 1995 and 1997-8 and sunspot maximum events of 1980 (Solar Cycle 21) and 1990-91 (Solar Cycle 22).

Earth is constantly bombarded by solar radiation, and occasionally radiation by supernovae. Fluctuation in radiation emitted by the Sun appears to stimulate massive changes in climate. East Africa, central Asia and Australia have a great natural variability in rainfall and this contributes to long periods of lethal droughts. Higher solar radiation is linked to droughts in equatorial east Africa. Kenya's Lake Naivasha in the Rift Valley has not completely dried out for at least 1000 years. It has laid down an annual record of water levels in its sediment which are a good indicator of drought and wet periods. High rainfall periods concentrate algae on the lake floor which decompose to organic compounds in the sediment. Long dry periods from 1000 to 1270, 1380 to 1420, 1560 to 1620 and 1760 to 1840 coincide with eras of famine, political unrest and mass migration. The climate reconstruction of east Africa shows the Little Climate Optimum and the Little Ice Age were not global. It is quite possible that climate changes driven by variations in solar radiation are far greater than even the most speculative catastrophic human-induced climate change scenarios.

Explosion of supernovae on our cosmic doorstep leave faint clues about events in the historical past. At a depth of 110 centimetres, ice at the South Pole contains a high nitrate content, nitrates formed when blast waves of ionising radiation struck the nitrogen-oxygen rich atmosphere. The ice at 110 centimetres depth formed from snow which fell in 1181 yet the medieval astronomers did not record a supernova in 1181. It is not understood why. Other recent supernoval explosions recorded in Antarctic ice cores were all observed by medieval astronomers. The Vela supernova in 1320, Tycho's star in 1572 and Kepler's star in 1604 all show prominent concentrations of nitrate in Antarctic ice at 80, 46 and 44 metres depth respectively. The Vela supernova was one of the closest supernoval explosions in our recent past. It lit up the skies and, although only a mere 640 light years away, the afterglow has recently been detected by the German-US ROSAT X-ray satellite.

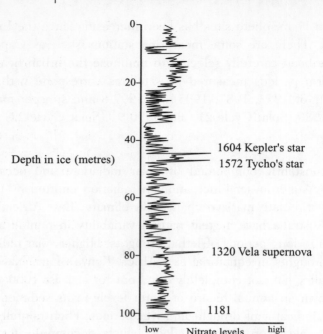

Cosmic fingerprints from supernovae preserved in Greenland ice.

In 1054 Chinese astronomers observed a bright star which was visible during daylight for 22 months. If newspapers had existed in 1054 they could have been easily read outside in the middle of the night. This bright star was a supernoval explosion. By contracting the Crab Nebula in the Constellation Taurus we go backwards in time and find that the Crab Nebula was a point in space in 1054. This point was a star which exploded and it is now a spinning neutron star, the headstone on the grave of a supernoval explosion.

Although the Sun has an influence on climate, it seems the influence of the Moon has been forgotten. Sediment cores of the last 100 000 years in the Atlantic Ocean show rhythmic fluctuations every 1500 to 1800 years between warm and cold eras. These cycles, called Bond Cycles, seem to be the pacemaker of climate change. The Moon resets the Earth's thermostat through its influence on tides. Strong tides increase the vertical mixing of water in the oceans, pulling cold water from the deeps to the surface. The cold surface water cools the atmosphere. Weak tides reduce mixing, keeping cold water at the bottom of the ocean out of contact with the atmosphere thereby allowing the atmosphere to warm.

It appears that the changing alignment of the Earth, Moon and Sun causes changes in the strength of the tides on the same timescale as Bond Cycles. During the Little Ice Age, tides reached their maximum strength in 1425. Since then tides have weakened, will be at their weakest in 2500 and will not peak again until 3100. Although there are many forces at work, the 1500 to 1800 year cycle may also have been a significant driving force for climate over the last 10 000 years.

In more recent times, there has been debate about greenhouse, a phenomenon of the atmosphere. It is suggested that greenhouse gas emissions trap heat in the lower atmosphere and the resultant surface warming of the Earth is called the greenhouse effect. Greenhouse gases do not warm the surface directly, the atmosphere must heat up first. If there is no prior warning of warming in the lower atmosphere, then there can be no consequent greenhouse effect attributable to it.

A 22-year-global coverage of satellite-derived atmosphere temperatures shows only modest warming in the Northern Hemisphere and a slight cooling in the Southern. A less complete coverage of atmospheric temperatures is available back to 1958 from balloon-mounted thermometers. It agrees well with the global satellite data for their period of overlap. In the twentieth century, there was surface warming until 1944 followed by 32 years of slight cooling before resumed warming from 1977. There was a single warming step in 1976–1977.

Most weather stations are where they have always been. Buildings have sprung up around them and forests have been cut down. Local temperatures are driven up, making analysis of data misleading for the computer models that are the basis for many weather and global climate predictions. If the atmosphere heats up like a giant greenhouse, then the troposphere should also be warming. It isn't. Furthermore, the effects of natural variability in orbit, solar activity, the lunar tides, ocean currents, ice sheet dynamics, volcanicity, sedimentation, mountain building, subsidence and continental drift are far greater for temperature changes than those calculated for the worst human-induced greenhouse scenario.

There is an inescapable conclusion: observed slight surface warming in the twentieth century is related to factors other than the greenhouse effect.

Something happened in 1976–7. Globally-averaged temperatures in the lower atmosphere jumped 0.3 °C, sea-surface temperature in the central equatorial Pacific jumped 0.6 °C, sea surface temperature in the southern California Current during the upwelling season increased 1.5 to 3 °C but there was reduced upwelling, the heat content of the upper 300 metres of the world's oceans increased, other measures of warming showed a sudden step-like warming and the surface sea temperature in the subtropical South Pacific peaked in 1976 and cooled about 2 °C over the following decade. Tree ring measurements for the last 2000 years show that fluctuating coolings and warmings are normal and the warming in the first half of the twentieth century is not unprecedented. The 1976–7 event shows a major re-ordering of ocean heat transport and coincides with the change in the rate of change of the length of the day. Maybe the global warming of that century is just a measure of variability on a dynamic evolving planet.

We live in the last days of our normal ration of 10 000 years of benign climate in a 100 000 year cycle driven by orbital changes. Orbital variations change the length of the day. The orbital driver of our current

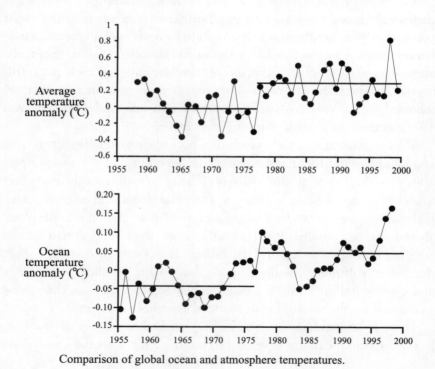

Comparison of global ocean and atmosphere temperatures.

greenhouse/icehouse cycle is well past its zenith and summer reflection of solar energy at higher latitudes of the Northern Hemisphere is now waning. The Armageddon we humans face is not a pleasant greenhouse warming but a bitter and prolonged icehouse. The fourteenth century was our wake-up call.

The Earth sings quietly to itself. It emits a gentle hum, far too low and too feeble for human ears to detect. The hum is a very messy noise of some 50 notes crammed into less than two octaves at pitches between 2 and 7 millihertz. Musically speaking, the Earth's singing is about 16 octaves below middle C. If the hum was sped up and amplified, it would be a painful mindless cacophony that would, by comparison, make modern jungle music sound positively Mozartesque. The hum is a free oscillation, rather like the ring that a bell makes well after the bell is struck.

The volume is about 10 per cent louder from December–February and June–August and varies during the course of a day. The hum is quite unlike the loud clear seismic signals from earth tremors and earthquakes, and probably derives from the fluctuation of atmospheric pressure. When air pressure rises, the atmosphere presses down slightly harder on the ground and the oceans. When the pressure drops, the surface gently rebounds. The planet is therefore like a gong being gently tapped at frequencies that create a constant hum telling us that the planet and its atmosphere are quietly getting on with the normal business of constant change.

9

THE GEOLOGY
OF TOMORROW

'Why, sometimes I've believed as many as six impossible things before breakfast.'

Lewis Carroll, *Through the Looking-glass*
Spoken by the White Queen.

Humans, a large terrestrial animal concentrated near sea level, are at great risk of environmental stress and extinction. We, like all other organisms that have ever been on Earth, are living at the limit of survival. The complex infrastructure we need for shelter and food ensure disease and starvation which have destroyed populations before, will do so again. Earthquakes, volcanoes and tsunamis will continue to take their toll on humans but will not drive an extinction unless a massive volcanic eruption is in tandem with another natural catastrophe such as a large impact. Climate will change anyway.

Sea level will continue to rise in a stepwise erratic pattern, as it has for the last 18 000 years, until the next icehouse. In the West Antarctic the recession rates of the fast flowing rivers of ice indicate a rapid erosion of the slow-moving inland ice sheet driven by the same factors that drove the 120-metre sea level rise over the last 14 700 years. Calculations based on declassified satellite imagery indicate this annual wastage to the oceans is equivalent to the 'missing' sea level rise component calculated from the hydrological cycle of approximately 1 mm per annum. The wild card in the whole global warming debate is the West Antarctic Ice Sheet. No discussion on climate change or sea level rise is possible without considering the major player in the game: the West Antarctic Ice Sheet.

Glaciologists identified in ice cores a massive collapse into the sea of the West Antarctic Ice Sheet some 7700 to 6600 years ago. Geologists working on coral reefs in Florida have identified a rapid sea level rise at the same time. This is called the coherence criterion in science. Independent evidence from one field of science supports independent evidence from another. This degree of coherence raises the confidence level of the scientific conclusions.

The collapse of the West Antarctic Ice Sheet has already raised sea level and it has another 6 metres to rise before the collapse is complete. Collapse was probably started by the massive post-glacial sea level rise and that resulting from the collapse of the West Antarctic Ice Sheet is a consequence of natural processes which commenced 7000 years ago. The Pine Island Glacier in West Antarctica has been thinning 1.6 metres per year due to ice dynamics and not atmospheric temperature changes. There is nothing humans can do to stop this process. It would not be surprising if sea level rose a few metres over the next century causing untold suffering in low-lying areas such as Bangladesh, Holland, north Germany and many non-coralline islands. Most coral atolls in the Pacific, Indian and Atlantic Oceans will do what they have done when sea level has risen in the past. They will just grow in order to accommodate the sea level rise and will not suffer inundation. Low-lying parts of England, where many atomic reactors are sited, will be inundated. Human-induced global warming may have a small subsidiary effect on this process but it is not a major factor. Sea level rise and fall is a geological fact of life, especially during the current period of very rapidly fluctuating climate.

If there is a 6-metre sea level rise from the complete melting of the West Antarctic Ice Sheet, sea levels will be restored to the position they were 123 000 years ago and disrupt coastal populations. If global warming occurs and sea level further rises, there will be further mass social

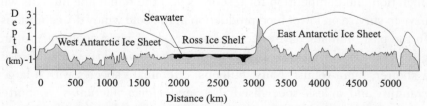

The Antarctic ice sheet showing that the West Antarctic Ice Sheet is underpinned by sea water.

disruption of populations of coastal humans, as has occurred in the past. The fossil record shows high sea levels drive greater biodiversity, especially in shallow water ecosystems. History shows warmer wetter times have led to great renaissances in human history. If the past is a key to the present, a sea level rise by ice melting or expansion of the oceans will initially put pressure on humans before a period of great prosperity and expansion, but will not lead to the extinction of *Homo sapiens*.

The ocean currents that give Europe its mild climate are changing as always. There is one body of scientific thought that suggests that a slight global warming, for whatever reason, will switch off the North Atlantic Drift. This current brings warm water to north-western Europe from the Gulf Stream as part of a global conveyor belt bringing warm surface water from the Gulf of Mexico to north-west Europe and sending deep cold water back. The belt is driven by two pumps where cold surface water sinks and returns south. One is in the Greenland Sea and the other is in the Labrador Sea. Over the last 20 years it appears the conveyor belt has been greatly reduced in power. The irony is that global warming could turn off the North Atlantic Drift and average temperatures in north-western Europe could plunge by more than 5 °C.

The history of recent climate change suggests planet Earth will soon lurch into another glaciation, possibly in only 300 or 400 years time but certainly before 2800. Furthermore, this history shows that such climate changes can be very rapid and can occur in less than three score and ten years. Past ice ages have led to famine, disease, population reduction and warfare but have not led to the extinction of humans. Depopulation will occur by disease pandemics. As in the past, urban communities will drift into subsistence agriculture and cities will be vacated. If the next glaciation is as intense as the last, the area now occupied by 60 per cent of the planet's population will be covered by ice. Much of the Northern Hemisphere will again be covered by ice sheets kilometres thick. Sea level will drop, forests will retreat, there will be massive migration and competition for resources and the remaining humans will have to survive on lower food production in the cold windy dry conditions. In the past, humans have speciated in periods of rapid cooling. A future glaciation may drive *Homo sapiens* to speciate into *Homo macdonaldsensis*, a shorter, more robust, hairy, bulbous, effeminate species with a larger cranium and a less specialised diet, and *Homo micturans*, a shorter gracile to emaciated-looking species prone to injury, liver problems, gout, diabetes and a poor diet.

The Holocene is the period when humans live on Earth. The planet will survive that brief period when we humans thought we were the dominant organism and would live forever. Bacteria will continue to dominate the Earth. Plant and animal species will not be conserved on the ever-changing dynamic Earth. Many species will evolve into new species and many other species will become extinct. New vacated habitats will then be filled by the newly evolved species. *Homo sapiens*, like other organisms over the history of time, will have left their mark on the geology of the planet and will probably evolve into another species.

It is only since Roman times that humans have had a profound effect on the surface of the Earth. This will be reflected in the future geology. For example, each westerner consumes more than 180 tonnes per annum of water and more than 20 tonnes per annum of sand, gravel, aggregate, cement, coal (or its energy equivalent) and metals. Almost none of these commodities are recycled. Over the last century, the *per capita* consumption of commodities has increased tenfold, the diversity of minerals and elements used has quadrupled. In order to maintain our life style, each year we mine more material than is washed down the world's river systems each year by natural processes. We consumers have a voracious appetite for the fruits of the Earth which has given us a high standard of living and increased longevity.

My forecast of the future is based on the history of the past written in stone. I speculate that the modern human period on Earth, which

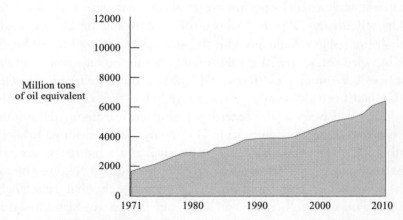

World energy consumption from 1971-2010. It reflects the massive increase in energy demand by developing nations, including China.

I call the Younger Holocene, will be defined in the future geological record by a period of devegetation, possible minor mass extinctions of terrestrial and marine macrofauna and accelerated weathering, erosion and sedimentation. A discontinuous sequence of muddy lake, delta, estuarine and deep ocean sediments formed in the Younger Holocene will be enriched in complex organic compounds, metals and daughter isotopes from nuclear fission. Rare metal-, hydrocarbon- and silicate-rich relics will be found in an ancient saline soil whereas the reworking of sandy sediments in rivers, deltas and continental shelves by multicellular organisms will destroy most human relics. Some relics, constructed of stone, bricks and concrete, will be preserved in the rock record. Whether humans make a small change to climate or not is irrelevant. Major natural climate cycles will continue to dominate the geological record and will swamp any projected human-induced climate changes.

There are a number of possible scenarios for minor mass extinctions of humans. The atmosphere offers little protection against asteroids or comets larger than 100 metres in size. Extraterrestrial bodies have a terminal velocity of 73 kilometres per second and it is only the larger bodies that puncture the atmosphere and the Earth's crust. Most of the smaller bodies explode or frictionally ablate during descent through the atmosphere. Reassuringly, the greater the size of an extra-terrestrial visitor, the less frequently it arrives. Figures such as one climate-modifying impact every 100 000 years are the most pessimistic published. Such extraterrestrial visitors are not at all uncommon.

On 1 February 1994, high above the western Pacific Ocean, a huge fireball from space exploded with the equivalent energy of a 40 kiloton bomb, twice the power of the Hiroshima bomb. So large was the blast that the US military satellites and military brass believed a nuclear device had been detonated. It took days before it was concluded that the Earth had been at the receiving end of an extraterrestrial invader. An asteroid airburst occurred on 18 January 2000 over the Yukon in northern Canada. The object was between 2 and 3 metres in size. The blast took place 25 kilometres above the ground, was equivalent to a 5 kiloton nuclear bomb and emitted so much light that street lights operating on solar cells turned off. The sonic boom was heard in British Columbia and Alaska. As the meteorite extinguished itself, the lights turned back on overloading the power grid. Such common events create

Asteroid diameter (metres)	Average interval between impacts (years)	Consequences of asteroid strike	Possible area of direct destruction for land impacts
Less than 40		Asteroids detonate in upper atmosphere	
75	1 000	Iron asteroids leave craters on the ground; stony asteroids explode in the lower atmosphere	Large city such as Washington, London or Moscow
160	4 000	Asteroids explode on impact with the Earth's surface; ocean impacts raise significant tsunamis	Large urban area such as New York or Tokyo
350	16 000	Impacts on land produce craters; ocean impacts cause ocean-wide tsunamis	Small state or nation such as Delaware or Estonia
700	63 000	Land impacts produce large craters; ocean impacts can cause tsunamis reaching the scale of the hemisphere	Medium-sized state or small nation such as Virginia or Taiwan
1 700	250 000	Land and ocean impacts throw enough dust into the atmosphere to affect climate and agriculture; ocean impacts cause global tsunamis	Medium-sized nation or large state such as France, Japan or California
3 000	1 000 000	Global climate change; global ejecta from the impact sparks widespread fires	Large nation such as Mexico or India
7 000	10 000 000	Global fires and probable mass extinction	Area approaching continental scale, such as Australia or the US
16 000	100 000 000	Large mass extinction that threatens the survival of all advanced life forms	An entire continent

Frequency, size and devastation from meteorite impacting.

some disquiet. US Defense Department satellites detected the incoming object on 18 January 2000 in the Yukon and unsuspecting townspeople suspected a terrorist attack. Since the 1970s military satellites have spotted more than 400 such events and, with a number of nuclear nations at odds with each other, it is conceivable an atmospheric extraterrestrial explosion could be cause for a trigger-happy nation to light the fuse for a nuclear conflagration.

A geomagnetic reversal, a switch of north and south poles, would cause a breakdown of social structures and infrastructure in the industrialised countries resulting in starvation and disease. Human populations near oceans could be destroyed or greatly stressed if a small extraterrestrial visitor lands in an ocean basin. In the Pacific basin there would be mass killing of the circum-Pacific population by massive tsunamis and the aftermath with the breakdown of infrastructure if a large piece of a Hawaiian volcano slips onto the ocean floor. The same could occur around the Atlantic basin if a piece of the Canary Islands slips into the ocean. Changes in the flow of the Gulf Stream could refrigerate northern Europe or another ice armada could destroy infrastructure and change climate. A major volcanic eruption in a highly populated area such as Mt Fuji, Japan or Seattle, US would cripple a major economy within weeks. A huge eruption like those which have occurred in the past at Toba, Indonesia, Taupo, New Zealand, and Kamchatka, Russia could destroy most of the planet's human infrastructure and cool the planet for decades, resulting in a minor mass extinction of humans. One of the best candidates for a major volcanic eruption is Taupo. The Taupo volcanic centre has been active for 300 000 years. Since the crater-forming Oruanui eruption 26 500 years ago, there have been 28 eruptions which have blasted out 0.1 to 45 cubic kilometres of debris. Taupo is still active and is unusual among large volcanoes in terms of the frequency of eruptions over the last few thousand years. Australia enjoyed its last volcanic eruption in 1948, offshore from Mt Gambier. Another eruption is overdue in south-eastern South Australia–Western Victoria. For the last 70 million years there has been volcanic activity in eastern Australia.

If a large extraterrestrial visitor such as an Apollo asteroid more than 20 kilometres in size impacts with Earth, there will be a major mass extinction of life on Earth. If such an impact induced massive volcanism,

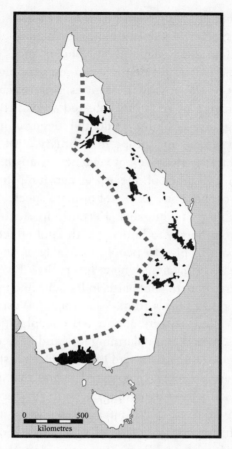

The eastern Australian volcanic province which has been erupting for the last 70 million years. The most recent eruptions have been in far north Queensland and south eastern Victoria.

extinction rates would be higher. In all probability, humans and many terrestrial and shallow marine organisms would disappear. Bacteria have survived all previous major mass extinctions and these super-adapted organisms would survive the next major meteorite impact. A close supernoval explosion or solar superflare would fry most terrestrial and shallow marine organisms. Again, bacteria would survive.

Contrary to popular belief, we actually live life right at the edge. The black plague of the fourteenth century killed half the people in Europe. The most intense minor mass extinction of Europeans by the black plague was from 1348-52. This occurred during the grip of the Little Ice Age when the community was already under great environmental pressure after hundreds of years of warm weather. The plague derived from another species, rats. Antibiotic-resistant plague bacteria have recently been found in Madagascar. The chances of humans being depopulated by a plague pandemic again are very high.

Globalisation of trade, growth of cities, intensification of agriculture and lack of spraying of mosquito-infested wetlands with DDT are all giving emerging diseases unprecedented opportunities. Outbreaks of foot-and-mouth disease in Europe in February 2001 are a direct result of international trade and a lack of vigilance. Many bacteria, viruses and prions occur in a number of species or can jump from one species to humans. AIDS occurs in a number of primate species and most probably jumped from chimps to humans. Recently in Australia, a bat-derived virus jumped from horses to humans with fatal effects. The nipah virus jumped from bats to pigs to people in Malaysia, mosquitoes spread a number of diseases (malaria, dengue fever, Ross River fever, West Nile virus), and rodents spread hantavirus in Panama and tularemia in Kosovo.

In September 1999 birds from Asia brought West Nile virus to New York. In all, 61 New Yorkers contracted encephalitis and 7 died. The West Nile virus spread at an alarming rate and has now infected crows, half the local geese and sparrows. On mosquito-infested wetlands in the eastern US, there are now 77 infected migratory bird species capable of carrying the virus to every corner of North America. Humans usually get the disease from mosquito bites when the population of infected city birds is sufficiently large to infect enough mosquitoes. In 1997 527 people in Bucharest, Romania, contracted West Nile virus and 50 died. As with other viruses, there is no specific treatment for the infection.

Probably the best known recent trans-species disease is Creutzfeld-Jacob Disease which was transferred as protein from sheep (scrapie) to cattle (mad cow disease) to humans (CJD). With the combination of a gestation period of up to 30 years, bungling and an information blackout, the effects of Creutzfeld-Jacob Disease were recognised far too late and the full effect of the disease is not yet known.

The Spanish flu pandemic of 1919-20 killed more people than World War I. This exotic strain appears to have jumped from pigs to humans in 1918. New strains of flu appear every year. Most are slight variants of existing viruses and no special problems are posed. Every few decades, a completely different virus appears, triggering a pandemic that can kill millions. The last two were in 1957 and 1968 and the killer strains were thought to have jumped from pigs or poultry to humans. The next pandemic is certain. It could begin anywhere and at any time. Will the next pandemic depopulate the world as did the Spanish flu of 1919?

If I was to make a prediction about the extinction of *Homo sapiens* on Earth, I would suggest that a bacterial or viral pandemic would be the most driving cause. If this pandemic occurred at the time of massive volcanicity, impacting by an extraterrestrial visitor or a mass killing of populations around an ocean basin by volcanic collapse, then extinction of humans would almost be assured. As with all other extinctions, pockets of *Homo sapiens* would still exist after the major mass extinction in isolated enclaves such as Tasmania, New Zealand, the Andes and the Tibetan Plateau. These pockets may speciate or drift into extinction if the gene pool is too small.

Over the next million years, it will be business as usual with earthquakes and volcanoes pretty well in the same places as they occur now. However, in 50 million years time, we'll need to draw a new map of the globe. A few isolated islands such as East Africa and Southern California will be dwarfed by the supercontinent of EurAfricoIndioAustralAsia and the smaller continents of the Americas and Antarctica. Australia would have drifted northwards and engulfed south-east Asia and Japan and will be stitched onto far eastern Siberia. There will again be no Mediterranean Sea. The sea between China and Japan will be a mountain range. A few remnant islands such as New Zealand will still exist in the great oceans.

The planet will be basking in its normal greenhouse conditions, sea levels will be restored to their normal far higher levels, atmospheric oxygen content will be higher and the shallow water ecosystems will be teeming with new and modified life forms. Humans will be a long-forgotten fossil relic. Bacteria will continue to do what they have always been doing for almost 4000 million years.

In current climate change discussions we hear about atmospheric gases such as carbon dioxide, methane and ozone. We hear nothing about the main greenhouse gas, water vapour. We hear little about the driving forces of climate change such as ice, ocean currents, mountain building, the closure or opening of seaways, continental drift, volcanoes, the changing speed of the Earth's rotation, orbital wobbles and sunspot activity. Planet Earth has a past, a present and a future. If we ignore the past, then we do so at our peril. We are then left with little hope of understanding the present Earth systems and no chance of predicting the future.

What we see and measure as changes to the Earth in our own lifetime constitute just one frame in the movie of the history of Earth. If we try to understand the whole movie by looking at just one frame, conclusions are meaningless. Yet, this view of the planet pervades in the modern world.

There appear to be two levels of communication regarding the history of our planet and climate change. In the scientific arena there is one level which shows, with a healthy dose of scepticism and uncertainty, the complex and fascinating intertwining of evolving natural processes. The future of our planet is already written in stone for all to read. However, there is another level run by the media and joined by opportunistic scientists chasing fame and funds, some politicians and many environmental and nefarious groups. This level presents a superficial dogmatic doom-and-gloom message for consumption by the non-scientific community. Almost every natural event, catastrophe or perceived problem is ascribed to human-induced climate change. The consensus view in the public is that we are heading for a human-induced greenhouse with shocking consequences. However, the science of the complex interplay of processes on our evolving planet is based on evidence, not consensus. Glib seven-second grabs of unsubstantiated statements of belief regarding climate change and car-sticker politics remind us that we really live in an Alice in Wonderland world.

In an attempt to understand the history of planet Earth, some people such as the creationists want science and theology to remain mired in the seventeenth century. Their created contradictory world gives the degree of security required by those who are fearful of the ever-expanding body of challenging scientific knowledge which doubles every 8 years. Most of those giving the doom-and-gloom environmental message for the consumption by a non-scientific audience are no different from creationists. There is an unswerving dogma promulgated with religious zeal and, as it is a matter of dogmatic belief, untestable. There is a hidden message that we must suffer for our perceived sins! Their message is unaffected by knowledge despite scientific knowledge being dis-passionate, reproducible, international and freely available for scrutiny. This body of knowledge is divided into data derived from observation, measurement, calculation, experiment and thought. Interpretation, called a theory, is based on these data. Inductive and deductive thinking processes are used. A scientific theory is just a neat way of explaining data and, with more data, the theory changes. A scientific theory, such as evolution, is not dogma but the knowledge of the day.

It is espoused by commentators that we now live in the information age. This may well be so but information is not synonymous with knowledge. Whole economies are information-based. By using the knowledge written in stone about the short and long geological past, we are able to understand the present and make more reliable predictions about the future. Humans have the knowledge and ability to postpone or even avoid extinction of *Homo sapiens*. Do we have the will or do we continue with our eyes wide shut? The choice is ours. Extinction or evolution.

Whatever we choose, the Earth will keep humming.

REFERENCES

Aberhan, M. and Fürsich, F. T., 2000: Mass origination versus mass extinction: the biological contribution to the Pliensbachian-Toarcian extinction event. *Journal of the Geological Society, London* 157, 55-60.

Ackermann, T. P., 1988: Aerosols in climate modelling. In: *Aerosols and climate* (Eds P. V. Hobbs and M. P. McCormick). Deepack, 335-348.

Agricola, Georgius, 1556: *De Re Metallica* (translated by E. C. Hoover and L. H. Hoover, 1950), Dover Publications Inc., New York.

Allen, J. R. L., 1994: *Paleoclimates and their modelling with special reference to the Mesozoic Era*. Chapman and Hall.

Allen, J. R. M., Brandt, U., Brauer, A., Hubberten, H.-W., Huntley, B., Keller, J., Kraml, M., Mackensen, A., Mingram, J., Negendank, J. F. W., Nowaczyk, N. R., Oberhänsli, H., Watts, W. A., Wulf, S. and Zolitschka, B., 1999: Rapid environmental changes in southern Europe during the last glacial period. *Nature* 400, 740-743.

Alley, R. B., 1998: Icing the North Atlantic. *Nature* 392, 335-337.

Alley, R. B. and Whillans, I. M., 1991: Changes in the West Antarctic Ice Sheet. *Science* 254, 956-953.

Alley, R. B., Meese, D. A., Shuman, C. A., Gow, A. J., Taylor, K. C., Grootes, P. M., White, J. W. C., Ram, M., Waddington, E. D., Mayewski, P. A. and Zelinski, G. A., 1993: Abrupt increase in Greenland snow accumulation at the end of the Younger Dryas event. *Nature* 362, 527-529.

Alley, R. B. and MacAyeal, D. R., 1994: Ice-rafted debris associated with binge/purge oscillations of the Laurentide Ice Sheet. *Paleoceanography* 9, 503-511.

Alvarez, W. L., 1986: Toward a theory of impact crises. *Eos* 649-655.

Alvarez, W., Asaro, F. and Montanari, A., 1990: Iridium profile for 10 million years across the Cretaceous-Tertiary boundary at Gubbio (Italy). *Science* 250, 1700-1702.

Alvarez, W., Smit, J., Lowrie, W., Asaro, F., Margolis, S. V., Claeys, P., Kastner, M. and Hildebrand, A. R., 1992: Proximal impact deposits at the Cretaceous-Tertiary boundary in the Gulf of Mexico: A study of DSDP Leg 77 Sites 536 and 540. *Geology* 20, 697-700.

Ames, D. E., Watkinson, D. H. and Parrish, R. R., 1998: Dating of a regional hydrothermal system induced by the 1850 Ma Sudbury impact event. *Geology* 26, 385-480.

Archer, A. W., 1996: Reliability of lunar orbital periods extracted from ancient cyclic tidal rhythmites. *Earth and Planetary Science Letters* 141, 1-10.

Baillie, M., 1998: *Exodus to Arthur*. Batsford

Barber, D. C., Dyke, A., Hillaire-Marcel, C., Jennings, A. E., Andrews, J. T., Kerwin,

M. W., Bilodeau, McNeely, R., Southon, J., Morehead, M. D. and Gagnon, J. M., 1999: Forcing of the cold event of 8200 years ago by catastrophic drainage of Laramide lakes. *Nature* 400, 344-348.

Barnard, P. D. M., 1973: Mesozoic floras. In: *Organisms and continents through time* (Ed. N. F. Hughes). Special Paper of the Palaeontological Association, London, 12, 175-187.

Barnola, J. M., Raynaud, D., Korotkevich, Y. S. and Lorius, C., 1987: Vostok ice core provides 160 000-year record of atmospheric CO_2. *Nature* 329, 408-414.

Barron, E. J. and Fawcett, P. J., 1995: The climate of Pangea: a review of climate model simulations of the Permian. In: *The Permian of Northern Pangea. Vol. 1. Paleogeography, Paleoclimates, Stratigraphy* (Eds. P. A. Scholle, T. M. Peryt and D. S. Ulmer-Scholle). Springer Verlag, 37-52.

Bentley, C., 1997: Rapid sea level rise soon from West Antarctic ice sheet collapse? *Science* 275, 1077-1078.

Benton, M. J., 1995: Diversification and extinction in the history of life. *Science* 268, 252-258.

Bentor, Y. K., 1989: Geological events in the Bible. *Terra Nova* 1, 326-338.

Berger, A., 1988: Milankovitch theory and climate. *Review of Geophysics* 26, 624-657.

Berger, A., Loutre, M. F. and Dekant, V., 1989: Astronomical frequencies for pre-Quaternary palaeoclimate studies. *Terra Reviews* 1, 474-479.

Berner, R. A., 1991: A model for atmospheric CO_2 over Phanerozoic time. *American Journal of Science* 291, 339-376.

Berner, R. A., 1994: GEOCARB II: A revised model for atmospheric CO_2 over Phanerozoic time. *American Journal of Science* 294, 56-91.

Bianchi, G. G. and McCave, N. I., 1999: Holocene periodicity in North Atlantic climate and deep-ocean flow south of Iceland. *Nature* 397, 515-517.

Bigg, G. R., Wadley, M. R., Stevens, D. P. and Joohnson, J. A., 2000: Glacial thermohaline circulation states of the north Atlantic: the compatibility of modelling and observations. *Journal of the Geological Society, London* 157, 655-665.

Bills, B. G., 1994: Obliquity-oblateness feedback: Are climatically sensitive values of obliquity dynamically unstable? *Geophysical Research Letters* 21, 177-180.

Bills, B. G., James, T. S. and Mengel, J. G., 1999: Climatic impact of glacial cycle polar motion: coupled oscillations of ice sheet mass and rotation pole position. *Journal of Geophysical Research* 104, B1, 1059-1074.

Bindschadler, R., 1997: Actively surging West Antarctic ice streams and their response characteristics. *Annals of Glaciology* 24, 409-414.

Bindschadler, R., 1998: Future of the West Antarctic Ice Sheet. *Science* 282, 428-429.

Bindschadler, R. and Vornberger, P., 1998: Changes in the West Antarctic Ice Sheet since 1963 from declassified satellite photography. *Science* 279, 689-691.

Bindschadler, R. A., Allkey, R. B., Anderson, J., Schipp, S., Borns, H., Fastook, J., Jacobs, S., Raymond, C. F. and Shuman, C. A., 1998: What is happening to the West Antarctic Ice Sheet? *Eos* 79, 264-265.

Bond, G., Broecker, W., Johnson, S., McManus, J., Labeyrie, L., Jouzel, J. and Bonattis, G., 1993: Correlations between climate records from North Atlantic sediments and Greenland ice. *Nature* 365, 143-147.

Bowler, J. M., 1996: Antarctic ice cap origins: global thermostat and sea level controls in evidence from Southern Australia. In *Program and Abstracts of the 1996 Selwyn Memorial Symposium*, Victorian Division—Geological Society of Australia, 16-19.

Bradley, R. S. and Jones, P. D., 1992: *Climate since AD 1500*. Routledge.

Brasier, M. D., 1992: Global ocean-atmosphere change across the Precambrian-Cambrian transition. *Geological Magazine* 129, 161-168.

Brasseur, G. and Granier, C., 1992: Mount Pinatubo aerosols, chlorofluorocarbons and ozone depletion. *Science* 257, 1239-1242.

Broccoli, A. J., 1994: Learning from past climates. *Nature* 371, 282.

Broecker, W. S., 1984: Terminations. In: *Milankovitch and climate* (Eds A. Berger, J. Imbrie, J. Hays, G. Kulka and B. Saltzman). D Riedel, Dordrecht, 2: 687-698.

Broecker, W., Bond, G. and McManus, J., 1993: Heinrich events: Triggers of ocean circulation change? In: *Ice in the climate system*. (Ed. W. Richard Peltier). NATO Workshop, Aussois, 1992. Springer Verlag, 161-166.

Broecker, W. S., Stutherland, S. and Peng, T-T, 1999: A possible 20th-century slowdown of Southern Ocean deep water formation. *Science* 286, 1132-1135.

Bromham, L., Phillips, M. J. and Penny, D., 1999: Growing up with dinosaurs: molecular dates and the mammalian radiation. *TREE* 14, 113-118.

Bryson, R. A. and Goodman, B. M., 1980: Volcanic activity and climatic changes. *Science* 207, 1041-1044.

Budd, W. F. and McInnes, B. J., 1979: Periodic surging of the Antarctic ice sheet—an assessment by modelling. *Hydrological Sciences Bulletin* 24, 1: 95-103.

Budyko, M. I., Golytsin, G. S. and Israel, Y. A., 1988: *Global climatic catastrophes*. Springer Verlag.

Buick, R., Groves, D. I. and Dunlop, J. S. R., 1995: Geological origin of described stromatolites older than 3.2 Ga: Comment and reply. *Geology* 23, 191-192.

Burroughs, W. J., 1997: *Does the weather really matter? The social implications of climate change*. Cambridge University Press.

Burton, K. W., Ling Hong-Fei and O'Nions, R. K., 1997: Closure of the Central American Isthmus and its effect on deep-water formation in the North Atlantic. *Nature* 386, 382-385.

Butler, R. F., 1992: *Palaeomagnetism: Magnetic domains to geologic terranes*. Blackwell.

Butler, R. W. H., McClelland, E. and Jones, R. E., 1999: Calibrating the duration and timing of the Messinian salinity crisis in the Mediterranean: linked tectonoclimatic signals in thrust-top basins of Sicily. *Journal of the Geological Society, London* 156, 827-835.

Caldeira, K. and Rampino, M. R., 1991: The Mid Cretaceous superplume, carbon dioxide, and global warming. *Geophysical Research Letters* 18, 987-990.

Calder, N., 1974: *The weather machine and the threat of ice*. British Broadcasting Corporation.

Campbell, I. H. and Griffiths, R. W., 1992: The evolution of the mantle's chemical structure. *Lithos* 30, 389-399.

Carey, S. W., 1976: *The expanding Earth.* Elsevier.

Carpenter, R., 1966: *Discontinuity in Greek civilisation.* Cambridge University Press.

Carr, M. H., 1987: Water on Mars. *Nature* 326, 30-35.

Cas, R. A. F. and Wright, J. V., 1987: *Volcanic Successions: Modern and Ancient.* Allen & Unwin.

Chang, S., 1994: The planetary setting of prebiotic evolution. In: *Early life on Earth* (Ed. S. Bengtson). Columbia University Press, 10-23.

Charles, C., 1998: The ends of an era. *Nature* 394, 422-423.

Chyba, C. F., 1993: The violent environment of the origin of life: Progress and uncertainties. *Geochimica et Cosmochimica Acta* 57, 3351-3358.

Cloud, P., 1968: Atmospheric and hydrostatic evolution on the primitive Earth. *Science* 160, 1135-1143.

Cloud, P., 1973: Paleoecological significance of the banded iron formation. *Economic Geology* 68, 1135-1143.

Cloud, P., 1988: *Oasis in Space. Earth history from the beginning.* W. W. Norton & Co.

Coe, R. S., Prévot, M. and Camps, P., 1995: New evidence for extraordinary rapid change of the geomagnetic field during a reversal. *Nature* 374, 687-692.

Colinvaux, P., 1996: Biogeography: low-down on a land bridge. *Nature* 382, 21.

Condie, K. C., 1997: *Plate tectonics and crustal evolution.* Butterworth Heinemann.

Conroy, G. C., 1997: *Reconstructing human origins.* W.W. Norton and Co.

Constantine, A., Chinsamy, A., Vickers-Rich, P. and Rich, T. H., 1998: Periglacial environments and polar dinosaurs. *South African Journal of Science* 94, 137-139.

Conway, H., Hall, B. L., Denton, G. H., Gades, A. M. and Waddington, E. D., 1999: Past and future grounding-line retreat of the West Antarctic Ice Sheet. *Science* 286, 280-284.

Covey, C. and Thompson, S. L., 1989: Testing the effects of ocean heat transport on climate. *Global and Planetary Change* 75, 331-341.

Coward, M. P., Broughton, R. D., Luff, I. W., Peterson, M. G., Pudsey, C. J., Rex, D. C. and Asifkhan, M., 1986: Collision tectonics in the NW Himalayas. *Geological Society of London Special Publication* 19, 203-220.

Creber, G. I. and Chaloner, W. G., 1985: Tree growth in the Mesozoic and early Tertiary and the reconstruction of climates. *Palaeogeography, Palaeoclimates, Palaeoecology* 52, 35-60.

Creer, K., 1965: An expanding Earth? *Nature* 205, 539-544.

Crowley, T. J. and North, G. R., 1991: *Paleoclimatology.* Oxford University Press.

Crowley, T. J. and Baum, S. K., 1993: Effect of decreased solar luminosity on late Precambrian ice extent. *Journal of Geophysical Research* 98, 16723-16732.

Dahl-Jensen, D., Mosegaard, K., Gundestrup, N., Clow, G. D., Johnsen, S. J., Hansen, A. W. and Balling, N., 1998: Past temperature directly from the Greenland Ice Sheet. *Science* 282, 268-271.

Davies, G. F. and Richards, M. A., 1992: Mantle convection. *Journal of Geology* 100, 151-206.

Denton, G. H. and Karlén, W., 1973: Holocene climatic variations—their pattern and possible cause. *Quaternary Research* 3, 155-205.

Deutsch, A., Greshake, A., Pesonen, L. J. and Pihlaja, P., 1998: Unaltered cosmic spherules in a 1.4 Ga-old sandstone from Finland. *Nature* 395, 146-148.

Dickens, G. R., 1999: Carbon cycle: The blast in the past. *Nature* 401, 752-755.

Dokken, T. M. and Jansen, E., 1999: Rapid changes in the mechanism of ocean convection during the last glacial period. *Nature* 401, 458-461.

Dones, L. and Tremaine, S., 1993: Why does the Earth spin forward? *Science* 259, 350-354.

Dorale, J. A., Edwards, L. R., Ito, E. and González, L. A., 1998: Climate and vegetation history of the Midcontinent from 75 to 25 ka: a speleothem record from Crevice Cave, Missouri, USA. *Science* 282, 1871-1874.

Dowdeswell, J. A., Elverhøi, A., Andrews, J. T. and Hebbeln, D., 1999: Asynchronous deposition of ice-rafted layers in the Nordic seas and North Atlantic Ocean. *Nature* 400, 348-351.

Driscoll, N. W. and Haug, G H., 1998: A short circuit in thermohaline circulation: a cause for Northern Hemisphere glaciation? *Science* 282, 436-438.

Druitt, T. H., Edwards, L., Mellors, R. M., Pyle, D. M., Sparks, R. S. J., Lanphere, M., Davies, M. and Barriero, B., 2000: Santorini Volcano. *Geological Society Memoir* 19.

Dunlop, D. J., 1995: Magnetism in rocks. *Journal of Geophysical Research* 100, 2161-2174.

Du Toit, A., 1937: *Our wandering continents*. Oliver and Boyd.

Ekart, D. D., Cerling, T. E., Montañez and Tabor, N. J., 1999: A 400 million year carbon isotope record of pedogenic carbonate: implications for paleoatmospheric carbon dioxide. *American Journal of Science* 299, 805-827.

Ellis, R., 1998: *Imagining Atlantis*. Alfred A. Knopp, New York.

Enzel, Y., Ely, L. L., Mishra, S., Ramesh, R., Amit, R., Lazar, B., Rajaguru, S. N., Baker, V. R. and Sandler A., 1999: High-resolution Holocene environmental changes in the Thar Desert, northwestern India. *Science* 284, 125-128.

Erwin, D. H., 1993: *The great Paleozoic crisis*. Columbia University Press.

Evans, D. A., Beukes, N. J. and Kirschvink, J. L., 1997: Low-latitude glaciation in the Palaeoproterozoic era. *Nature* 386, 262-266.

Eyles, N., 1993: Earth's glacial record and its tectonic setting. *Earth Science Reviews* 35, 1-248.

Fairbanks, R. G., 1989: A 17 000-year glacio-eustatic sea level record: influence of glacial melting rates on the Younger Dryas event and deep ocean circulation. *Nature* 342, 637-642.

Fawcett, P. J., Barron, E. J., Robinson, V. D. and Katz, B. J., 1994: The climatic evolution of India and Australia from the late Permian to mid-Jurassic: comparison of climate model results with the geologic record. *Geological Society of America Special Paper* 288, 139-157.

Flohn, H., 1987. The role of ice sheets in climatic history. In: *The physical basis of ice sheet modelling*. Proceedings of the Vancouver Symposium (IAHS Publication 170), 321-341.

Flower, B. P., 1999: Warming without high CO_2. *Nature* 399, 313-314.

Fortey, R., 1998: *Life: An unauthorised biography*. Harper Collins.

Foster, D. A., Murphy, J. M. and Gleadow, A. J. W., 1994: Middle Tertiary hydrothermal activity and uplift of the northern Flinders Ranges, South Australia: Insights from apatite fission-track thermochronology. *Australian Journal of Earth Sciences* 41, 11-17.

Foster, R. J., 1974: Eocene echinoids and the Drake Passage. *Nature* 249, 751.

Frakes, L. A., 1979: *Climates throughout geologic time*. Elsevier.

Frakes, L. A., Francis, J. E. and Syktus, J. I., 1992: *Climate modes of the Phanerozoic*. Cambridge University Press.

François, L. M. and Goddéris, Y., 1998: Isotopic constraints on the Cenozoic evolution of the carbon cycle. *Chemical Geology* 145, 177-212.

Franck, S., Kossacki, K. and Bounama, C., 1999: Modelling the global carbon cycle for the past and future evolution of the earth system. *Chemical Geology* 159, 305-317.

Frears, B., 1997: Caroline carbon dioxide, Otway Basin. *MESA Journal* 5, April 1997, 22-25.

Fresnel, B., Pécsi, M. and Velichko, A. A., 1992: *Atlas of paleoclimates and paleoenvironments of the northern hemisphere*. Fischer.

Frogley, M. R., Tzedakis, P. C. and Heaton, T. H. E., 1999: Climate variability in Northwest Greece during the last Interglacial. *Science* 285, 1886-1889.

Gabriel, J., 1999: Among the Norse tribes. A remarkable account of Ibn Fadlan. *Aramco World* 50, 6, 36-42.

Geller, M., 1988: Solar cycles and the atmosphere. *Nature* 332, 584-585.

Gerlach, T., 1991: Etna's greenhouse pump. *Nature* 351, 352-353.

Gibbs, M. T., Bluth, G. J. S., Fawcell, P. J. and Kump, L. R., 1999: Global chemical erosion over the last 250 my: variations due to changes in palaeogeography, palaeoclimate, and palaeogeology. *American Journal of Science* 299, 611-651.

Gilliland, R. L., 1982: Solar, volcanic and CO_2 forcing of recent climate changes. *Climatic Change* 4, 111-131.

Glikson, A., 1993: Asteroids and early Precambrian crustal evolution. *Earth Science Reviews* 35, 285-319.

Glikson, A., 1999: Eugene and Carolyn Shoemaker's Australian impacts exploration: 1981-1997. *Australian Geologist* 15-18.

Glikson, A. Y., 1999: Oceanic mega-impacts and crustal evolution. *Geology* 27, 387-390.

Goldreich, P., 1966: History of the lunar orbit. *Reviews in Geophysics* 4, 411-439.

Gostin, V. A., Haines, P. W., Jenkins, R. J. F., Compston, W. and Williams, I. S., 1986: Impact eject horizon within late Precambrian shales, Adelaide Geosyncline, South Australia. *Science* 233, 198-200.

Grady, M. M., 1999: Meteorites and micro-fossils from Mars. *Geoscientist* 9, 1, 4-7.

Gray, V., 2000: The cause of global warming. *Energy and Environment* II, 613–629.

Grevemeyer, I., Herber, R. and Essen, H-H., 2000: Microseismological evidence for a changing wave climate in the northeast Atlantic Ocean. *Nature* 408, 349–352.

Griffin, D. L., 1999: The late Miocene climate of northeastern Africa: unravelling the signals in the sedimentary succession. *Journal of the Geological Society, London* 156, 817-826.

Grossman, E. E. and Fletcher, C. H., 1998: Sea level higher than present 3500 years ago on the northern main Hawaiian Islands. *Geology* 26, 289-384.

Grosswald, M. G., 1993: Extent and melting history of the Late Weichselian ice sheet, the Barents-Kara continental margin. In: *Ice in the climate system.* (Ed. W. Richard Peltier). NATO Workshop, Aussois, 1992. Springer Verlag, 1-20.

Grosswald, M. G. and Hughes, T. J., 1995: Paleoglaciology's grand unsolved problem. *Journal of Glaciology* 41, 138, 313-332.

Grousset, F. E., Labeyrie, L., Sinko, J. A., Cremer, M., Bond, G., Duptrat, J., Cortijo, E. and Huon, S., 1993: Patterns of ice-rafted detritus in the glacial North Atlantic (40-55°N). *Paleoceanography* 8, 2, 175-192.

Guilderson, T. P. and Schrag, D. P. 1998: Abrupt shift in subsurface temperatures in the tropical Pacific associated with changes in El Niño *Science* 281, 240–243.

Gutzmer, J. and Beukes, N. J., 1998: Earliest laterites and possible evidence for terrestrial vegetation in the Early Proterozoic. *Geology* 26, 193-288.

Habermehl, M. A., 1980: The Great Artesian Basin, Australia. *BMR Journal of Australia Geology and Geophysics* 5, 9-38.

Handler, P., 1989: The effect of volcanic aerosols on global climate. *Journal of Volcanology and Geothermal Research* 37, 233-249.

Haq, B. U., Hardenbol, J. and Vail, P. R., 1987: Chronology of fluctuating sea levels since the Triassic. *Science* 235, 1156-1167.

Harrison, T. M., Copeland, P., Kidd, W. S. F. and Yin, A., 1992: Rising Tibet. *Science* 255, 1663-1670.

Hegerl, G., 1998: Climate change: the past as a guide to the future. *Nature* 392, 758-759.

Heinrich, H., 1988: Origin and consequences of cyclic ice rafting in the Northeast Atlantic Ocean during the past 130 000 years. *Quaternary Research* 29, 142-152.

Hill, A., Ward, S., Deino, A., Curtis, G. and Drake, R., 1992: Earliest *Homo. Nature* 355, 719-722.

Hill, R. I., Campbell, I. H., Davies, G. F. and Griffiths, R. W., 1992: Mantle plumes and continental tectonics. *Science* 256, 186-193.

Holdsworth, G., 1990: Sunspot cycles and climate. *Nature* 346, 705.

Holland, H. D., 1984: *The chemical evolution of the atmosphere and oceans.* Princeton University Press.

Hong, S., Candelone, J. P., Patterson, C. C. and Boutron, C. F., 1994: Greenland ice evidence of hemispheric lead pollution two millennia ago by Greek and Roman civilizations. *Science* 265, 1841-1843.

Hsü, K. J., 1972: When the Mediterranean dried up. *Scientific American* 227, 6, 27-36.

Huber, B. T., 1998: Tropical paradise at the Cretaceous poles? *Nature* 282, 2199-2200.

Hubert-Ferrari, A., Barka, A., Jacques, E., Nalbant, S. S., Meyer, B., Armijo, R., Tapponnier, P. and King, G. C. P., 2000: Seismic hazard in the Marmara Sea region following the 17 August 1999 Izmit earthquake. *Nature* 404, 279-273.

Hudson, J. D., 1989: Palaeoatmospheres in the Phanerozoic. *Journal of the Geological Society, London* 146, 155-160.

Hughes, T., 1975: The West Antarctic ice sheet: instability, disintegration, and limitation of ice ages. *Review of Geophysics and Space Physics* 13, 4, 502-526.

Hughes, T., 1987: Ice dynamics and deglaciation models when ice sheets collapse. In: *North America and adjacent oceans during the last deglaciation.* (Eds W. F. Ruddiman and H. E Wright Jnr). (Volume K of *The Geology of North America*) Geological Society of North America, Boulder, Colorado, 183-220.

Hughes, T., 1992: Abrupt climatic change related to unstable ice-sheet dynamics: toward a new paradigm. *Palaeogeography, Palaeoclimatology, Palaeoecology* 97, 203-234.

Hut, P., 1987: Comet showers as a cause of mass extinctions. *Nature* 329, 118-125.

Issar, A. S., 1995: Climate change and the history of the Middle East. *American Scientist* 83, 350-355.

Ito, T., Masuda, K., Hamano, Y. and Matsui, T., 1995: Climate friction: A possible cause for secular drift of Earth's obliquity. *Journal of Geophysical Research* 100, 15147-15161.

Jacobs, J. A., 1992: *Deep interior of the Earth.* Chapman and Hall.

Jacobsen, H. P. and Raymond, C. F., 1998: Thermal effects on the location of ice stream margins. *Journal of Geophysical Research* 103, B6, 12 111-12 122.

Jacobsen, T. and Adams, R., 1958: Salt and silt in ancient Mesopotamian agriculture. *Science* 126, 1251-1258.

Jenkins, G. S., 1996: A sensitivity study of changes in Earth's rotation rate with an atmospheric general circulation model. *Global and Planetary Change* 11, 141-154.

Jenkins, R. J. F., 1984: Ediacaran events: boundary relationships and correlation of key sections, especially in 'Armorica'. *Geological Magazine* 121, 635-643.

Johnsen, S. J., Clausen, H. B., Dansgaard, W., Fuhrer, K., Gundestrup, N., Hammer, C. U., Iversen, P., Jouzewl, J. and Steffensen, J. P., 1992: Irregular glacial interstadials recorded in a new Greenland ice core. *Nature* 359, 311-313.

Jones, P., 1998: It was the Best of Times, it was the Worst of Times. *Science* 280, 544-545.

Jouzel, J., 1999: Calibrating the isotopic paleothermometer. *Science* 286, 910-911.

Kandler, O., 1994: The early diversification of life. In: *Early life on Earth* (Ed. S. Bengtson) Columbia University Press, 152-160.

Kasting, J. F., 1993: Earth's early atmosphere. *Science* 259, 920-926.

Kaufman, A. J., 1997: An ice age in the tropics. *Nature* 386, 227-228.

Keigwin, L. D. and Pickart, R. S., 1999: Slope water current over the Laurentian Fan on interannual to millennial time scales. *Science* 286, 520-523.

Kennedy, M. J., 1996: Stratigraphy, sedimentology, and isotopic geochemistry of Australian Neoproterozoic postglacial cap dolostones: deglaciation, ^{13}C excursions, and carbonate precipitation. *Journal of Sedimentology Research* 66, 1050-1064.

Kerrick, D. M. and Caldeira, K., 1998: Metamorphic CO_2 degassing from orogenic belts. *Chemical Geology* 145, 213-232.

Killworth, P., 1998: Something stirs in the deep. *Nature* 396, 720-721.

Kirschvink, J. L., 1992: Late Proterozoic low-latitude global glaciation: The snowball Earth. In: *The Proterozoic Biosphere: A multidisciplinary Study* (Eds J. W. Schopf and C. Klein). Cambridge University Press, 51-52.

Klemm, J. and Hättestrand, C., 1999: Frozen-bed Fennoscandian and Laurentide ice sheets during the Last Glacial Maximum. *Nature* 402, 63-66.

Koch, P. L., Hoppe, K. A. and Webb, S. D., 1998: The isotope ecology of late Pleistocene mammals in North America. *Chemical Geology* 152, 119-138.

Krabill, W., Frederick, E., Manizade, S., Martin, C., Sonntag, J., Swift, R., Thomas, R., Wright, W. and Yungel, J., 1999: Rapid thinning of parts of the South Greenland ice sheet. *Science* 283, 1522-1524.

Kroon, D., Shimmield, G., Austin, W. E. N., Derrick, S., Knutz, P. and Shimmield, T., 2000: Century- to millennial-scale sedimentological-geochemical records of glacial-Holocene sediment variations from the Barra Fan (NE Atlantic). *Journal of the Geological Society, London* 157, 643-653.

Kuhn, J. R., Libbrecht, K. G. and Dickie, R. H., 1988: The surface temperature of the Sun and changes in the solar constant. *Science* 242, 908-911.

Kuhn, W. R., Walker, J. C. G. and Marshall, H. G., 1989: The effect on Earth's surface temperature from variations in rotation rate, continent formation, solar luminosity, and carbon dioxide. *Journal of Geophysical Research* 94, 11129-11136.

Kutzbach, J. E. and Gallimore, R. G., 1989: Pangean climates: Megamonsoons of the Megacontinent. *Journal of Geophysical Research* 94, 3341-3357.

Labonne, M., Othman, D. B. and Luck, J.-M., 1998: Recent and past anthropogenic impact on a Mediterranean lagoon: lead isotope constraints from mussel shells. *Applied Geochemistry* 13, 885-892.

Laird, K. R., Fritz, S. C., Maasch, K. A. and Cumming, B. F., 1996: Greater drought intensity and frequency before AD 1200 in the Great Northern Plains, USA. *Nature* 384, 552-554.

Lamb, H. H., 1968: *Climatic history and the future*. Princeton University Press.

Lambeck, K., 1980: *The Earth's variable rotation: Geophysical causes and consequences*. Cambridge University Press.

Larson, R. L., 1991: Geological consequences of superplumes. *Geology* 19, 963-966.

Lehman, S., 1993: Climate change: ice sheets, wayward winds and sea change. *Nature* 365, 108-109.

Leblanc, M., Morales, J. A., Borrego, J. and Elbaz-Poulichet, F., 2000: 4500-year-old mining pollution in southwestern Spain: Long term implications for modern mining pollution. *Economic Geology* 95, 655-662.

Lehman, S., 1997: Sudden end of an interglacial. *Nature* 390, 117-119.

Lehman, S. and Keigwin, L. D., 1992: Sudden change in the North Atlantic circulation during the last deglaciation. *Nature* 356, 757-762.

Le Roux, J. P., 1994: Impacts, tillites, and the breakup of Gondwanaland: a second discussion. *Journal of Geology* 102, 483-485.

Li, L. and Keller, G., 1998: Abrupt deep sea warming at the end of the Cretaceous. *Nature* 26, 961-1056.

Linsley, B. K., Wellington, G. M. and Schrag, D. P., 2000: Decadal sea surface temperature variability in the subtropical South Pacific from 1726 to 1997 AD. *Science* 290, 1145–1148.

Long, J., 1998: *Dinosaurs of Australia and New Zealand and other animals of the Mesozoic Era.* UNSW Press.

MacAyeal, D. R., 1993a: A low-order model of the Heinrich event cycle. *Paleoceanography* 8, 767-773.

MacAyeal, D. R., 1993b: Binge/purge oscillations of the Laurentide ice sheet as the cause of the North Atlantic's Heinrich events. *Paleoceanography* 8, 775-784.

Mahlman, J. D., 1997: Uncertainties in projections of human-caused climate warming. *Science* 278, 1416-1417.

Mann, M. B., Bradley, R. S. and Hughes, M. K., 1999: Northern hemisphere temperatures during the last millennium: inferences, uncertainties and limitations. *Geophysical Research Letters* 26, 759–762.

Marenco, G. F., 1977: The epoch of Triassic magmatism in Siberia. *International Geology Review* 19, 1089-1099.

Marinatos, S., 1939: The volcanic destruction of Minoan Crete. *Antiquity* 13, 425-439.

Marty, B. and Tolstikhin, I. N., 1998: CO_2 fluxes from mid-ocean ridges, arcs and plumes. *Chemical Geology* 145, 233-248.

Mann, M. E., Bradley, R. S. and Hughes, M. K., 1998: Global-scale temperature patterns and climate forcing over the past six centuries. *Nature* 392, 779-787.

Mann, M. E., Bradley, R. S. and Hughes, M. K., 1999: Northern hemisphere temperatures during the last millennium: inferences, uncertainties and limitations. *Geophysical Research Letters* 26, 759-762.

Marcus, S. L., Chao, Y. and Gegout, P., 1998: Detection and modelling of nontidal oceanic effects on Earth's rotation rate. *Science* 281, 1656-1659.

Martin, E. E. and MacDougall, J. D., 1995: Sr and Nd isotopes at the Permian/Triassic boundary: A record of climate change. *Chemical Geology* 125, 73-99.

Matthews, S. W., 1976: What's happening to our climate? *National Geographic* 150, 5, 576-615.

Maurrasse, F. J. M. and Sen, G., 1991: Impacts, tsunamis, and the Haitan K/T boundary layer. *Science* 252, 1690-1693.

McKay, D. S., Gibson, E. K., Thomas-Keprta, K. L., Vali, H., Romanek, C. S., Clemett, S. J., Chillier, X. D. F., Maechling, C. M. and Zare, R. N., 1996: Search for past life on Mars: possible relic biogenic activity in Martian meteorite ALH84001. *Science* 273, 924-930.

McGuire, W. J., Howarth, R. J., Firth, C. R., Solow, A. R., Pullen, A. D., Saunders, S. J., Stewart, I. S. and Vita-Finzi, C., 1997: Correlation between rate of sea-level change and frequency of explosive vulcanism in the Mediterranean. *Nature* 389, 473-476.

McLaren, D. J. and Goodfellow, W. D., 1990: Geological and biological consequences of giant impacts. *Annual Review of Earth and Planetary Sciences* 18, 123-171.

McLennan, S. M., 1988: Recycling of the continental crust. *Pure and Applied Geophysics* 128, 683-898.

Meier, M. F., and Post, A., 1969: What are glacier surges? *Canadian Journal of Earth Sciences* 6, 807-818.

Melchiorre, E. B., Criss, R. E. and Rose, T. P., 1999: Oxygen and carbon isotope study of natural and synthetic malachite. *Economic Geology* 94, 245-260.

Melchiorre, E. B., Criss, R. E. and Rose, T. P., 2000: Oxygen and carbon isotope study of natural and synthetic azurite. *Economic Geology* 95, 623-630.

Melosh, H. J., 1989: *Impact cratering. A geologic process.* Oxford University Press.

Merline, W. K., Close, L. M., Dumas, C., Chapman, C. R., Roddier, F., Ménard, F., Slater, D. C., Duvert, G., Shelton, C. and Morgan, T., 1999: Discovery of a moon orbiting the asteroid 45 Eugenia. *Nature* 401, 565-568.

Michaels, P. J. and Knappenberger, P. C., 1996: Human effect on global climate? *Nature* 384, 522-523.

Miller, S. L., 1953: A production of amino acids under possible primitive Earth conditions. *Science* 117, 528-529.

Miller, S. L. and Bada, J. L., 1988: Submarine hot springs and the origin of life. *Nature* 334, 609-611.

Mitford, N., 1969. *The Sun King: Louis XIV at Versailles.* Sphere Books.

Moore, P., 1998: *Patrick Moore on Mars.* Cassell.

Mörner, N-A., 1984: Planetary, solar, atmospheric, hydrospheric and endogene processes as origins of climate changes on Earth. In: *Climate Changes on a Yearly to Millennial Basis* (Eds N-A. Mörner and W. Karlén). D. Reidel, Dordrecht, 483-507.

Mörner, N-A., 1991: Trans-polar VGP shifts and Earth's rotation. *Geophysics, Astrophysics, Fluid Dynamics* 60, 149-155.

Mörner, N-A., 1993: Global change: the high-amplitude changes 13-10 ka ago. *Global and Planetary Change* 7, 243-250.

Mörner, N-A., 1996: Earth rotation, ocean circulation and palaeoclimate: the North Atlantic-European example. In: *Late Quaternary Palaeoceanography of the North Atlantic*

Margins (Eds A. J. Andrews, W. E. N. Austin, H. Bergsten and A. E. Jennings). Geological Society Special Paper No 111, London, 359-370.

Mory, A. J., Iasky, R. P., Glikson, A. Y. and Pirajno, F., 2000: Woodleigh, Carnarvon Basin, Western Australia: a new 120 km diameter impact structure. *Earth and Planetary Science Letters* 177, 119-128.

Naurzbaerv, M. M. and Vaganov, B. A., 2000: Variations of early summer and annual temperature in east Taymir and Putoran (Siberia) over the last two millennia inferred from tree rings. *Journal of Geophysical Research* 105, 7371–7326.

Newsom, H. E. and Taylor, S. R., 1989: Geochemical implications of the formation of the Moon by a single giant impact. *Nature* 338, 29-34.

Nisbit, E. G., 1986: RNA, hydrothermal systems, zeolites and the origin of life. *Episodes* 9, 83-90.

Norris, R. D. and Röhl, U., 1999: Carbon cycling and chronology of climate warming during the Palaeocene/Eocene transition. *Nature* 401, 775-778.

Oberberck, V. R., Marshall, J. R. and Aggarwal, H., 1993: Impacts, tillites, and the breakup of Gondwanaland. *Journal of Geology* 101, 1-19.

Oglesby, R. J. and Ogg, J. G., 1988: The effect of large fluctuations in obliquity on climates of the Late Proterozoic. *Paleoclimates* 24, 293-316.

Oro, J., 1994: Early chemical stages in the origin of life. In: *Early life on Earth* (Ed. S. Bengtson). Columbia University Press, 48-59.

Paillard, D., 1998: The timing of Pleistocene glaciations from a simple multiple-state climate model. *Nature* 391, 378-381.

Pannella, G., 1972: Paleontologic evidence of the Earth's rotational history since the Precambrian. *Astrophysics and Space Science* 16, 121-237.

Pantic, N. and Stefanovic, D., 1984: Complex interaction of cosmic and geological events that effect the climate throughout geologic history. In: *Milankovitch and climate* (Eds A. Berger, J. Imbrie, J. Hays, G. Kulka and B. Saltzman). D Riedel, Dordrecht, 2: 251-264.

Park, J. and Oglesby, R. J., 1991: Milankovitch rhythms in the Cretaceous: A GCM modelling study. *Palaeogeography, Palaeoclimatology, Palaeoecology* 4, 329-356.

Park, J. K., 1997: Palaeomagnetic evidence for low-latitude glaciation during deposition of the Neoproterozoic Rapitan Group, Mackenzie Mountains, N.W.T., Canada. *Canadian Journal of Earth Sciences* 34, 34-49.

Parker, E. N., 1999: Sunny side of global warming. *Nature* 399, 416-417.

Peltier, W. R. and Hyde, W., 1984: A model of the Ice Age cycle. In: *Milankovitch and climate* (Eds A. Berger, J. Imbrie, J. Hays, G. Kulka and B. Saltzman). D Riedel, Dordrecht, 2: 565-580.

Petit, J. R., Jouzel, J., Raynaud, D., Barkov, N. I., Barnola, J.-M., Basile, I., Bender, M., Chappallaz, J., Davis, M., Delayque, G., Delmotte, M., Kotlyakov, V. M., Legrand, M., Lipenkov, V. Y., Lorius, C., Pépin, L., Ritz, C., Saltzman, E. and Stievenard, M., 1999: Atmospheric history of the past 420,000 years from the Vostok ice core, Antarctica. *Nature* 399, 429-436.

Pflug, H.-D., 1996: Umweltgeologische Daten zum Treibhauseffekt und anderen Klimaeinflüssen. *Giessener Geologische Schriften, Festschrift Knoblick* 56, 223-254.

Pirazzoli, P. A., 1996: *Sea-level changes: the last 20,000 years.* John Wiley & Sons.

Plotnick, R. E., 1980: Relationship between biological extinctions and geomagnetic reversals. *Geology* 8, 578-581.

Poag, C. W. and Aubrey, M.-P., 1995: Upper Eocene impactites of the U.S. east coast: depositional origins, biostratigraphic framework and correlation. *Palaios* 10, 16-43.

Preiss, W. V., 1987: *The Adelaide Geosyncline.* Bulletin 53, Geological Survey of South Australia.

Prueher, L. M., Rea, D. K., Picard, S., Garcia, J-P, Lécuyer, C., Sheppard, S. M. F., Cappetta, H. and Emig, C. C., 1998: Rapid onset of glacial conditions in the subarctic North Pacific region at 2.67 Ma: Clues to causality. *Geology* 961-1056.

Prinn, R. G. and Fegley, B., 1987: The atmosphere of Venus, Earth and Mars: A critical comparison. *Annual Review of Earth and Planetary Sciences* 15, 171-212.

Rabinowitz, D. L., Helin, E., Lawrence, K. and Pravdo, S., 2000: A reduced estimate of the number of kilometre-sized near Earth asteroids. *Nature* 403, 165-166.

Rampino, M. R. and Self, S., 1992: Volcanic winter and accelerated glaciation following the Toba super-eruption. *Nature* 359, 50-52.

Raup, D. M., 1991: *Extinction. Bad genes or bad luck.* W. W. Norton & Co.

Raymo, M. E. and Ruddiman, W. F., 1992: Tectonic forcing of late Cenozoic climate. *Nature* 359, 117-122.

Raymo, M. E., Ganley, K., Carter, S., Oppo, D. W. and McManus, J., 1998: Millennial-scale climate instability during the early Pleistocene epoch. *Nature* 392, 699-702.

Retallack, G. J., 1980: Late Carboniferous to Middle Triassic megafossil floras from the Sydney Basin. *Geological Survey of New South Wales Bulletin* 26, 383-430.

Retallick, G. J., Seyedolali, A., Krull, E. S., Holser, W. T., Ambers, C. P. and Kyte, F. T., 1998: Search for evidence of impact at the Permian-Triassic boundary in Antarctica and Australia. *Geology* 26, 979-982.

Retallack. G. J., 1999: Permafrost palaeoclimate of Permian palaeosols in the Gerringong volcanic facies of New South Wales. *Australian Journal of Earth Sciences* 46, 11-22.

Retallack, G. J. and Krull, E. S., 1999: Landscape ecological shift at the Permian-Triassic boundary in Antarctica. *Australian Journal of Earth Sciences* 46, 785-812.

Retallack, G. J., 1999: Post-apocalyptic greenhouse paleoclimate revealed by earliest Triassic palaeosols in the Sydney Basin, Australia. *Geological Society of America Bulletin* 111.

Ribes, E., Ribes, J. C. and Barthalot, R., 1987: Evidence for a larger Sun with a slower rotation during the seventeenth century. *Nature* 126, 52-66.

Rieder, R., Economou, T., Wänkhe, H., Turkevich, A., Crisp, J., Brückner, J., Dreibus, G. and McSween, H. Y., 1997: The chemical composition of Martian soil and rocks returned by the mobile alpha proton X-ray spectrometer: preliminary results from the X-ray mode. *Science* 278, 1771-1774.

Ringot, E. J., 1998: Fast recession of a West Antarctic glacier. *Science* 281, 549-551.

Robinson, A. B., Baliunas, S. L., Soon, W. and Robinson, Z. W., 1998: Environmental effects of increased atmospheric carbon dioxide. *Medical Sentinel* 3, 5, 171-178.

Rosanova, C. E., Lucchitta, B. K. and Ferrigno, J. G., 1998: Velocities of Thwaites Glacier and smaller glaciers along the Marie Byrd coast, West Antarctica. *Annals of Glaciology* 27, 47-53.

Rossignol-Strick, M., Paterne, M., Bassinot, F. C., Emeis, K. C. and De Lange, G. J., 1998: An unusual mid-Pleistocene monsoon period over Africa and Asia. *Nature* 392, 269-272.

Rosman, K. J. R., Chisolm, W., Boutron, C. F., Candelone, J.-P., Jaffrezo, J.-L. and Davidson, C. I., 1998: Seasonal variations in the origin of lead in snow at Dye 3, Greenland. *Earth and Planetary Science Letters* 160, 383-389.

Rothwell, R. G., Thomson, J. and Kaehler, G., 1998: Low sea-level emplacement of a very large late Pleistocene 'megaturbidite' in the Western Mediterranean Sea. *Nature* 392, 377-380.

Rowden-Rich, R. J. M. and Wilson, C. J. L., 1996: Models for strain localisation in Law Dome, Antarctica. *Annals of Glaciology* 23, 396-401.

Rubincam, D. P., 1995: Has climate changed the Earth's tilt? *Paleoceanography* 10, 365-372.

Rudnick, R. L., 1995: Making continental crust. *Nature* 378, 571-578.

Runcorn, S. K., 1979: Palaeontological data on the history of the Earth-Moon system. *Physics of the Earth and Planetary Interiors* 20, 1-5.

Runnels, C. N., 1995: Environmental degradation in ancient Greece. *Scientific American* 27, 3, 96-99.

Russell, M. J., Ingham, J. K., Zedef, V., Maktav, D., Sunar, F., Hall, A. and Fallick, A. E., 1999: Search for signs of ancient life on Mars: expectations from hydromagnesite microbialites, Salda Lake, Turkey. *Journal of the Geological Society, London* 156, 869-888.

Ryan, W. B. F. and Pitman, W. C., 1998: *Noah's Flood: The new scientific discoveries about the event that changed history.* Simon & Schuster.

Santer, B. D., Taylor, K. E., Wigley, T. M. L., Johns, T. C., Jones, P. D., Karoly, D. J., Mitchell, J. F. B., Oort, A. H., Penner, J. E., Ramaswamy, V., Schwarzkopf, M. D., Stouffer, R. J. and Tett, S., 1996: A search for human influences on the thermal structure of the atmosphere. *Nature* 382, 39-46.

Scherer, R. P., Aldahan, A., Tulaczyk, S., Possnert, G., Engelhardt, H. and Kamb, B., 1998: Pleistocene collapse of the West Antarctic ice sheet. *Science* 281, 82-85.

Schmidt, P. W. and Williams, G. W., 1995: The Neoproterozoic climatic paradox: Equatorial palaeolatitude for Marinoan glaciation near sea level in south Australia. *Earth and Planetary Science Letters* 134, 107-124.

Schopf, J. W., 1994: The oldest known records of life: Early Archean stromatolites, microfossils, and organic matter. In: *Early life on Earth* (Ed. S. Bengtson). Columbia University Press, 193-206.

Schwarzacher, W., 1993: *Cyclostratigraphy and the Milankovitch theory*. Elsevier.

Scrutton, C. T., 1978: Periodic growth features in fossil organisms and the length of the day and month. In: *Tidal friction and the Earth's rotation* (Eds P. Brosche and J. Sdermann). Springer Verlag, 154-196.

Seilacher, A., 1994: Early multicellular life: Late Proterozoic fossils and the Cambrian explosion. In: *Early life on Earth* (Ed. S. Bengtson). Columbia University Press, 389-400.

Sepkoski, J. J., 1989: Periodicity in extinction and the problem of catastrophism in the history of life. *Journal of the Geological Society*, London 146, 7-19.

Severinghaus, J. P., Sowers, T., Brook, E. J., Alley, R. B. and Bender, M. L., 1998: Timing of abrupt climate change at the end of the Younger Dryas interval from thermally fractionated gases in polar ice. *Nature* 391, 141-146.

Seyitoglu, G. and Scott, B. C., 1992: Late Cenozoic volcanic evolution of the northeastern Aegean region. *Journal of Volcanology and Geothermal Research* 54, 157-176.

Shepherd, A., Wingham, D. J., Mansley, J. A. D. and Corr, H. F. J., 2001: Inland thinning of Pine Island Glacier, West Antarctica. *Science* 291, 862–864.

Sigurdsson, H., Carey, S. and Devine, J. D., 1990: Assessment of mass, dynamics, and environmental effects of the Minoan eruption of Santorini Volcano. In *Thera and the Ancient World—Proceedings of the Third International Congress* (Eds Hardy, D. A. et alia). London, Thera Foundation, 2, 100-112.

Simkin, T., 1993: Terrestrial volcanism in space and time. *Annual Review of Earth and Planetary Sciences* 21, 427-452.

Simonson, B. M., Davies, D., Wallace, M., Reeves, S. and Hassler, S. W., 1998: Iridium anomaly but no shocked quartz from Archean microkrystite layer: Oceanic impact ejecta? *Geology* 26, 198-208.

Sloan, R. E., Rigby, J. K., van Valen, L. M. and Gabriel, D., 1986: Gradual dinosaur extinction and simultaneous ungulate radiation in the Hell Creek Formation. *Science* 232, 629-633.

Sonett, C. P., Morfill, G. E. and Jokipp, J. R., 1987: Interstellar shock waves and [10]Be from ice cores. *Nature* 330, 458-460.

Spray, J. G., Kelley, S. P. and Rowley, D. B., 1998: Evidence for a late Triassic impact event on Earth. *Nature* 392, 171-173.

Stanley, G. D., 1992: Tropical reef ecosystems and their evolution. *Encyclopedia of Earth Sciences*, Volume 4, 375-388.

Stauffer, B., Blunier, T., Dällenbach, A., Indermühle, A., Schwander, J., Stocker, T. F., Tschumi, I., Chappellaz, J., Raynaud, D., Hammer, C. U. and Clausen, H. B., 1998: Atmospheric CO_2 concentration and millennial-scale climate change during the last glacial period. *Nature* 392, 59-62.

Stoffers, P., 2000: Elemental mercury at submarine hydrothermal vents in the Bay of Plenty, Taupo Volcanic Zone, New Zealand. *Geology* 27, 931-934.

Storey, B. C., 1995: The role of mantle plumes in continental breakup: Case histories from Gondwanaland. *Nature* 377, 301-308.

Stuiver, M. and Quay, P. D., 1980: Changes in atmospheric carbon-14 attributed to a variable Sun. *Science* 207, 11-19.

Sutton, A. N., Blake, S., Wilson, C. J. N. and Charlier, B. L. A., 2000: Late Quaternary evolution of a hyperactive rhyolite magmatic system. Taupo volcanic centre, New Zealand. *Journal of the Geological Society, London* 157, 537-552.

Tajika, E., 1998: Climate change during the last 150 million years: reconstruction from a carbon cycle model. *Earth and Planetary Science Letters* 160, 6695-6707.

Taylor, E. L., Taylor, T. N. and Cunéo, R., 1992: The present is not the key to the past: a polar forest from the Permian of Antarctica. *Science* 257, 1657-1677.

Taylor, S. R. and Esat, T. M., 1996: Geochemical constraints on the origin of the Moon. *Geophysical Monographs* 95, 33-46.

Tett, S. F. B., Stott, P. A., Allen, M. R., Ingram, W. J. and Mitchell, J. F. B., 1999: Causes of twentieth-century temperature change near the Earth's surface. *Nature* 399, 569-572.

Tonkin, P. C., 1998: Lorne Basin, New South Wales: evidence for a possible impact origin? *Australian Journal of Earth Sciences* 45, 669-671.

Toscano, M. A. and Lundberg, J., 1998: Early Holocene sea-level record from submerged fossil reefs on the southeast Florida margin. *Geology* 26, 3, 255-258.

Touveny, N., de Beaulieu, J-L., Bonifay, E., Creer, K. M., Gulot, J., Icole, M., Johnsen, S., Jouzel, J., Reille, M., Williams, T. and Williamson, D., 1994: Climate variations in Europe over the past 140 kyr deduced from rock magnetism. *Nature* 371, 503-506.

Treiman, A., 1999: Martian life 'still kicking' in meteorite ALH84001. *Eos* 205-209.

Trendall, A., 2000: The significance of banded iron formation (BIF) in the Precambrian stratigraphic record. *Geoscientist* 10, 6, 4-7.

Tsedakis, P. C., 1999: The last climatic cycle at Kopais, central Greece. *Journal of the Geological Society, London* 156, 425-434.

Tuchman, B. W., 1979: *A distant mirror: the calamitous 14th Century*. Penguin Books.

Tudge, C., 1995: *The day before yesterday. Five Million Years of Human History*. Pimlico.

Turner, P., 1980: *Continental red beds*. Elsevier.

Twidale, C. R., 1998: Antiquity of landforms: an 'extremely unlikely' concept vindicated. *Australian Journal of Earth Sciences* 45, 657-668.

Urban, F. B., Cole, J. E. and Overpeck, J. T., 2000: Influence of mean climate change on climate variability from a 155-year tropical Pacific coral record. *Nature* 407, 989–995.

Vail, P. R. and Mitchum, R. M., 1979: Global cycles of relative changes of sea level from seismic stratigraphy. *American Association of Petroleum Geologists Memoir* 29, 469-472.

Vallianou, D., 1996: New evidence of earthquake destructions in late Minoan Crete. In *Archaeoseismology* (Eds Stiros, R. and Jones, R. E.). Fitch Lab Occasional Paper 7, Athens, 153-167.

Vaganov, E. A., Hughes, M. K., Kirdyanov, A. V., Schweingruber, F. H. and Silkin, P. P., 1999: Influence of snowfall and melt timing on tree growth in subarctic Eurasia. *Nature* 400, 149-151.

Veevers, J. J., 1990: Tectonic-climatic supercycle in the billion year plate-tectonic eon: Permian Pangean icehouse alternates with Cretaceous dispersed-continents greenhouse. *Sedimentary Geology* 68, 1-16.

Verschuur, G. L., 1996: *Impact—The threat of comets and asteroids*. Oxford University Press.

Vines, G., 1999: Mass extinctions. *New Scientist* 11th December 1999, Supplement 126, 1-4.

Vinnikov, K. Y., Robock, A., Stouffer, R. J., Walsh, J. E., Parkinson, C. L., Cavalieri, D. J., Mitchell, J. F. B., Garrett, D. and Zakharov, V. F., 1999: Global warming and Northern Hemisphere sea ice extent. *Science* 286, 1934-1937.

Vreeland, R. H., Rosenzweig, W. D. and Powers, D. W., 2000: Isolation of a 250 million-year-old halotolerant bacterium from a primary salt crystal. *Nature* 409, 897-900.

Walker, J. C. G. and Zahnle, K. J., 1986: Lunar nodal tide and distance to the Moon during the Precambrian. *Nature* 320, 600-602.

Walsh, J. E., 1991: The Arctic as bellwether. *Nature* 352, 19-20.

Walsh, K. J. and Sellers, W. D., 1993: Response of a global climate model to a thirty percent reduction of the solar constant. *Global Planetary Change* 8, 219-230.

Walter, M. and des Marais, D. J., 1993: Preservation of biological information in thermal spring deposits: developing a strategy for the search for fossil life on Mars. *Icarus* 101, 129-143.

Wegener, A., 1912: Die Entstehung der Kontinente. *Geologische Rundschau* 3, 276-292.

Wetherill, G. W., 1985: Occurrence of giant impacts during the growth of terrestrial planets. *Science* 221, 877-879.

Wetherill, G. W., 1990: Formation of the Earth. *Annual Review of Earth and Planetary Sciences* 18, 205-256.

Wetherill, G. W., 1994: Provenance of the terrestrial planets. *Geochimica et Cosmochimica Acta* 58, 4513-4520.

Whitfield, J., 1999: Earth sciences: mercurial vents. *Nature* 401, 755.

Williams, G. E., 1975: Late Precambrian glacial climate and the Earth's obliquity. *Geological Magazine* 112, 441-465.

Williams, G. E. and Goode, A. D. T., 1978: Possible western outlet for an ancient Murray River in South Australia. *Search* 9, 443-447.

Williams, G. E., 1986: Precambrian permafrost horizons as indicators of palaeoclimate. *Precambrian Research* 32, 233-242.

Williams, G. E., 1993: History of the Earth's obliquity. *Earth Science Reviews* 24, 1-45.

Williams, G. E., 1998: Precambrian tidal and glacial eustatic clastic deposits: implications for Precambrian Earth-Moon dynamics and palaeoclimate. *Sedimentary Geology* 120, 55-74.

Wilson, C. R., 1998: Oceanic effects on Earth's rotation rate. *Science* 281, 1623-1624.

Wilson, L., 1999: Volcanic meteorites? *Geoscientist* 10, 2, 4-6.

World Climate Report 2000: Major advances required 5, 10.

World Climate Report 2000: Sea-ing nothing new under the Sun 5, 14.

World Climate Report 2000: Earth track 6, 9.

Yiou, P. and Ghil, M., 1993: Nonlinear paleoclimatic variability from Quaternary records. In: *Ice in the climate system* (Ed. W. R. Peltier). NATO workshop, Aussois 1992. Springer, 557-558.

Young, G. M., 1991: The geologic record of glaciation: Relevance to climatic history of Earth. *Geoscience Canada* 18, 100-108.

Zielenski, G. A., Mayewski, P. A., Meeker, L. D., Whitlow, S., Twickler, M. S., Morrison, M., Meese, D. A., Gow, A. J. and Alley, R. B., 1994: Record of volcanism since 7000 BC from the GISP 2 Greenland ice core and implication for the volcano-climate system. *Science* 264, 948-951.

INDEX